Teilhard de Chardin's
The Phenomenon of Man
Explained

Louis M. Savary

Paulist Press
New York / Mahwah, NJ

Library of Congress Cataloging-in-Publication Data
Names: Savary, Louis M., author.
Title: Teilhard de Chardin's The phenomenon of man explained : uncovering the scientific foundations of his spirituality / Louis M Savary.
Description: New York ; Mahwah, NJ : Paulist Press, 2020. | Summary: "This book establishes the connection between the evolutionary scientific ideas of The Human Phenomenon and the Christian spirituality and theology of The Divine Milieu"—Provided by publisher.
Identifiers: LCCN 2019044787 (print) | LCCN 2019044788 (ebook) | ISBN 9780809154487 (paperback) | ISBN 9781587688409 (ebook)
Subjects: LCSH: Teilhard de Chardin, Pierre. Phénomène humain. | Cosmology. | Evolution. | Philosophical anthropology. | Teilhard de Chardin, Pierre. Milieu divin.
Classification: LCC B2430.T373 P5637 2020 (print) | LCC B2430.T373 (ebook) | DDC 194—dc23
LC record available at https://lccn.loc.gov/2019044787
LC ebook record available at https://lccn.loc.gov/2019044788

ISBN 978-0-8091-5448-7 (paperback)
ISBN 978-1-58768-840-9 (e-book)

Published by Paulist Press
997 Macarthur Boulevard
Mahwah, New Jersey 07430
www.paulistpress.com

Printed and bound in the
United States of America

Contents

Contents

Preface

To TRULY UNDERSTAND the value and purpose of the book *The Phenomenon of Man*, you must first understand the mind and heart of the man who wrote it.

Pierre Teilhard de Chardin (1881–1955) was born in the Auvergne area of France. He was a middle child among ten in a devout patrician Catholic family. His father was an amateur geologist, his mother a deeply spiritual woman. From his father, Teilhard developed a love for Earth, from his mother a love for God. These two loves grew together and matured in the young Pierre. He learned to love both matter and spirit, both science and religion.

After attending a Jesuit high school, Teilhard became a Jesuit, a member of the Catholic religious order called the Society of Jesus. In the seminary, he studied both science and religion. He received a degree in theology and, after ordination, went on to earn a doctorate in geology.

In his career as a geologist, he participated in many geological digs, especially in China, where he was part of the team that discovered Peking man. During his lifetime, he published over 1,500 scholarly articles in scientific journals in his field. He was highly regarded as a scientist.

As a religious person, Teilhard manifested certain mystical qualities that are evident in his book on spirituality, *The Divine Milieu*, and in his many essays on spiritual and theological topics. He once described himself as passionately in love with the world and passionately in love with God.

For many people in Teilhard's era, these two loves were viewed as contradictory. Evolution offered a good example of this radical separation. Scientists affirmed evolution as a great scientific discovery, and dismissed religion as outdated, superstitious, and meaningless. At the same time, religious leaders refused to accept evolution because, to them, it contradicted the testimony of Sacred Scripture and challenged the word of God.

During Teilhard's adult life, in Europe and the United States, the conflict between modern science and religion grew fierce. Science was committed to evolution and Christianity was committed to a literal interpretation of the Bible, so much so that Pope Pius X condemned as heretical what he called "modernism." According to the pope, modernism's heresies included most current scientific theories, especially the theory of evolution.[1] The pope demanded that every priest and theology professor swear an oath against modernism and, in effect, deny Darwinian evolution.

Even Charles Darwin, a good Christian, had been hesitant to publish his evolutionary findings for fear that his theories would upset his Christian colleagues and clerics. Half a century later, Teilhard tried in vain to explain, to both his fellow scientists and to church officials, how he was able to integrate modern science and evolution with his Christian faith.

For the most part, both sides adamantly rejected his integrative perspective. His church, to which he had sworn fidelity, prohibited him from publishing any of his spiritual or theological writings. He shared typewritten copies of some of his manuscripts with a few supportive Jesuit friends and scientific colleagues. The rest of the world never saw his writings, except for his scientific papers, until after his death in 1955.

In addition to two complete books, *The Divine Milieu* and *The Phenomenon of Man*, Teilhard's posthumously published essays fill eight or nine collected volumes.

Ideas for *The Phenomenon of Man* were already germinating in Teilhard's mind in the 1920s. He completed its first draft in 1939. Teilhard wrote *Phenomenon* as a scientific treatise for his fellow scientists. When he presented this scientific manuscript to the church for publication approval, the officials in the Holy Office found it unacceptable. Scientists never got to read his ideas until after his death.

For me, writing *Teilhard de Chardin's* The Phenomenon of Man *Explained* has been the most daunting project I have ever attempted. Teilhard writes not only as an intellectual genius, but also as a poet, and a spiritual mystic. *Phenomenon* is his masterpiece. When its first English edition appeared in 1959, reviewers gave it the highest praise and compared Teilhard to some of the world's most famous thinkers. One reviewer described *Phenomenon* as "the most significant achievement in synthetic thinking since that of Aquinas." Another said Teilhard was "a great scientist with the deep metaphysical disquietude of a St. Augustine or a Pascal." These reviewers were themselves giants in their own fields. They included Sir Julian Huxley, Arnold J. Toynbee, Abraham J. Heschel, and Karl Stern.

Unfortunately, most readers could not make heads or tails of the book. Few ever read it cover to cover.

The challenge I gave myself was to make Teilhard's masterpiece accessible to any intelligent and curious reader. It would have to be a relatively short book—not a heavy five-hundred-page tome. It would have to be theoretical yet practical, fascinating yet factual, lofty yet useful, challenging yet understandable. It would show how familiar experiences can prove revelatory.

Phenomenon Explained does not attempt to develop every idea and insight in Teilhard's text. Its purpose is to present Teilhard's key findings and clarify his approach in such a way that the reader may then pick up Teilhard's own text and feel at home with it.

Many times in frustration I have been tempted to give up the project as impossible, even though I have been teaching, writing about, and trying to "live" Teilhard's insights for half a century. From time to time, I would wake up at three or four in the morning with a new insight or a simpler way to explain a complex idea. It became clear to me that it was important that I continue.

Teilhard wants to take you through an epic journey, from the birth of the cosmos, through the stages of development from prelife to life on our planet, to the clear emergence of the human phenomenon and the birth of thought and society. He also wants to show you how the trajectory of evolution points to an even further stage of human development.

By learning to perceive this multibillion-year process as he sees it, he believes we can learn how to release the true spirit of humanity and begin to tap into its currently unimaginable potential. Although Teilhard wrote his *Phenomenon* almost a century ago, it is still powerfully revelatory today.

Louis M. Savary
Tampa, Florida

Acknowledgments

I OWE SPECIAL THANKS to several professional friends for their patience and kindness in reviewing my manuscript and for their insightful comments. Sr. Kathleen Duffy, SND, physics professor at Chestnut Hill University in Philadelphia and editor of the scholarly journal *Teilhard Studies*. Edward Vacek, SJ, theology professor at Loyola University, New Orleans. Roger Haight, SJ, professor at Columbia University and former president of the Catholic Theological Society of America.

Susie Timchak and Peter Esseff reviewed the manuscript and offered scores of helpful suggestions for making the text more grammatically accurate and easily readable. Boundless love to my faithful wife who keeps me on task and reminds me that, as long as I am breathing, I have work to do for God.

Thanks to publisher Harper & Row, who early on had the foresight to recognize Teilhard's important contributions to both science and religion and to make available most of his writings in English.

Deep gratitude to Paul McMahon and Donna Crilly, my very supportive editors at Paulist Press, and to their editorial team who believe that books on Teilhard's thought, accessible to the ordinary reader, deserve to be published and kept in print for future generations.

Following Paulist Press protocol for scriptural references, I have used the NSRVCE (Catholic Edition) throughout. It is easily accessed on the internet at https://www.biblegateway.com/versions/New-Revised -Standard-Version-Catholic-Edition-NRSVCE-Bible/.

Overview

Teilhard: Rewriting Natural History

IN HIS BOOK *The Phenomenon of Man*, Teilhard is doing something very original and daring in the scientific world. He is *re-envisioning and reshaping the science of natural history*. He is trying to *evolve* the very science that introduced evolution to the scientific world. *Phenomenon* shows in detail how he reperceives and reconfigures natural history from his new perspective.

Museums of natural history have been around for centuries. Their purpose is to track and trace the story of life on our planet as far back as possible. Geologists and paleontologists continue to find ancient fossils to be catalogued. Until now, the billion-year evolving story of animal nature has been categorized and classified primarily by their physical characteristics—teeth, arms, hands, feet, skull shape, cranial volume, eye positions, and so on.

Teilhard wants to advance the field of natural history beyond a discipline of *classification*. His *Phenomenon* is intended to *evolve* this scientific field, not revolutionize it. Revolution means to destroy the system that is in place and replace it with something totally new. In contrast, evolution means to take everything in the present system as a foundation and raise it to a new level.

Evolution in scientific fields is not new. Isaac Newton did it for mathematics, Einstein did it for physics, Darwin did it for biology, Marie Curie did it for chemistry, David Hilbert did it for geometry, and so on.

Teilhard wants to re-envision natural history from a new perspective, specifically, to show that evolution is moving progressively in a certain direction and has always been moving this way.

Evolution with a Direction

The issue Teilhard faces is that biologists acknowledge that evolution is continually changing the face of the world by producing ever-new species of plants, insects, and animals. But most believe that evolution's myriad mutations and adaptations present no discernibly clear direction or purpose. For them, nature just keeps generating new species to replace other species that go extinct.

Teilhard claims that, as long as naturalists use physical characteristics alone to trace the emergence of human life on Earth, they cannot fully account for the species *Homo sapiens* anywhere in their classifications. No amount of analysis of bones or any other physical characteristics can explain how the species *Homo sapiens* became capable of self-reflective thinking. Nor can bones explain how humans began creating languages, mathematics, art, literature, philosophy, theology, sciences, and technology.

Given this massive evidence of reasoning, creativity, and self-reflection among humans, *Homo sapiens* in the traditional naturalist system is simply an anomaly, a freak of nature. With outstanding human specimens in history like Aristotle, Aquinas, Leonardo, Galileo, and Napoleon, plus physical evidence of human creativity and ingenuity like the Greek Parthenon, the Louvre Museum, the Library of Congress, and the New York Stock Exchange, the human race simply doesn't fit anywhere in the naturalist classification system.

In *Phenomenon*, Teilhard proposes to use a different kind of measurement to track the history of life. This new way to measure change clearly reveals evolution's progressive path. It shows how *Homo sapiens* is a natural outcome of the evolutionary process.

Teilhard's new measuring device is complexity. For him, the *amount of neurological complexity and level of consciousness in various species provides a clear way of revealing and measuring nature's trajectory of evolutionary development.*

He shows how everything in the museums of natural history contributes to and confirms his new measurement approach. What he adds to the evolution of matter is the *evolution of mind*. From this perspective, he says, the phenomenon of *Homo sapiens* is no longer a random anomaly in evolution, but its most natural outcome.

If we graph evolution's history—plotting the rise in complexity over time on a graph's x-axis (time) and y-axis (degree of complexity)—complexity's path reveals a *clear direction* in the evolution of life.

These, then, are Teilhard's two ambitious intentions in writing *Phenomenon*.

First, he proposes *complexity as a new basis of measurement for the scientific field of natural history*. Traditionally, the sciences used two fundamental ways to measure reality—*space* and *time*. To these, Teilhard adds a third fundamental way of measuring reality—*complexity*.

Second, he proposes to *use this new way of measuring to track the developmental path of evolution itself*.

What Teilhard does in *Phenomenon* is as significant a breakthrough in natural history as quantum theory was in physics or radioactivity was in chemistry or imaginary numbers were in mathematics. A century later, his book is still basically "unknown" in the scientific community.

In *Phenomenon*, Teilhard takes you through the reasoning he uses to rewrite natural history and the ongoing story of evolution. Because much of his argument relies on the categorization and physical classification of traditional natural history, you will encounter much terminology foreign to anyone except biologists, botanists, geologists, anthropologists, and other related natural scientists. It's not essential that you research every category of evidence to which he refers. The important thing is to follow his line of reasoning.

Pre-Notes

For the Reader of
The Phenomenon of Man
Explained

- It's not important to have studied Teilhard's *The Phenomenon of Man* before you read *Phenomenon Explained*. If you have a copy of Teilhard's own text, you may follow it as you read these pages. Or, you may wait and read Teilhard's original work afterward.
- Quotes from *The Phenomenon of Man* are taken from Bernard Wall's English translation in the Harper Colophon 1965 edition. I am well aware that inclusive language is noticeably absent in Teilhard's writings, as reflected in Wall's English translation that I am using. It is the dog-eared version of *Phenomenon* that I have read, reread, annotated, and underlined for over forty years. Remember that inclusive language was not a part of the social consciousness until the last quarter of the twentieth century, when textbook writers first began to change their book titles from *Biology of Man* to *Human Biology*. Teilhard was certainly "inclusive" in his life and theology. If he were writing today, I'm sure his language would more accurately reflect this evolved worldview. As you read the word *man* in numerous Teilhard quotations cited in the text, please be forgiving. I trust you will not be offended or feel the need to criticize Teilhard or his first English translator, both of whom were of

a different time and wrote with utmost sincerity and love. Cited page numbers following quotation from *The Phenomenon of Man* are from this edition.

- For readers using the more recent 2003 English "inclusive" translation by Sarah Appleton-Weber, titled *The Human Phenomenon*, I provide corresponding page numbers in *italics*.[1]

- The Harper 1965 edition of *Phenomenon* begins with a long introduction by Sir Julian Huxley (11–28). No need to read it beforehand. Huxley's comments are best appreciated after reading *Phenomenon Explained*.

- In Teilhard's preface (29–30, *1–2*) and foreword (31–36, *3–7*) almost every sentence is important. His opening pages provide essential information and orientation for understanding the rest of his text. They present clearly Teilhard's perspective and purpose.

- A short glossary of certain Teilhardian and scientific terms is provided in the back of the book. I give the meaning of the word when it first appears. If you encounter the word later, the glossary can help refresh your memory. The index can guide you back to its first appearance.

- From time to time, I will suggest how the scientific ideas he proposes provide a fresh perspective on spirituality. For example,

Spiritual Implications

For the scientist, Teilhard is re-envisioning the science of natural history. For the believer, he is re-envisioning God's creation story. And he wants to share it. In this book, Teilhard introduces us to a Creator God that no one before him had ever pictured or described. He tells a creation story that no believer has ever proposed before.

Teilhard assumes that creation must be a self-expression of God. Yet, God who is pure *Spirit* sets in motion a universe that is pure *Matter*. God who is pure *Life itself* sets in motion a universe that is *Lifeless*. God who is pure *Love* sets in motion a universe full of nothing but *Inert Particles*.

Pre-Notes

And yet, some of these myriad inert particles have become you and me—humans who are spiritual beings—who think, make free choices, and create things that never existed before. How did this happen? How did a universe of pure Matter become Spirit?

That is the mystery Teilhard sets out to explore in *Phenomenon*.

For Teilhard personally, whether scientists agree or not, *Phenomenon* is a book about God's revelation. As Teilhard writes in *The Divine Milieu*,

> By means of all created things, without exception, the divine assails us, penetrates us, and molds us. We imagined it [the divine] as distant and inaccessible, when in fact we live steeped in its burning layers.

Teilhard's Preface

(29–30, 1–2)*

TEILHARD'S PREFACE provides an essential orientation to the rest of *Phenomenon*. Though it is only two pages long, it reveals the book's intended audience, its subject matter, the process he follows, his purpose, and an alternate group of potential readers. A quick look at each topic.

- *Audience*. He informs us on the very first page of his preface that the book is "purely and simply a scientific treatise," written primarily for scientists, not for philosophers or theologians. So, we are not to expect a book on theology or spirituality. He is proposing to scientists a new method for categorizing and classifying the data of natural history.
- *Subject Matter*. Teilhard titled his book *Le phénomène humain* (*The Human Phenomenon*). It is important to grasp up front what Teilhard sees as the subject matter of his research. A *phenomenon* is something that can be seen, observed, and measured. It is something *apparent and tangible*.

For Teilhard, the "human phenomenon" includes much more than the *individual human being*. As a biological, thinking creature, more evolved than any other creature on Earth, the individual is the proper subject matter of biology and psychology.

---

* Numbers in parentheses in regular type refer to pages in the original Harper edition of *The Phenomenon of Man*. *Italicized* numbers refer to pages in the 2002 translation by Sarah Appleton-Weber.

1

The "human phenomenon" also includes much more than the *collective being* that we call *humanity*. As a whole, humanity possesses much more capability, potential, and purpose than any individual man or woman. As a collective, humanity is the proper subject matter of sociology, social psychology, and anthropology.

When Teilhard talks about the "human phenomenon," he sees much, much more than the seven-plus billion people living and interacting on Earth. As part of the human phenomenon, he includes *everything observably human*. These are part of his human phenomenon as he sees it: the New York City subway system in full operation; tractors harvesting corn in Nebraska; a noisy Ford Motor plant; St. Mark's Cathedral in Venice; a fan-filled soccer stadium in Brazil. If Teilhard were alive today, as part of the human phenomenon he would include a rocket lifting off at the Kennedy Space Center, the International Space Station orbiting Earth, and scores of communication satellites circling our planet connecting billions of cells phones in every city and town on Earth.

Of course, he includes you and me as *individual humans* in his vision, as well as the great collective being that we call *humanity*, a whole that is far greater than the sum of its individual parts. For Teilhard, the human phenomenon also includes *everything that humanity has discovered and made*, everything that was never on Earth before *Homo sapiens*, everything that nature by itself could never have produced. For instance, nature by itself could never have made your refrigerator, your car, your toothpaste, credit cards, wristwatches, shoes, and so on. An endless list. Because humans invented and made these things, they are all part of the human phenomenon as Teilhard sees it. So, when he uses shorthand words like *man* or *humanity*, he "sees" and includes all the above. *Homo sapiens*, he insists, deserves to be studied in its entirety.

In this fuller light, the human phenomenon is clearly recognized as something truly new that has appeared on Earth. For Teilhard, this study of the human phenomenon belongs in a category by itself. He sees it as a new scientific field. It includes the evolution of mind as well as the evolution of matter.

- *Process.* The analytic process Teilhard follows in *Phenomenon* is to situate humanity sequentially along evolution's path from its beginnings. Humanity's initial stages begin with the formation of atoms and molecules early in the universe's almost fourteen-billion-year history. Physically, each of us is completely composed of some of those primordial atoms, since science assures us that every subatomic particle that exists today throughout the cosmos came bursting into existence in that first moment of space/time.

- *Purpose.* In *Phenomenon*, Teilhard wants to show the *unique significance* of the emergence of the human species in Earth's maturation process. He offers two reasons to account for the uniqueness of the human phenomenon plus two undisputed facts.

The reason humans deserve to be recognized as uniquely significant, he says, are because we manifest (1) *reflective thinking* and (2) a *complex social life*. Teilhard insists that without studying humanity's inner life and its social complexity, it is impossible "to give a fully coherent account of the phenomenon of man" (29, 2).

The two scientific facts are the following:

- *We humans are the last species to emerge in the long evolutionary line.*
- *We have emerged from within that long line.*

Humanity was not created out of nothing; rather it emerged organically from what went before. What he wants to show in *Phenomenon* is this:

- "Man is not simply a new species of animal…he represents, he initiates, *a new species of life*."[1]

Teilhard insists that the human being that emerged "belongs to another level, another form, another species of life in the universe." And the study of humanity and human evolution, Teilhard insists, is a brand-new science.

He is saying to his fellow scientists, "I am going to approach humanity in a new and different way. I invite you to put your specialized scientific expertise aside for a while and consider my way of studying humanity."

- *Other Readers.* Teilhard feels his *scientific* reflections also offer "ample room for farther-reaching speculations of the philosopher and the theologian" (29, 1). He invites readers interested in spirituality to use his scientific insights and conclusions as a basis upon which to build their spirituality and spiritual practices. In that regard, I shall provide some suggestions as we progress.

For convenience, here is a quick summary of Teilhard's preface.

Summary

Q: For what audience is Teilhard writing *Phenomenon?*

A: *Scientists.*

Q: What is the book's subject matter?

A: *The human phenomenon—every aspect of human life.*

Q: How does he describe the thesis of his book?

A: *To show that the study of humanity in its entirety is a new science.*

Q: What process does he use to do this?

A: *He uses a scientific process of observation to follow humanity's evolution starting from the first moments of the universe.*

Q: What is his purpose for doing this?

A: *He wants to show the uniqueness of human life. In his words, "Man is not simply a new species of animal…he initiates a new species of life."*

Q: What are two assumptions Teilhard makes in his study?

A: *That humans manifest (1) reflective thinking and (2) a complex social life.*

Q: Does he have other readers in mind that might be interested in *Phenomenon?*

A: *Yes, specifically, philosophers and theologians.*

Teilhard's Foreword
"Seeing" (31–36, 3–7)

Outline

TEILHARD'S FOREWORD to *Phenomenon* is only six pages long, but he introduces the reader to many new concepts and processes that are essential to understanding his approach. Among them are the following:

- Learning to "see" reality his way.
- The concepts *metamorphosis* and *endomorphism*.
- Three fundamental insights that are key to his theory.
- Seven senses of seeing.
- The concepts *anthropogenesis* and *cosmogenesis*.

To cover these topics, we need more than six pages.

Another Purpose of *Phenomenon*: Learning to See

The foreword's title is "Seeing." Teilhard wants to teach his readers how to "see" the way he sees since most people can't see what he sees. They have never been taught to see in his way.

Teaching his readers to "see" becomes a secondary but important purpose for writing *Phenomenon*. Unless you learn to "see" in his new way, you will miss the main point of his book—developing a new way of looking at reality. He says readers need "new eyes." Don't assume you already possess Teilhard's "eyes."

His insistence on learning to "see" is reminiscent of what Jesus said about the crowds. They watched his healings and listened to his teachings, yet they never got his real meaning. "Seeing they do not perceive, and hearing they do not listen, nor do they understand" (Matt 13:13).

Teilhard suggests that many scientists may have never truly looked and seen the human phenomenon. In his foreword's very first sentence, he writes, "This work may be summed up as an attempt *to see and to make others see* what happens" when we really observe this phenomenon we call humanity in its beginnings and becoming, and in its transformation of Earth (31, 3). For Teilhard, everything depends on the ability to observe and see. His way of seeing involves reflective thought and *consciousness*.

Some Fundamental Insights

On his opening page, Teilhard casually drops a series of tightly interlocked insights. For most of us—even scientists—they may take a bit of reflection to absorb. But they are key to his theory.

1. *"Fuller being is [implies, requires] closer union."* Teilhard notes that this insight forms "the kernel and conclusion of this book" (31, 3), so it must be important. How do we increase union or make it "closer"? He answers,
2. *"Union increases only through an increase in consciousness, that is to say, in vision"* (31, 3). For Teilhard, "vision" refers to the new conscious ability to "see" in the way he describes in these opening pages and the way he presents "seeing" in *Phenomenon*.
3. *"If to see is really to become more [conscious], if vision is really fuller being, then we should look closely at man in order to increase our capacity to live"* (33, 4).

When Teilhard says "we should look closely at man," he means the entire trajectory of human evolution leading up to *Homo sapiens* and beyond. As we consciously move that trajectory forward toward higher consciousness, we will "increase our capacity to live."

The truth and value of these assertions will become evident only as we integrate much of the knowledge in Teilhard's *Phenomenon*. You might want to take a few moments now to reflect on these three statements. It will help you to begin to grasp the connection he sees between vision and consciousness, between union and fuller being.

Consciousness, for our purposes, may be simply described as *awareness accompanied by an appropriate response*. Simple awareness is not enough to qualify as consciousness. Awareness might mean I am looking but not really seeing. Only when I give an appropriate response to what I see can I verify that I have looked *and seen*. Appropriate responses might include words, actions, decisions, insights, logical implications, or even a choice *not* to act.

For Teilhard, conscious seeing is of the utmost importance. He gives two reasons for this. First, if you don't adapt your "eyes" to see the information presented in Teilhard's book the way he sees it, you will miss his purpose and conclusions and possibly misunderstand and misuse what he says. You'll be like the nonmusician who looks at a page of music manuscript. He can clearly see the musical notes on the staff and all the other musical symbols on the page, but he has no idea what they mean. Or the English speaker who can look at a page of Arabic writing and even admire its form and beauty, yet cannot comprehend it.

Second, "learning to see" in general is an important life skill that everyone needs. As far as Teilhard is concerned, "the whole of life lies in that verb" *seeing* (31, 3). Human life and maturity is essentially about continually improving one's ability to see and perceive, to respond and act appropriately.

Every living creature, from the most primitive to the most sophisticated, survives by *seeing*. For Teilhard, seeing is akin to consciousness, since it requires both being aware of one's surroundings and responding appropriately. He says, "To see or to perish is the very condition laid upon everything that makes up the universe" (31, 3). We judge the intelligence of an animal by its ability to grasp more and more of its surroundings with conscious awareness. For survival—and even more so for growth—it is vital to be able to see, understand, learn, and act appropriately.

Phenomenon's Focus of Study

In his foreword Teilhard poses the question, Why do I make the phenomenon of humanity the focus of my scientific study? He offers two reasons.

First, he sees *humanity as the central element of the evolving world.* What we humans do or don't do, he realizes, has powerful effects on the success or failure of all future evolutionary processes on Earth.

Second, he sees *humanity as the key to Earth's future.* We humans are the only species that can use our consciousness and imagination to envision a forward-moving future. Either we accept responsibility for inventing ways to create the future that we envision, or we can abdicate our responsibility in this regard and "perish."

Objectivity and Subjectivity

Traditional scientists ask, How can human individuals claim to research objectively the entire human phenomenon? How can humanity study itself, since it is both the *object* of the inquiry and the *subject* doing the research? To objective scientists, conducting such a self-study would be paradoxical. They would insist that subject and object must remain physically and emotionally separate. A scientific observer cannot become involved with what is observed. Otherwise, the scientist cannot be "objective."[2]

Teilhard insists that the mutual influence of observer and observed is not paradoxical. In his method of inquiry, "object and subject marry and mutually transform each other in the act of knowledge" (31, 4).

For Teilhard, to "marry" the object of your inquiry means you are in love with it and become one with it. In that union, your *object* of inquiry, *humanity,* becomes the *subject* of inquiry—the partner in the quest. Just as mutual transformation happens to the two partners in a loving marriage, a mutual transformation happens in a loving scientific inquiry. Transformation happens to both partners, the observing subject (you) and the "subject matter" of inquiry (humanity).

For Teilhard, the act of "seeing" in his sense is in fact an act of loving union between observer and observed. In Teilhard's loving mode of "seeing," seeing is itself transformative. Teilhard here is describing a nondualistic way of thinking.

A Nondualistic Mindset

For longer than three thousand years, in our Western culture dualistic thinking continues to be the way we are taught to think and see. To be objective, we are told, you must remain "separate" from the thing you are looking at. A dualist thinker believes an observer is separate from the object of observation and is convinced that such dualistic thinking is being "objective." Those used to thinking dualistically find it difficult to shift to a nondualistic mindset.

The dualistic thinker tends to see a thing and label it as either this or that. The nondualistic thinker tends to see, not either/or, but *both/ and*. Teilhard is asking readers to begin seeing in a nondualistic way. He would say, "This and that participate in the same reality. You and I participate in the same reality. If I am changed as I look at something, the something I look at is changed in that act."

Some people say that Earth was made from stars and that we humans are physically made up of the stardust that shaped the Earth. In effect, we have become *conscious* stardust that has learned to study the stars. We have learned to study what we are made of. It's as though, through us humans, the stars that shaped us are coming to know themselves. That is an example of nondualistic thinking.

In their book *The Universe Story*, Brian Swimme and Thomas Berry express such a nondualistic way of thinking when they write, "The [human] eye that searches the Milky Way galaxy is itself an eye shaped by the Milky Way. The mind that searches for contact with the Milky Way is the very mind of the Milky Way galaxy in search of its own depths."[3]

The poet Walt Whitman was a nondualistic thinker. When he admired a beautiful sunset, he saw himself as "a space the Milky Way fashioned to feel its own grandeur."

Once we learn to "see" in Teilhard's loving way, where everything is connected and mutually affecting everything else, we enter a new state of consciousness. When we see something through loving eyes, we are transformed. And, in that personal transformation, the object of our study (humanity) is also transformed. In other words, the "changed" observer is also part of the "changed" observed.

Teilhard claims that with the new ability to "see" in this nondualistic way both a *metamorphosis* and an *endomorphism* occur in us. These are two important concepts. Both provide ways to see with new eyes.

Metamorphosis and Endomorphism

Metamorphosis describes a *change in the form, state, or nature* of a thing or a person into a different one, usually from a lower state to a higher (*meta*) state. It is the same being, only its form or state changes. For example, an insect is transformed from an immature form (caterpillar) to an adult form (butterfly). Or, a certain man undergoes a metamorphosis from being a football player to becoming a businessman. Or, a scientist goes from being an agnostic to becoming a believer.

When someone undergoes a metamorphosis to a new state of being—a new career, a new role, a new level of maturity, and so on—many things in life take on new significance. For example, boys and girls in high school begin to find themselves attracted to each other in ways that probably never occurred in grammar school. They have undergone a metamorphosis. The metamorphosed graduate student in chemistry looks at his field differently from the high school student taking chemistry as a required course. New parents look at their own baby in ways they have never looked at others' babies. Teilhard is saying that when you undergo a metamorphosis, like falling in love with the universe as he did, you undergo a metamorphosis and begin to see everything with new eyes.

Endomorphism describes a *mapping of one set of objects onto another set of the same size*, so that the new mapping reveals what could not be recognized in the first mapping. For example, a sewer map of a town (one mapping) may be overlaid with a transparent street map of the same town (another mapping of the same reality). Such a pairing would enable a plumber to identify the precise street address to track the source of a leak in the town's water system. Your new loving eyes, in effect, place a new map over the object of your inquiry, and with this new map you see humanity again for the first time, that is, in a new way.

In *Phenomenon*, Teilhard begins by taking various mappings (or descriptions) of the human family that each of the physical sciences—biology, physics, chemistry, geology, anthropology, psychology, sociology, and so forth—traditionally uses. He then overlays these maps with a new map that shows the intellectual, technological, and social life of humanity. Teilhard hopes this new mapping will enable the scientific reader of his book to "see" a different picture of the same human family. He hopes his new mapping will enable scientists to see new meaning and purpose for the human species. ·

With your new nondualistic eyes, Teilhard will also invite you to imagine a further endomorphism. This is a *time-sequence mapping* overlaying all these other scientific mappings. This will be a "moving picture" map—using time-lapse photography. The map will start from the Big Bang, filming humanity from its earliest origins in elemental makeup as it continues to morph through billions of years of evolution up to the present day. Teilhard's *Phenomenon* creates for his readers a kind of new time-lapse mapping (*endomorphism*).

Adopting Teilhard's "new eyes" is not an easy shift for many people to make. But the more completely we can enter his new mindset, the more we will be able to see the beginning and becoming of the human phenomenon the way Teilhard sees it.

One of the unique qualities of being a human is that we can change our perspective. We can adopt a new mindset. Unlike animals, we can choose to look at our life and our surroundings from new perspectives. Using each new perspective (or mapping, or endomorphism), we can look at the same object or event in different ways so that it "lights up and yields its secrets" (32, 4). The more perspectives we can take as we look at an object or event, the richer and more all-encompassing the object or event appears. This is the power of having "new eyes" and using new mappings.

Unlike animals, we humans can also mentally follow stages in the construction of a new house *in process* and identify what is being built and how close it may be to completion. With our minds we can also mentally follow many other kinds of structures and the processes by which they are organized, for instance, the writing of a book, the development of a mathematical system, the analysis of a military strategy, the expansion of a business organization, or the investigation of a complex biological process. These are processes an animal cannot comprehend. In *Phenomenon*, Teilhard invites us to watch the process of the human phenomenon emerging and to recognize its uniqueness.

Teilhard identifies this *ability to see structure and process* as a "biological property of thought" (33, 4). By "biological," he refers to the neurological complexity of the human brain (a biological organ). This more complex brain is a physical prerequisite of human thought. Thus, humans are able to think abstractly and identify form, process, and structure.

Teilhard is interested in teaching us the importance of this "biological property" of our minds because we humans are influential agents at the center of a material universe in transformation. The universe, and especially Earth, is "under construction" by the forces of evolution (33, 4). Whether we realize it or not, from now on we humans are workers partly responsible for that evolutionary construction and for the future of our species and of Earth itself.

The Seven "Senses" of Your New Eyes (33–34, 5)

Teilhard presents a lesson in "seeing." We all know that if you wish to develop ability in playing a musical instrument, there are certain skills, exercises, and techniques you must develop and practice daily. For Teilhard, if you wish to develop your capacity to see with new eyes, there are certain activities you must practice daily. He calls them seven "senses." He lists them in order of difficulty. The first few senses are relatively easy to practice, but remain essential, never to be skipped in daily practice, even as you develop your abilities in the more difficult senses. Here are the seven senses. I have added some suggestions for practicing each one.

1. *Sense of space.* To develop this sense, you would practice recognizing and identifying size, patterns, movement, direction, especially the "immensity in greatness and smallness" in things (33, 5). You might sit by a window where you can look outdoors or turn around and observe objects in your room. To develop the "sense of space,"

begin by identifying and comparing sizes, spaces, distances, and so on. You can easily practice this skill wherever you happen to be.

2. *Sense of time.* Here, you would practice recognizing past, present, future, duration, and change. You may think of objects around you or people in your family or community. What does "past" mean to a child five years old? What in your life has endured and what has just passed by? Take any technological object, like the telephone or automobile, and ask how it has changed and metamorphosed over time.

3. *Sense of number.* Here, you practice recognizing and using all forms of counting, measuring, and repetition. For example, you may make a list of twenty things in your life that involve number or measurement. How many kinds of measurement are used in a kitchen? In a clothes closet? In an automobile? In school? At church?

4. *Sense of proportion.* Here, you practice making comparisons and contrasts in size, shape, time, rhythm, scale, dimension, and number—from the infinitesimal to the immense, from the simple to the complex. When you are in your kitchen, see if you can identify five or ten shapes that may also be found in your bedroom or office or bathroom. Estimate the number of minutes or hours you spend in each room in your home. Which room do you enter and exit most in a day? Which the least? Which doors do you open and close the most? The least?

5. *Sense of quality.* Here, instead of focusing on number, quantity, similarity, or proportion, you look for qualities of grace, taste, creativity, artistry, richness, sophistication, distinctiveness. Among your family and friends, name one who manifests "grace" or gracefulness. Another who manifests "taste" in food, clothing, music, or literature. Another whom you would call "creative." Another who exhibits "sophistication." And one whom you would label as "distinctive."

6. *Sense of development.* Here, the task is to recognize novelty, inner movements, ripeness, maturation, complexity, the stages of development of different individuals. You

also learn to identify and name those emergent properties in each new stage that were not there before. It would be helpful if you could recognize stages of maturity in yourself. If you are a parent or grandparent or a schoolteacher, you may be able to notice stages of inner growth happening to the children in your life. Can you list some properties or abilities or sensitivities that you notice in a certain child today that weren't present a year ago? The more emerging abilities you can name, the better.

7. *Sense of the organic.* Here, you focus on recognizing how things are interconnected and interdependent, how union happens, what happens to the whole as the parts change, and what happens to the parts when the whole changes. Notice how a family dynamic changes when one member departs (for college, for a job in another town, or because of divorce or death). What happens to the family as a *whole* as one or more of its members are separated from it? What happens to the members who remain? Have they changed or developed new abilities or responsibilities? What occurred to change the individuals who left the whole?

Some Observations on Teilhard's Seven Senses

Note, for example, that the emergence of this seventh *sense of the organic* happens only among humans. With the sense of the organic, humanity finally becomes ecologically conscious of issues important to the planet such as global warming, species extinctions, the detrimental effects of fossil fuels, carbon footprints, renewable energy, and the need for the conservation of natural resources. Also, in our day, people have come to realize that they as individuals are organically related to humanity as a whole, that humanity is organically related to all life on Earth, and that all life on Earth is organically related to the evolving universe.

You may also notice that these seven senses of "seeing" emerged into awareness throughout Earth's history probably in much the same seven-step sequence as Teilhard presents them. Many animals develop ability in the first three "senses" (time, number, and proportion). Some of the primates develop a sense of quality and a sense of development. Humans uniquely enjoy developing the sense of the organic.

In much the same way that professional musicians continue to develop skill and subtlety in playing their musical instruments, people can continually develop their expertise in using each of the seven senses. As human culture advances and scientific awareness continues to improve, we humans will continue to refine our ability to use each of these seven senses of seeing. In fact, we need never stop improving our ability in each.

These seven senses, says Teilhard, "illuminate our vision" (34, 5). Each provides a different spotlight or perspective on the whole human phenomenon. All seven ways of seeing need to be activated and practiced for us to be able to "see" as fully as Teilhard invites us to see.

As we open up and develop each of the seven senses, the environment appears differently. It's as if each emerging sense provides a different mapping of the human phenomenon, each mapping overlaying the ones before it. These are *endomorphisms*. With each new mapping, we make new connections, notice new relationships, and identify emerging processes that we never noticed before.

As we develop these seven senses, they enable us to see more comprehensively what is all around us. Moreover, we discover that we are being transformed *within*. In a very real sense, we are no longer who we used to be. Our "new eyes" invite us to become something new within. We may still appear the same on the outside or in a photograph, but we have been transformed within. We have undergone a *metamorphosis*.

Anthropogenesis and Cosmogenesis

Teilhard introduces three terms (34, 5), which he invented, that he will use frequently throughout his text:

- *cosmogenesis*
- *anthropogenesis*
- *geogenesis*

15

All three terms end in *-genesis*. The word *genesis* refers to something in process, something that had a conception and a birth, and continues going through stages of development to maturity. When you see a word ending in *-genesis*, think of "beginning and becoming."

Many academic names end in *-ology*, such as sociology, psychology, and physiology. The ending *-ology* means "the study of." Just as *anthropology* is the study of (*-ology*) different aspects and qualities of humanity, *anthropogenesis* specifically refers to humanity's developmental or evolutionary process, its beginning and becoming. When we study the entire human phenomenon in light of its beginning and becoming, we recognize that the species *Homo sapiens* had a time of conception and a time of birth. It is presently growing and developing, but it has not yet reached its maturity or fulfillment. So, in the domain of anthropogenesis, we may talk about the infancy of humanity, its childhood, its adulthood, its function in the world, its responsibilities, its challenges, and its fulfillment.

Similarly, *cosmology* is the study of (*-ology*) the universe, its makeup, its contents, its movements, its history, its diversity, and so forth. *Cosmogenesis* refers specifically to the universe's developmental or evolutionary process. So, someone interested in *cosmogenesis* would talk about the conception, birth, and infancy of the universe, the laws that govern evolution and how they function at different stages in the evolutionary process.

The conception, birth, and infancy of Earth (*geogenesis*) reveal a chronological sequence of emerging properties. A person studying geogenesis would be interested primarily in the *sequence of appearance* of life-forms on Earth and the *emerging properties and abilities* of each new life-form. For example, notice that rocks came first; but a rock cannot move by itself. Plants came next; though a plant or vine can move by itself, it must remain connected to its roots. An animal may move freely from place to place but must remain grounded. A bird can also move through the air by flying. A primate can learn to recognize as many as a few hundred words. Only a human can write a book.

Humanity's development (*anthropogenesis*) cannot be separated from Earth's development (*geogenesis*), and Earth's development cannot be separated from the universe's development (*cosmogenesis*). Teilhard's *Phenomenon* is a study of all three processes as they are nested within each other.

Cosmogenesis focuses on the universe in its beginnings and process of becoming what it is meant to be.

Geogenesis focuses on planet Earth in its beginnings and process of becoming what it is meant to be.

Anthropogenesis focuses on humanity in its beginnings and process of becoming what it is meant to be.

It is important to grasp the difference between geology and geogenesis as well as the difference between anthropology and anthropogenesis. Perhaps it will be easier to talk first about an apple pie.

Suppose a customer has finished eating dinner in a restaurant and desires a piece of apple pie for dessert. The customer is interested only in the finished product. He or she wishes to eat a piece of the apple pie displayed on the pastry shelf. When a slice of pie is delivered to the table, the customer may focus on the makeup and quality of the crust, the contents of the filling, the taste of the pie, and the spices flavoring it. In the examination of the pie, the customer is practicing "pie-ology."

However, the baker in the kitchen practices "pie-genesis." To get the pie ready for eating, the baker must focus on the pie's "process of becoming what it was meant to be," from start to finish. The baker needs to be familiar with every step of the pie's genesis, from collecting and assembling the pie's ingredients, to measuring the ingredients into a mixing bowl, rolling out the crust, preparing the filling, adding the sweetener and spices, and baking the pie at the proper temperature for the exact amount of time.

Each person or company that provides the pie's ingredients—flour, baking powder, butter, apples, cinnamon, and so on—is focused only on providing the specific ingredients for which they are responsible. Another company made the pie dish, another manufactured the stove, the local power company provides the electricity. None of these people or companies—only the baker—is focused on the "genesis" (or "becoming") of the pie. Only the baker knows how to carry out the process needed to ensure that the pie will become the delicious dessert it was meant to be.

Now, apply this to *anthropogenesis*. Teilhard was aware that many different branches of science study the "ingredients" of humanity—biological, chemical, physical, social, psychological, and so forth.

These scientists are focused only on providing data and information about the specific "ingredients" of the human phenomenon for which they are responsible. None of these traditional sciences is focused on the genesis of humanity, that is, humanity's process of becoming what it is meant to become.

Teilhard wants us to learn how to focus on *the whole human phenomenon in its process*, much like the baker focuses on the whole apple pie in its process of becoming what it is meant to be.

You may argue that the baker enjoys, ahead of time, a clear picture of what the apple pie should look like when it is done. But no one knows what humanity should look like when it has fully matured. Teilhard believes he knows the direction humankind is going. He knows that some scientists believe that humanity's process is purely random and has no clear direction, purpose, or completion. They would not acknowledge such a reality as Teilhard's *anthropogenesis*.

Teilhard suggests that such scientists may have assumed randomness without having studied the long process humanity has been going through in its genesis and gestation. He would say that those scientists have not yet looked at humanity as a process—in the comprehensive way a baker would look at making an apple pie.

Teilhard's New Science

In a very real sense, Teilhard is proposing the creation of a new science called *anthropogenesis*. Graduates in the field of anthropogenesis would become like "bakers" of the human race. With his "new eyes," Teilhard, the first anthropogenesist, discovered that humanity has been clearly in a process of "becoming what it was meant to become" for billions of years.

The list of the most basic "ingredients" for humanity (oxygen, water, metals, and minerals) was being assembled from the first moments of the Big Bang. These moments marked the start of *cosmogenesis* as well as *anthropogenesis*. Other necessary ingredients for humanity's recognizable appearance were being prepared as our planet Earth developed (*geogenesis*), specifically in the emergence of cellular life. With the appearance of the primates, the "baking" process of humanity was well underway. By then, the pie was already in the oven.

In observing this process over eons of time, Teilhard begins to recognize and identify some "genesis" laws that are not measurable by a yardstick or a clock, but only by new forms of measurement, *complexity*, and *consciousness*. Teilhard uses these two new forms of measurement throughout *Phenomenon*.

In *Phenomenon*, Teilhard is trying to get scientists to look at the human phenomenon in the way a baker looks at preparing and baking an apple pie. His new way of looking at natural history focuses not on ingredients, structure, makeup, or functions of a human being, but at the *process* that humanity (as a collective living reality) has been going through since the Big Bang. As Teilhard discovers laws of genesis that govern evolution, it becomes evident to him that humanity is developing in a clearly recognizable direction. This direction can be identified by using the measuring tools of complexity and consciousness.

In re-envisioning natural history as a genesis, *Phenomenon* becomes, in effect, the first textbook in the science of anthropogenesis. Calling *Phenomenon* a "textbook" provides a simple and easy way to describe it. A textbook typically offers a structured way of learning about a subject. A textbook introduces a student into a new way of thinking. It provides a new mapping of some areas of reality that are the focus of study. It enriches consciousness. We might wish that Teilhard had included "Questions and Exercises" at the end of each chapter to help his "students" more fully grasp the material they have just read.

A branch of knowledge is considered more valuable insofar as it can be used to enrich other fields of study. For example, arithmetic is truly valuable, since it is a basic mental skill that enriches many other fields of study such as mathematics, physics, engineering, architecture, economics, accounting, statistics, music, and other fields that use measurement or computation.

But why would someone take a class in anthropogenesis? Teilhard believed that his "textbook" in anthropogenesis would be useful to people in the physical sciences as well as the social and psychological sciences. He saw anthropogenesis as especially valuable for enriching and providing a new mapping for the fields of philosophy, religion, and spirituality. This is one reason I have chosen to show how *Phenomenon* provides knowledge and insight to enrich spirituality. Or, as a mathematician might express it, "*Phenomenon* provides a new endomorphism (mapping) for spirituality."

When *Phenomenon* was first published, scientists in different fields read it without the necessary "new eyes." Each one read it with "-ology eyes" that they had developed as biologists, physicists, chemists, sociologists, psychologists, and so on (32, 6). Only with genesis-recognizing eyes would his scientific readers "get" what he was saying.

To begin Teilhard's course in anthropogenesis, the first challenge is to develop "new eyes." That is why "seeing"—and thinking—in Teilhard's way is so important.

Teilhard would say that until now scientists and philosophers have focused on anthropology and cosmology. He is interested in getting them to recognize the fields of *anthropogenesis* and *cosmogenesis*. When they look with "new eyes" at the human phenomenon, they will recognize that anthropogenesis tells a story of the human phenomenon more comprehensively than any other individual science.

Spiritual Implications

As a Jesuit priest, Teilhard's spirituality was shaped by the *Spiritual Exercises* of Ignatius Loyola, the founder of the Society of Jesus (the Jesuits). Ignatius lived in an age when, for a Christian, the goal of the spiritual life was to "avoid sin, save one's soul, and get to heaven." To do this, you were to learn *to love yourself and your neighbor* the way God loves you, unconditionally.

For Teilhard, the goal of the spiritual life is much larger than saving our individual souls. He realizes that God has a larger plan—a cosmic project. Teilhard called it cosmogenesis, geogenesis, and anthropogenesis. God intends for us humans to work on that project while we are alive on Earth. *Phenomenon* describes the evolutionary plan that Teilhard discovered. God's project calls for the human race as a whole to keep evolving in awareness of its purpose. God's project invites us to use all our compassion, creativity, and ingenuity to transform the entire planet with unconditional love.

Each of us in our lifetime has a purpose to fulfill in God's project. For humanity to fulfill the greater purpose of transforming the planet in love, we, individually and collectively, need to learn to see the world the way God sees it and *to love the whole world* (the cosmos) the way God loves it. In our day, in ways that St. Ignatius could never have grasped, God wants us to be involved in creating the future of anthropogenesis and geogenesis.

Teilhard's Foreword

To accomplish this transformation of the world, we need to develop a new set of spiritual exercises. Its first stage would involve "learning to see" as Teilhard describes it in the foreword. To keep anthropogenesis moving forward in the right way today, Teilhard encourages us as part of our metamorphosis to develop his "seven senses." He sees them not only as scientific exercises but also as spiritual exercises to be integrated into our spiritual lives. If we practice Teilhard's seven senses, we begin to see, appreciate, and integrate into our consciousness an ever-enlarging horizon of experiences that we may never have noticed before.

For Teilhard, the whole of life—including its spiritual dimensions—lies in that verb "to see."[4] Teilhard would tell you that he developed the ability to see what God is doing in the world by studying the phenomenon of the human family from its earliest beginnings. He developed "new eyes" not from his theological textbooks, though they provided hints on how and where to look. He learned about the kingdom of God from studying humanity in its evolving procession. He studied humanity's development not merely biologically, but also in its mental and social dimensions, especially in the growth of human reflective thought and consciousness. He learned to see using all seven levels.

What does "learning to see" mean in the spiritual life? If we measure the development of animals by their increasing ability to recognize and interpret their physical surroundings, shouldn't we measure the development of spiritual maturity in people by their increasing ability to recognize and see spiritual events in their surroundings?

Jesus said again and again that the kingdom of heaven is at hand; it is operating dynamically here and now in us and all around us. Teilhard shows us how to *see* this divine project—how to recognize and acknowledge God's activity and involvement happening all around us.

The most important reason for us to learn to "see" with our new eyes is that we humans are "the leading shoot of evolution" (36, 7).

Teilhard says that our spiritual challenge is to keep the evolutionary trajectory moving forward toward ever-higher consciousness. In this way, he assures us, we will increase our capacity to live—to deepen and expand our experience of life.

If you develop the new way of seeing that Teilhard proposes, you are going to "fall in love with the universe" as he did. That process will transform your way of relating to God, to other humans, and to the rest of the natural world.

21

If you asked Teilhard what you should do with your life, he would say that, whether you are a scientist or not, whether you are a believer or not, your full-time job—every human's responsibility—is to do everything you can to keep anthropogenesis and geogenesis moving forward.

BOOK ONE

BEFORE
LIFE CAME

Chapter 1

The Stuff of the Universe
(39–71, 11–38)

Warning!

IN *PHENOMENON*, Teilhard is always pointing out what he sees through "his eyes," with his unique vision. In the first moments of the universe, he is observing two major cosmic origins that form the subject matter of his book.

- *Cosmogenesis*, the beginning and becoming of the universe.
- *Anthropogenesis*, the earliest beginnings and becoming of humanity.

Teilhard envisions atoms being formed shortly after the Big Bang,[1] approximately 13.8 billion years ago. For him, the first moments of the universe mark the beginnings, or the first phase, of both cosmogenesis and anthropogenesis. As he pictures the first moments of the universe's birth, he is also "seeing" the moments when humanity was first conceived in the womb of space/time. You will not find his perspective presented in any textbook in physics, cosmology, chemistry, or biology.

Teilhard realizes that some of those very original elements are, in fact, living and acting in his body and brain right now. What is astounding to him is that those same ancient atoms active in his human cortex at this moment enable him to use his mind to look back and reflect upon the very beginnings of the universe.

Teilhard wants you to realize that, at the Big Bang, you are witnessing the first moments in the long genesis and development of humanity—the origins of the stuff of which you and I are ultimately made.

In *Phenomenon*, he writes about being lost in wonder and bewilderment at atomic particles over 13 billion years old finding their purpose in every human on Earth today. Bits of reality as old as creation itself are enabling him—as well as you and me—to think, laugh, climb stairs, drive cars, enjoy music, and worship God. He is in awe that some of these primordial particles are firing neurons in his own cortex as he formulates the next sentence in his manuscript.

The eyes with which he reviews his manuscript are themselves a product of anthropogenesis. Those eyes began their evolution in fish, then reptiles, birds, and animals. His eyes are a result of millions of tiny mutations and adaptations that took place through countless millennia in Earth's development.

When Teilhard talks of "elemental matter," he is talking about the earliest structural beginnings of anthropogenesis. This is the elemental matter—all the bits and pieces of atoms—that eventually contributed to create Teilhard himself, as well as you and me. With Teilhard's eyes, we are ready to explore how we began.

1. Elemental Matter (40–43, *12–14*)

SIMPLEST ELEMENTS

Teilhard reminds us that the reason for pushing a thing's beginnings back into the dim past is to get at its simplest elements. Doing such a search is important when we wish to understand what that thing is made of and where it originated (39, *11*).

For example, a piecrust's main ingredient is flour. The baker may be interested only in tracing the flour back to the supermarket where he purchased it. But that flour came from a wheat field.

The wheat farmer conducts a deeper search. He is concerned with the genesis and gestation of the year's crop that started from wheat seeds that he bought from a catalog. The anthropologist would trace wheat's genesis back even further, to the time, perhaps as far back as six thousand years ago in Europe, where wheat was first domesticated and used in baking. The chemist, digging even deeper into the wheat itself, might analyze the grain down to its basic chemical components of complex carbohydrates. This is how one traces a phenomenon, like piecrust, back to its ultimate origins.

In *Phenomenon*, Teilhard wants to do something similar. He wants to trace the human phenomenon back to its ultimate origins and its fundamental elements—as far back as the time when the universe burst into existence. Teilhard knows what humanity is now. We are over seven billion people busily moving about on Earth, each of us enjoying self-reflective consciousness. Teilhard's project is to trace our human beginnings along the evolutionary journey by which we have arrived at this highly complex and conscious stage. Where and when did the process begin? Of what are we ultimately made (39, *11*)?

The answer is that every cell and atom of our body is made up of particles and atoms that began their existence at the Big Bang. That's where the ingredients for every one of us began—about 13.8 billion years ago. Those were the first moments of anthropogenesis. That's where we all started. What we are made of is far older than dirt. Only by beginning at the beginning can we truly understand the gestation process that got us to "here and now."

In his study of the human phenomenon, Teilhard wants to begin with *elemental matter*, the first "stuff" of which we are made.

In his text, Teilhard clearly admits that he is not a professional physicist or chemist. He is only a geologist or, as he calls himself, a "naturalist" (39, *11*). As a curious naturalist, he keeps up with scientific studies in many fields. Because of reported scientific discoveries, he says, he can assert three facts about elemental matter. He writes, "The stuff of tangible things [matter] reveals itself with increasing insistence as radically particulate yet essentially related, and lastly, prodigiously active" (40, *12*).

More simply, he is saying that matter manifests in three ways, as (1) *plurality*, (2) *unity*, and (3) *energy*. These are the three earliest "faces of matter." Because they are matter's "faces" they make their *appearance* and can be studied *as a phenomenon*. A phenomenon is something we can observe. Thus, the important word *phenomenon* in his book's title. We are *observing* the earliest origins of humanity.

It is important to remember the names of these three faces of matter—*plurality*, *unity*, and *energy*. Teilhard will show how these three faces are manifested again and again at each level of growing complexity, as seen on Earth. Whenever Teilhard talks about *plurality*, *unity*, and *energy* in *Phenomenon*, he is not talking abstractly the way physicists and chemists do. The three faces are "observable" phenomena. He is observing and highlighting a consistent basic pattern in the universe. Later, at different evolutionary stages, he may call these three faces by different names. But, despite the names he uses, those faces of matter will still be variations of plurality, unity, and energy.

Later, in book 3, Teilhard will show how, billions of years after the Big Bang, these same three will become the three "faces of humanity." In some ways we humans turn out to be not very different from elemental matter in our own expressions of plurality, unity, and energy.

WHAT TEILHARD KNEW AND WHAT HE DIDN'T KNOW

Before we jump into his analysis of the three faces of matter, recall that Teilhard had finished his *Phenomenon* manuscript by 1940. Since then, science has accumulated much knowledge about the origins of the universe and planet Earth.

For example, Teilhard's text is vague and rather ambiguous about how the universe grew from its starting point to look like what it now has become. Reading his text, we can see that he favored describing cosmic development as an evolutionary process (47n, 17n). This was a daring position, because almost every cosmologist of the 1920s and 1930s preferred to depict the universe in an "eternal steady state," where the orbits of all planets, stars, and galaxies were fixed from the beginning and would remain unchangeable forever. The idea that the universe began as an explosive singularity initiating an evolutionary process of continual change seemed abhorrent to cosmologists at that time.

In 1949, a decade after Teilhard finished *Phenomenon*, British astronomer Fred Hoyle first used the term *Big Bang* as a humorous, and some say cynical, way of describing how the universe came into existence. Today, the Big Bang theory is what virtually every physicist and astronomer believes.

As far as contemporary science now knows, nothing in the cosmos operates in an "eternally steady state." We realize that stars, like our Sun, are born and die. Some depart in a final burst of blindingly bright energy called a nova. Others are sucked into powerful sewer-like black holes. These dark cosmic vacuum cleaners wait patiently near the centers of each galaxy to devour unfortunate stars that approach too closely, only to disappear forever. We now know that nebulae are the cosmic mothers that give birth to new stars in the universe—at the rate of about one every three minutes. These stellar children then turn around and gradually drain their mother nebula of all energy.

According to current theory—Teilhard knew only the basics of it—at the first moment of space/time, the Big Bang spewed out numberless subatomic particles. Among those particles, Teilhard would know of protons, neutrons, electrons, and photons. Since his day, physicists have identified dozens more elementary subatomic particles, some probably existing even in the earliest days of the universe.

In addition, Teilhard knew nothing about so-called *dark matter* and *dark energy*. Scientists estimate that these two elements make up over 90 percent of the known universe. Even our highly advanced detection technologies have not yet been able to see, capture, or analyze either of these two omnipresent yet elusive elements.

For Teilhard's purposes in *Phenomenon*, however, it is enough to know that every cell of our human body is made up of trillions of atoms, molecules, chemical compounds, and cells, each of which is built primarily of protons, neutrons, and electrons. To truly understand the phenomenon of humanity, says Teilhard, it is essential to understand these subatomic particles. They are elemental matter. We need to know how they act and how they interact, because it turns out that we humans are like them and act like them. The three faces of matter are

- *plurality*
- *unity*
- *energy*

Plurality is the first commonality, the first "face" of matter.

Plurality (40–41, 12)

In this first subheading, "Plurality," Teilhard highlights the profoundly "particulate" nature of ordinary human experience. We humans are plural—billions of us—like the first particles. We also think of the world as plural, as made up of countless distinct elements. We tend to see things as separate and individuated—from raindrops and snow-flakes to grains of sand and kernels of corn, from billions of individual animals walking our planet to trillions of individual stars orbiting in our galaxy. *Plurality.*

Many scientists focus on plurality—and stop there. They seem to delight in breaking things down into their ultimate individual parts. In their laboratories, scientists persist in cutting up even things that seem to be indivisible. They keep subdividing the simplest tangible things into their more microscopic elements—like chemical compounds into molecules, molecules into atoms, and atoms into subatomic particles. The word *atom* really means "indivisible." Yet, particle physicists have dissected the atom, predicting, finding, and naming a staggering number of subatomic particles. *Plurality.*

Teilhard sums up this issue of plurality and microscopic diversity. He writes,

> Bewildering in its multiplicity and its minuteness, the sub-stratum of the tangible universe is in an unending state of disintegration [able to be broken down into smaller and smaller elements] as it goes downward. (41, *12*)

Unity (41–42, 12–13)

The plurality of elements in a human body at the atomic and subatomic levels is far beyond our everyday human experience. When we look at the ordinary things around us, we don't see atomic particles, molecules, or cells. As we grasp reality with our senses, we see wholes. We experience hearing a dog bark, kicking a stone, smelling fresh-mown grass, gazing at the moon, and biting into a slice of pizza.

Our sense experience is important. It tells us that there is more to the countless miniscule particles than their individuality, their par-ticulateness. What is far more evident is that *individual particles keep joining together to form connections and unions* (42, *12*). They become dogs, stones, grass, and pizzas. Individual particles forming wholes is a clear pattern. Things have been connecting and joining together from the beginning of the universe. It seems to be a kind of law of matter that *individual elements attract other elements in order to join together to form connections.* Teilhard likes to call connections by the French word *unions*. The process of *Attraction leading to Union* is a basic structural pattern in the universe.

For example, early in the universe's history the first union of subatomic particles became atoms of *hydrogen*. In its most basic form, a hydrogen atom is made up of one proton in its nucleus and one electron orbiting around that nucleus. *Helium*, the second element, has two protons and two neutrons in its nucleus and two orbiting electrons.

Everything we see around us seems to be individuated—drops of water, grains of salt, leaves on trees, peas in a pod, and so on—yet each is made up of lesser bits of matter that have been attracted to each other to form a structured *unity*. Subatomic particles do not want to remain separate. They are driven to connect with other subatomic particles to form unions that we call atoms. For Teilhard, this insight—the drive to form unities—is key to understanding everything about the universe. He realizes that *attraction is the most fundamental force in the universe.* Attraction plays a basic role in Teilhard's science of anthropogenesis.

This is Teilhard's powerful insight: *attraction* is the force that built and shaped the universe into what we experience today. Everything wants to keep connecting with something else to form new unities. *Attraction leads to Connection.* The inner drive to form new connections never stops. What can we observe about these new unities in the world of atoms?

HOMOGENEITY

Teilhard notes two characteristics of these various unities or unions (atoms) formed by subatomic particles. They manifest *homogeneity* and *collectivity*. Teilhard identifies in atoms three kinds of homogeneity, that is, *uniformity in basic structure and composition.* He names the three

- *structural homogeneity*
- *specific homogeneity*
- *basic homogeneity*

First, there is a kind of universal or *structural homogeneity* in the basic makeup of every atom in the universe. Each individual atom's structure is similar. That structure includes a nucleus containing protons and neutrons surrounded by orbiting electrons. Every atom in the

31

universe is built like every other atom. It turns out, as we shall see, that such structural homogeneity is manifest at every level of complexity, right up to the human brain. Everyone's brain is similarly structured. We live in a universe of *structural homogeneity*.

Second, Teilhard also recognizes a *specific homogeneity* within each of the hundred or more atoms in the table of chemical elements. For example, every atom of a specific isotope of iron on Earth has the same number of protons and neutrons in its nucleus and the same number of orbiting electrons around that nucleus. *Specific homogeneity* reinforces the emergence of a consistently structured universe. Any atom of hydrogen can substitute for any other atom of hydrogen, since every hydrogen atom is structured identically. Likewise, any atom of helium can substitute for any other atom of helium. Specific homogeneity continues to operate at higher levels. For example, the brains of animals in each species are similarly structured. Brains of dogs are similarly structured. Brains of parrots are similarly structured. Brains of alligators are similarly structured. Brains of laboratory rats are similarly structured. *Specific homogeneity*.

Third, the most *basic homogeneity* is seen in the fact that, among subatomic particles, each proton, neutron, and electron throughout the universe enjoys the same properties as every other proton, neutron, and electron. This sameness means that each proton is potentially interchangeable with every other proton in the universe, every neutron is similarly interchangeable, and so is every electron. *Basic homogeneity* produces a universe whose *elements are continually interchangeable and rearrangeable*. Such a malleable system is essential and sufficient for evolution to occur.

COLLECTIVITY

Collective Unity. The law of Attraction never stops working. The drive to connect and form higher unities does not stop with subatomic particles being attracted to form atoms. It describes only the first of many levels of attraction toward higher degrees of unity. Next comes the drive for atoms to connect in order to form *molecules*, followed by the drive among molecules to form higher unities called *compounds*.

The drive in matter to form ever-higher unities never ceases. This drive to ever-higher unities is another basic principle in Teilhard's anthropogenesis.

Teilhard notes that these collective unities of chemical elements tend to form in two distinct ways:

- *aggregates*, collections of the same chemical element
- *molecules*, combinations of different chemical elements

First, collective unities that are *aggregates may be formed by atoms of identical atomic structure.* For example, a piece of iron contains nothing but atoms of the element iron; a nugget of silver contains nothing but atoms of the element silver; and a carat of gold contains nothing but atoms of the element gold. These nuggets do not get a new chemical name other than their atomic name, such as *iron* (Fe), *silver* (Ag), or *gold* (Au). Nor do they manifest any new property or ability as a collective unity.

Second, other collective unities combine *different chemical elements* and become *molecules,* such as water or table salt. Water is a unity made up of atoms of hydrogen and oxygen, written H_2O. It deserves the new name—*water*—because it possesses properties that neither hydrogen (a gas) nor oxygen (a gas) possess. Water can nourish, lubricate, cleanse, aid cooking, and can morph into ice—or vapor.

Table salt, NaCl, forms a collective unity by combing atoms of sodium (Na) and chlorine (Cl). This combination deserves the new name—*table salt*—because it possesses properties that neither sodium (an abrasive irritant) nor chlorine (a poisonous gas) possesses. Salt can flavor food, season pickles, preserve fish, melt ice, and so on.

Without saying so, Teilhard is laying the groundwork for some basic evolutionary laws, such as the *universal drive of Attraction leading to Connection and unity.* Subatomic particles are attracted to each other to form *atoms.* Atoms of one kind are attracted to atoms of other kinds to form *molecules.* Molecules are attracted to other molecules to form chemical *compounds.*

Teilhard wants us to observe that each new level of union or unity possesses its own *new identity* (42, 13). A molecule of water—a liquid— has its own identity; it is not the identity of hydrogen or of oxygen, both of which by nature are gases. Table salt has its own identity; it is not the identity of sodium, a highly volatile alkali metal that eats away at things; nor is it the identity of chlorine, a poisonous gas.

One can begin to see a universal drive in all things *from Attraction to Connection,* and new identities forming with each new connection.

An obvious result of any connection is that its structure is more complex than the elements that make it up. The new structure possesses new properties and capacities. It also generates energy.

Teilhard recognizes that these three factors—*plurality, unity,* and *energy*—are not separate faces of matter, but closely related. Plurality is driven (or attracted) to form unities with new identities, and unities appear to be nature's way of releasing new energy.

Energy (42–43, 13–14)

The third characteristic of elemental matter is its *energy,* or potential. Teilhard notes that physics offers a simple definition of energy. Energy is "a capacity for action or, more exactly, for interaction" (42, 13). As examples of a capacity to action, water can lubricate; table salt can flavor food; carbon dioxide gives life to plants and trees; carbon in petroleum helps to power cars and trucks; iron nourishes your blood; calcium and magnesium energize your brain; oxygen feeds your lungs.

We know that matter has energy stored up within it according to Einstein's famous equation $E = mc^2$, where E stands for energy, m stands for matter, and c stands for the speed of light. The most familiar validation of Einstein's equation was in the development of nuclear energy. The atomic bomb proved that there is a tremendous amount of explosive *energy* locked up in the physical *matter* of one uranium atom.

However, the same formula tells us that each atom possesses only a limited amount of energy. In doing their work, atoms and molecules use up their energy and eventually become inert, that is, they are unable to do any more work.

As Teilhard reflects on the three main points of this first section—*plurality, unity,* and *energy*—he expresses his wonder at what they imply. He is awed at the consistency in the structure of individual atoms and molecules (*plurality*), and the wide variety of connections that these particles make (*unity*), as well as the different kinds of abilities or uses each new union possesses and the diversity of each union's potential (*energy*).

He notes too that physics predicts a disappointing future for our planet. Physicists say that all elemental matter is eventually going to become inert, because we and nature itself will eventually consume all Earth's energy. They paint a pessimistic picture of our long-term future (43, *14*).

But Teilhard sees hope as we look at *total matter*.

2. Total Matter (43–46, *14–16*)

DIFFERENT PERSPECTIVES

Until now, Teilhard has been talking about microscopic bits of matter—particles, atoms, and molecules. Now he wants to put *all that matter together*, the whole of matter, the biggest picture of the early universe. He looks at the entire physical universe all at once as "total matter." To do this involves using panoramic vision. For Teilhard, learning how to develop new perspectives and shift perspectives are necessary skills.

For example, suppose my wife and I are buying a house for our family. I ask several inspectors to come through the house. Each expert walks around focused on one aspect of the house. The carpenter looks at the condition of the wooden framework, the plumber inspects the pipes, the electrician tests the wiring, the roofer evaluates the shingles, and so on. Each one looks at what they are trained to look at. Each gives me a report from their different professional perspectives, which is certainly helpful.

Then I ask my wife to make an evaluation of the house from her perspective. Her viewpoint as she walks through the house is totally different from those of the experts. She looks at the house and property *as a living space for our family*. She observes the layout of the kitchen, the big backyard, the view from our bedroom window, the size of the closets, the convenient location of the washer/dryer, and so forth. She brings a new point of view to the house. She looks at it as a home, *as a whole, as a totum.*

Similarly, Teilhard reported how the world looks through the eyes of various specialists—such as the physicist, the chemist, the biologist, the anthropologist, and the astronomer. Now, he wants to look at the early *universe as a whole*. He is shifting to a different and all-inclusive perspective. Teilhard is observing the beginnings of humanity the way my wife looks our new home.

In this section, Teilhard again develops the three elements—*plurality*, *unity*, and *energy*. Instead of looking at the elemental forms of atoms, molecules, and compounds, Teilhard refocuses and examines the *plurality*, *unity*, and *energy* of the universe as *a single, immense interrelated reality*. He studies the totality of the elements in the universe and in our planet *as one whole*. For him, the whole universe is "the only real indivisible." As Teilhard puts it, "Considered in its physical, concrete reality, the stuff of the universe cannot divide itself but, as a kind of gigantic 'atom,' it forms in its totality...the only real indivisible" (43, 14). And because of the "wholeness of its whole," it is a *system*, a *totum*, and a *quantum*. What was *plurality* in the previous section here becomes *system*, what was *unity* there becomes a *totum* (whole), and what was *energy* there becomes a *quantum*. They represent the same "three faces" of matter, but at a higher level of complexity.

The universe as a whole is recognized as a *system* because it is made up of a great number of interacting parts (*plurality*) that all work together for a shared purpose.

It becomes a *totum* (or a new whole) because as a whole (*unity*) the universe possesses many qualities and functions that none of its parts possesses.

It becomes a *quantum* (with widely variable sources of energy) because, as a whole, it can perform new kinds of action (new *energy*) in transforming itself and the parts within it. Thus,

- *plurality* is now expressed as *system*
- *unity* is now expressed as *totum*
- *energy* is now expressed as *quantum*

Teilhard looks at each of the three aspects, or "faces," of this whole, as *system*, *totum*, and *quantum*.

The System (Its Interactive Parts) (43–44, 14–15)

When we look at *plurality*—separate elements—taken together as a whole and those elements interacting among themselves, we observe a *system* at work. For example, an automobile has many parts that work together to provide a system of transportation. A computer has many parts that work together to provide a system to access and process information. A human body has many parts that work together to form a person.

In this section, instead of looking at the *plurality* of elements in a house—its separate dimensions of plumbing, electrical wiring, roofing, walls, foundation, woodwork, and so forth—we would be looking at them all together as a *system*, that is, as interacting to provide a place for a family to live, love, and grow.

Here, instead of looking at the *plurality* of individual physical elements in a human child—such as skin, bones, blood, nerves, eyes, ears, nose, and organs—we would be looking at them all together, and would see a human *system* that integrates all of its individual, interacting parts. This whole is the child that the parents need to care for and nurture.

We need to look at planet Earth in the same way. We have already seen how scientists in different fields analyze the different elemental *pluralities* of Earth—soil, seas, forests, mountains, lakes, plants, trees, animals, insects, flowers, birds, fish, reptiles, atmosphere, weather patterns, and humans. Teilhard says we also need to take the perspective of looking at Earth as a *single system* and focus on how everything is interacting and working together. This is the viewpoint of *geogenesis*, the evolutionary "becoming" of Earth, and *cosmogenesis*, the "becoming" of the universe (cosmos) itself.

These are the eyes Teilhard wants us to use when looking at any system, whether it is a house, a child, a city, our planet, or the universe. He wants us to see its interdependent parts and observe how they interact *on behalf of the system*.

He also wants us to learn to recognize ever-larger systems and the interactions of their parts. For example, our Sun with its many orbiting planets and moons form a *solar system*. All the stars interacting in the Milky Way galaxy form a *galactic system*. All the hundreds of billions of galaxies interacting in the universe form a *universal system*.

While physicians, technicians, and scientists are focused on more specialized individual systems like plumbing systems in a building, or nervous systems in a person, Teilhard wants us to begin to comprehend larger and larger systems. This is the only way to see the cosmic whole (*totum*).

All parts of the universe are completely interdependent upon all the rest.

Each element of the cosmos is positively woven from all others....All around us, as far as the eye can see, the universe holds together, and only one way of considering it is really possible, that is, to take it as a whole, in one piece. (44, *15*)

THE *TOTUM* (THE WHOLE) (44–45, *15*)

When we looked at *unity* in the first section of this chapter, we identified the basic building blocks—protons, neutrons, and electrons—of every atom in the universe. We focused attention on the anatomy of each single chemical atom. In this section, Teilhard wants us to look at all those numberless atoms in the universe as they interact together, as a whole (*totum*) that has been forming and transforming itself since the Big Bang. The universe, he notes, is "something quite other than a mere entanglement of highly-articulated interconnections" (44, *15*). That *totum* is a being that has its own life, its own genesis (*cosmogenesis*). It also has its own processes distinct from any of its parts, its interacting subsystems, and their functions. In Teilhard's science of anthropogenesis, the *totum* reveals the anatomy of a living universe. That *totum* is also developing its own *collective mind*. But the emergence of mind is a topic for a later part of the book.

Teilhard observes another principle. Any *totum* (or whole) *has a unique life—a life of its own*. No individual part of an automobile can provide a system of transportation, only the whole auto can. No individual part of a computer can access the internet, only the whole computer can. No part of your human body can write a letter to a friend. You may claim that it is your arm that writes the letter. Try an experiment: cut your arm off, put some paper and a pen on the desk, and see if your arm by itself can write a letter. No, it is only you—your whole personal system, mind and body, working together (your *totum*)—that can write a letter.

At every level of complexity, Teilhard notes, new wholes are formed. At the microscopic level, each atom forms a new whole whose parts are protons, neutrons, and electrons. Each molecule forms a new whole whose parts are a combination (or union) of different atoms. Compounds are even more complex new wholes. They are combinations of different molecules. At the macroscopic level, each solar system forms a new whole, an interactive combination of planets and their moons. Galaxies form interactive combinations of billions of solar systems.

Teilhard points out that, at each level, the new wholes being formed take on many different combinations and appearances. The table of chemical elements identifies over a hundred different atomic structures. Each of these wholes has its specific qualities and uses. These chemical elements, joined together in various ways, form countless combinations of *molecules*, such as water, table salt, aspirin, alcohol, aspartame, caffeine, plus all the carbohydrates in our food. And none of these molecular wholes duplicates another in its structure, abilities, and functions. Each is unique.

Certain molecules bond together as *compounds*, such as acetone, ammonia, chloroform, glucose, lactose, and millions of other composites. None of these different compounds imitates any other. They all qualify as wholes in themselves. Yet, they are codependent upon each of their parts for their continued existence. And, they are all inextricably interrelated within the *totum* that is the universe. Moreover, they all possess energy and abilities. Ammonia has its abilities, which are different from the abilities of chloroform. Caffeine is used to stimulate, while aspartame is used to sweeten.

All these energies and abilities interact with each other in the *totum* and form a coherent symphony of movement and energy that Teilhard calls "the quantum."

THE QUANTUM (45–46, 16)

In the previous section, *energy* was expressed as the ability of atoms to act and interact, among themselves. We now look at all the atoms in the universe acting in concert. This is energy the way the entire universe *as a whole* expresses it.

Think of an orchestra performing a symphony. Each musician has a specific part to play and certain kinds of energy to contribute to the functioning of the whole. When all the instrumental sounds and melodic movements are coordinated into the single continuous yet ever-changing musical performance of a symphony, we experience the *quantum*—many sources of energy interacting with a shared purpose.

Teilhard asks us to observe the universe's quantum. This is the energy put out by the whole universe as it continually interacts to express itself and transform itself. *This is the energy driving the evolutionary process*. It is a different kind of energy from the energy of elemental matter, the matter (*m*) defined in Einstein's formula, $E = mc^2$.

Teilhard says that to identify energy expended in the universe's quantum process, we need to *redefine the concept of energy*—as well as energy's availability and its source (45, 16).

Energy—Redefining Energy

Teilhard begins by explaining how he redefines energy. If we consider any single atom with its nucleus and orbiting electrons, its energy has a microscopically small sphere of action. Now, says Teilhard, "let's turn our attention to the entirety [the *totum*] of these infinitesimal centers [atoms] which share the universal sphere among themselves" (46, 16). Each atom on Earth expresses its own unique effects, but acting in concert—all atoms acting together—express themselves "in a global capacity for action" (46, 16). They act, not as single musicians, but together as an orchestra creating a single complex musical self-expression. The orchestra releases a more powerful source of energy than the sum of all the individual musicians by themselves. It possesses a source of energy that is uniquely its own.

For example, we could watch each of the symphony musicians in their own homes practicing his or her part of the symphony. The oboe part sounds different from the trumpet part, and the notes the violins play are different from those assigned to the flutes. Each instrument creates its own energy. Yet only when all the musicians come together to perform the symphony do we experience the orchestra's unique energy and power. We experience the *symphony*. This more powerful expression of energy comes from the *interactions* of the parts. It is an energy that emerges uniquely from the whole. The whole—and only the whole—can provide the source for this new energy.

As individual humans, among billions on Earth, we each experience ourselves expending energy in ways similar to each orchestral musician. Each human being, just as each performer, has unique capacities and abilities to act and interact to express energy. Together, the human family can also act in concert in various smaller or larger groups and organizations, such as families, religious congregations, sports teams, research teams, congressional assemblies, or nations.

We are still learning to live and work together as symphony musicians. We still hit some sour notes. We humans are just learning how to be citizens of Earth, not merely citizens of a nation. Humanity as a *totum* needs to learn to perform like a symphony orchestra, to take action *as humanity itself* and to generate energy *as humanity itself.*

DURATION (46, 16)

This collective quantum of energy—atomic and human, individual and group—takes on its full significance within anthropogenesis, says Teilhard, but only when we realize that *all activity takes time to complete.* This "time to complete" is what Teilhard calls *duration.* Bringing anthropogenesis to its fullest potential is a process that will take a very long time, perhaps millions of years.

Duration may be described as *the amount of time taken to complete a process.* In an evolving universe, duration is an essential quality or dimension to consider (47, 17). Each of us is conscious of duration and we are used to thinking in terms of duration. We know that a symphony is not performed in a minute, nor is a car assembled in an hour. Nor does a child become an adult in a day. Every action consumes time. Every process takes a period of time to complete. Whether an activity takes a millisecond or a millennium to finish its process, it takes time.

Notice how Teilhard's concept of duration changes our perspective on the evolving universe. Evolution is focused less on measuring by clock time and more on measuring by process time (47, 17). For example, measured by clock time, civil law generally defines an adult as a person on his or her eighteenth birthday—or, in some cases, one's twenty-first birthday. Measured by process time (or duration), some people qualify emotionally as adults at fourteen or fifteen, others only at twenty-four or twenty-five. A few remain emotionally stunted and never make it through the process into adulthood. Teilhard's duration refers to this process-time way of measuring.

To understand the genesis of any whole and its activity more fully, Teilhard says, we must include the variable of "time" along with the variable of "space." When we think of the whole (*totum*) and its activity, we can no longer think of its sphere of influence as space by itself. The true milieu of our activity is *space/time* (47, 17). Every activity happens in space, but it also has duration. Any process takes up space, but it also takes up time.

- Physics is a science of space and *clock time.*[2]
- *Anthropogenesis* is a science of space and *process time.*

Only in space/time could there be a cosmogenesis and an anthropogenesis. Anthropogenesis is also a science of phases and development.

Only in space/time can we recognize, identify, and name each new phase of anthropogenesis. During its first phase of oneness, anthropogenesis was characterized by unions of elemental matter—particles and early atoms. Then, anthropogenesis moved into its second phase, interwoven with—yet still hidden within—all the new *wholes* of matter taking shape in space/time, including molecules, mountains, and moons.

SUMMARY

Physicists define energy simply as *the ability of matter to act and interact, to do work.* Their emphasis is on physical action. Teilhard says this definition of energy, even regarding physical matter, needs to be enriched and expanded.

In exploring interactive systems, Teilhard shows that there are other resources of energy, even at the physical level. In showing this, he lays the groundwork for his later exploration of *nonphysical energy.* Examples of expression of nonphysical energy include planning, conceptualizing, organizing, reasoning, choosing, agreeing, supporting, hoping, and so on. In later chapters, he will show that there are vast amounts of nonphysical energy potentially available to humanity, individually and as a whole.

For Teilhard, love, a nonphysical source of energy, is the most pervasive and powerful energy in the universe. He is not ready to prove that claim here, but eventually he wants to show that *the energy of love is prefigured in nonliving, physical matter.*

What he does show in this section is the following:

- Energy is available anywhere and everywhere that an atom of matter happens to be.
- Energy's sphere of action is unlimited, and it can operate anywhere in the universe.
- Energy has multiple sources, not merely fossil fuels and solar power.

- Energy's multiple sources can act in concert to produce new energy and new results.
- Energy needs time (duration) to express itself.

In *Phenomenon*, Teilhard wants to show that energy's ultimate purpose is to drive cosmogenesis and anthropogenesis forward.

Spiritual Implications

These notes on spirituality, placed after major sections of *Phenomenon*, are my personal additions to Teilhard's text. I offer them because I am sure they were present in Teilhard's mind as he wrote his scientific text. As a Christian, he believed that God created the universe and imbued it with the laws of Attraction and Union as well as the various faces of plurality, union, and energy.

When Teilhard describes being lost in wonder and bewilderment at sub-atomic particles from the Big Bang, he is really writing as a mystic standing in the presence of God. He is in awe at the marvelous way that, through the discoveries of science, he has been given a new perspective on the mystery of creation. Science offers a fascinating creation story that the ancient biblical writers could never have imagined, understood, or believed. For Teilhard, the information provided by science is like divine revelation coming to the human race in an entirely new way—not through religious prophets but through scientific research and discovery.

By studying and integrating the discoveries made by scientists over the past two hundred years, Teilhard was able to formulate important insights for our age. To those who read *Phenomenon* as scientists, he offers a new way to look at natural history and the process of evolution. To those who read *Phenomenon* as believers, he offers a new way to convey the divine secret at the heart of the world. And, he wants to share it.

Without saying so, Teilhard invites his readers who are believers to marvel in wonder and amazement at the ultimate structures of reality. On the surface, he is talking about subatomic particles. But with his "eyes" he sees these ancient particles in totally new ways. He is hoping that, through his words, we too will make the unspoken connections he makes. The astonishing fact is that those bits of reality as old as creation itself are enabling you and me today to tell a joke, chat with a neighbor, send a text message, sing a song, and make a grocery list.

He is telling us to put on new eyes and look at the millions of things going on all around us. See the many forms of life that live among us and interact with us. Look and recognize what God has put in motion. Picture beetles and bicycles, cats and computers, dogs and dump trucks, fruit flies and furnaces. Every one of them, like us, is made up of these primordial subatomic particles. In *Phenomenon*, he is offering pages of evolutionary information to stimulate reverence at the fascinating, loving creativity of God's mind.

Most scientists reading *Phenomenon* see Teilhard as re-envisioning and rewriting natural history—a daring task. To those who believe, *Phenomenon* shows how God is guiding creation. For Teilhard, cosmogenesis and anthropogenesis are works of God. They are God's project, God's reason for creating the universe in the first place. Those who know Teilhard realize that, without ever saying so, he is inviting us to recognize how it had to be God who implanted the drive to attraction and connection in those original subatomic particles.

Consider how much we humans are like those first subatomic particles. Just as they were attracted to one another to form connections, we are attracted to one another to form relationships. Like subatomic particles, we humans do not want to remain individuated and alone. We are drawn to form bonds with other things, with plants, animals, and other people. We want to feel connected, to experience deep Union. In traditional spirituality, we are taught how important it is to form a deep connection with God. This is good.

But the drive we feel to build relationships and to form deeper and deeper unions with others is central to the meaning and purpose of all creation.

God is also about energy. God created a universe so that we can discover and utilize the energy potential of Union. The innate drive to form connections is not only in human beings, it is in every smallest particle of matter in the universe. We cannot stop this innate drive to connect, to bond, to join, to stick together. We cannot stop our God-implanted energy to create and transform ourselves and our world that is released in these relationships.

We start by forming simple two-person unions such as best friends or married couples. Some spouses build families. Some friends form larger unions such as clubs or sports teams. Families are attracted together to form neighborhoods. Groups are attracted together to form villages and tribes. Communities unite to form educational centers like schools and universities or religious congregations. Unities possess unique energy and abilities that none of their members possess.

Teilhard might ask you to reflect upon the question, Why do we humans feel attracted to form partnerships with each other? Can it be because of the drive to connect that is active in the subatomic particles living within us?

Teilhard wants us to notice how these new connections or unions among humans have their own special characteristics that distinguish each relationship from its members. A deep relationship may possess abilities that neither of the partners has. A sports team can do things, like execute a play or win a game, which no individual team member can do.

From Teilhard's perspective, God is calling each relationship to serve God's work in the world in a unique way. God calls relationships to be of service to others, just as God calls individuals.

If God's thrust is behind creation and its movements, God's focus is on creating wholes or ever-larger systems. Shouldn't our eyes and interest be focused on learning to recognize and honor the development and potential of ever-larger systems? How would it affect our spirituality if we were to focus our attention on nurturing bigger wholes like humanity or nature, rather than just on our own spiritual growth and salvation?

3. The Evolution of Matter (46–52, 16–21)

In the eighteenth century, when modern physics was in its youth, its scientific goal was "to find a mathematical explanation of the world imagined as a system of stable elements in a closed equilibrium" (46, 16). Since then, science has gone through many developmental stages in its thinking. Today, science recognizes that the universe as a whole and all its parts are in continual transformation. Instead of being fixed and stable in its orbits and cyclic seasons, the universe is continually creating and re-creating its story, its history. Its story is of a whole-in-process.

The universe's story keeps progressing. Cosmogenesis and anthropogenesis both have a future. That future may be dismal or glorious, but it is inevitable. The *totum* (the whole universe) that Teilhard is talking about continues interacting as a system in its inbuilt evolutionary process.

Teilhard wants to study the present state of this whole-in-process from two different scientific perspectives:

- *qualitatively*, in terms of observable appearance
- *quantitatively*, according to identifiable numerical laws

He wants to see what each perspective reveals.

THE APPEARANCE (THE QUALITATIVE PROCESS) (47–50, 17–19)

The most obvious observable phenomenon in the evolution of matter, says Teilhard, manifests as "growing complexity." Amount or level of complexity is one way of describing or measuring a system. Roughly speaking, *the complexity of a system is measured by the sum of its component parts plus the number of their possible interactions.*

Here is an example. A jazz trio has three players (parts) plus a number of ways of interacting. A symphony orchestra may have as many as eighty players and far more ways of interacting than the jazz trio. So, the orchestra operates at a much higher level of complexity than the jazz trio.

In chemistry, this "complexity" phenomenon is clearly seen in the gradual emergence of more and more complexity in the table of chemical elements. As one studies the chemical table, its elements grow in complexity from the simplest atoms of hydrogen to the more and more complex atoms of uranium, polonium, and the like. The same is true in biology. Life first appears as single-celled creatures but, in time, living forms continue to grow evermore complex. The pattern of increasing complexity continues right up to human beings, the most complex organisms we know of. Each person contains trillions of cells.

Complexity is not the same as complicated. Complexity describes a well-ordered system of elements. "Complicated" refers to the intellectual confusion and emotional difficulty one may have in making sense of a collection of elements.

At the same time, we know that, no matter how complex an organism becomes, every atom in that organism is composed of a nucleus (protons and neutrons bonded together) surrounded by orbiting electrons. This consistency in structure is maintained in every single atom, from the simplest hydrogen atom with only one proton in its nucleus to the radioactive atoms with over a hundred protons in the nucleus.

The Law of Complexification

This discovery of the universal consistency of every atom's makeup, says Teilhard, "is the beacon that lights the history of the universe to our eyes" (48, *18*). It also clearly reveals a great law of evolution, the law of *complexification*. That is, the *totum* of matter reveals itself to us as an immense system *in a state of genesis*. It continues to develop by becoming evermore complex, or concentrated in its interactions. "Historically," Teilhard explains, "the stuff of the universe goes on becoming concentrated into ever more [complex] organized forms of matter" (49, *18*). As the universe continues to evolve, new (sub)systems emerging within it become more concentrated, more interactive, and more organized, that is, they grow more complex.

THE NUMERICAL LAWS
(THE QUANTITATIVE PROCESS) (50–52, *19–21*)

First, Teilhard looked at the whole universe *qualitatively* in terms of its observable appearance and identified the law of complexification. Now, he looks at it *quantitatively*, to identify its measurable laws.

From a quantitative perspective, he reminds us of two powerful principles derived from physics:

- *conservation of energy*
- *dissipation of energy*

These two principles describe characteristics of matter that the universe must deal with. They are basic laws in the science of physics.

We use fossil fuels to generate a continual increase in our ability to create technology to meet the expanding needs of evolution. All technical advances require an expenditure of material energy, energy that cannot be recaptured or reused. Wood, coal, petroleum, or propane gas are burned in campfires, furnaces, factories, outdoor grills, or cars. The burning consumes the fuel's energy. As Teilhard puts it,

"Nothing is constructed except at the price of an equivalent destruction" (51, 20).

According to science, the physical world cannot create new energy. There is only so much coal or oil buried beneath the Earth. We can only spend what is available while it lasts. The principle of *conservation of energy* is all about how we use the quantity of fuel available on the planet.

The principle of the *dissipation of energy* is slightly different. It is concerned with what happens to fuel after it is used. The *dissipation law* says that once physio-chemical fuel is used to do work or create a new synthesis, such fuel is used up. It *cannot be reconstituted or reused*, because in being consumed it has become dead ashes or an inert gas. As it is being used, the fuel breaks down into simple components that have little or no energy left in them.

Teilhard says, "From the real evolutionary standpoint, something is finally burned in the course of every [higher] synthesis in order to pay for that synthesis" (51, 20). Evolution has its costs. Furthermore, the quantity of physical fuel we can ever use to do our work was, as it were, "given in the beginning," so we need to conserve it.

But what do these two principles have to do with the progress of evolution?

The two major evolutionary processes—*geogenesis* (the continued development of planet Earth) and *cosmogenesis* (the continued development of the universe)—require great expenditures of physical energy. Evolutionary development on Earth is a necessary but costly operation. Energy from fossil fuels help drive what Teilhard calls the "rocket ship" of evolution. This energy enables a continuous thrust upward that produces innovations in transportation, communication, medicine, and technology.

But, according to the physical laws—the *conservation and dissipation of energy*—it looks like that rocket ship of evolution cannot keep climbing forever. As the last of Earth's existing quantity of fuel is exhausted, the rocket ship seems doomed to fall back to its death.

Although this dismal prediction is inherent in the laws of physics, Teilhard says, there are other resources available to *anthropogenesis* that allow us to be much more optimistic than the physicists. He will show us some of those resources.

Spiritual Implications

Again, here is a sample of how I imagine Teilhard, as a believing Christian, was thinking as he wrote the previous section.

When Teilhard considers the "matter" of our planet and the many laws that govern it, he realizes its personal significance to him. For Teilhard, Christianity, and especially Catholicism, is a religion of matter because God himself became matter in Jesus of Nazareth. Like Teilhard and us, Jesus's body is made up of some of those elementary particles from the Big Bang. When Teilhard looks at the humblest things of Earth—mud, dirt, and rocks—he makes connections to Christ as the incarnation of the Word of God. Most of us do not recognize these connections. Teilhard sees God's self-revelation to us in all forms of matter. For him, in addition to the inspired writings of scripture, physical matter becomes a source of divine revelation. In a book of his essays called *The Future of Man*, Teilhard writes,

> By definition and in essence, Christianity is the religion of the Incarnation: God uniting Himself with the world which He created, to unify it and, in some way, to incorporate it in Himself. To the believer in Christ, the Incarnation reflects the history of the universe.[3]

Objects from our deep human past, especially fossils discovered by paleontologists, are precious to Teilhard. They are ancient forms of matter present to us today as tangible witnesses of God's self-revelation and involvement in the very beginnings of our human story.

Objects from our more recent past reveal how the human story has become richer, more complex, and more conscious of God's continual presence in matter. Icons and statues, relics and bones, incorrupt bodies encased in glass, the blood of martyrs, tombstones and crypts, abbeys and cathedrals, scholarly tomes and sculptures, altars and baptismal fonts. The Eucharist. All reflect God's presence in matter.

Objects from our present civilization, those that are all around us, are continuing expressions of God's self-revelation in matter. At present, matter may be found expressed in art, music, science, architecture, literature, and liturgy. This is matter we can touch, see, hear, taste, and smell. Rituals with swinging censers and the smell of incense, colorful paintings and sensuous sculptures, missals and hymnals, Gregorian chant and pipe organs, colleges and school systems, orphanages and hospitals. Each is made of matter.

For Teilhard, these are family treasures of Christ's family. Each piece of tangible matter offers a revelation of something in our character, something in a faith shared with millions alive today, millions who have gone before, and millions still to come. This is the matter of our story. It is the divine story God is telling us through matter. And it matters.[4] All these tangible things show that the story of matter is moving forward.

Working together, like a symphony, all this matter has released the energy that has helped shape the mind and heart of human life today.

Chapter 2

The *Within* of Things
(53–66, 22–32)

Without and *Within*

I N THIS CHAPTER, Teilhard introduces several new concepts and terms that he continues to use throughout his book. They are essential to "seeing" the genesis of the human phenomenon as he perceives it.

Most importantly, Teilhard begins to use two prepositions as nouns:

- the *without*
- the *within*

For him, everything has a *without* and a *within*. (In Appleton-Weber's new translation, *The Human Phenomenon*, she has chosen to use the words "outside" for *without*, and "inside" for *within*.)

By the *without* of things, Teilhard is referring to their *physical, tangible, visible, dimensions* such as size, shape, weight, density, structure, movement, velocity, and lifespan. By the *within* of things, he is referring to their *inner life*, actions and events that are intangible and invisible to others. For example, as humans, we have a *without*, expressed in our bodies, organs, brains, blood, nervous systems, limbs, movements, and speech. But we also have a *within*, an inner life. Anyone can observe our *without*, but they cannot see our *within*—our thoughts, emotions, daydreams, plans, choices, and so on.

We know that plants and animals also have an inner life, though not self-reflective as ours. For anyone who doubts that plants have a *within*, I recommend an older but marvelous book by Peter Tompkins and Christopher Bird, *The Secret Life of Plants: A Fascinating Account of the Physical, Emotional, and Spiritual Relations between Plants and Man.*

In this chapter, Teilhard goes beyond affirming the *within of plants.* He argues that just about *everything that exists* has a basic *within*, though it may not be as evident as it is in animals and humans. It is quite difficult, but possible, for us to imagine that a rock has a *within*, or that a lake has a *within*, or that an automobile, a musical instrument, and a shoe has a *within*. Teilhard pushes us much deeper. He wants to show that even each cell, each molecule, and each atom has a *within*.

For example, look at each atom. Its electrons are spinning around a nucleus. That is its *without*. But physicists tell us that the protons and neutrons within the nucleus are holding themselves together using what physicists call the "strong nuclear force." That invisible expression of energy is a hint of its *within*.

The concept of *within* is central to Teilhard's thought. It offers him another way of looking at the universe. He uses the *within* of things to trace a fresh evolutionary path and process that science has never considered. For him, the *within* reveals the "rest of the story," the "inside story" of evolution. It is the story of the emergence of the "I" or "me" experience, what philosophers call *subjectivity.*

Teilhard wants to approach the "phenomenon of man" gradually by, first, studying the inner life of nonliving things. In doing so, he opens our perspective to horizons previously unexplored. Studying anthropogenesis by exploring the *within* of all things provides a new and richer story of the cosmic journey than the one that natural science currently offers.

Teilhard begins painting an expanded picture of human history by enriching it with the interwoven cosmic evolutionary history of these two realities, the *without* and the *within.* In *Phenomenon*, he is writing nothing less than a new cosmic story.[1] In this chapter, he wants to show something important, namely, that not only the story of the *without* but also the story of the *within* begins with the Big Bang.

This chapter's three sections present three assertions that Teilhard makes about the *within* of things.

1. A *within exists in things*, if only because things have interactive moving parts and connections plus an inner "reserve" of energy.
2. Some elements of the *within* are *qualitative*.
3. Other elements of the *within* are *quantitative*.

1. Existence of the *Within* (54–58, 23–25)

Humans and animals enjoy a full inner life characterized by awareness and consciousness. Our pets seem to share many inner experiences with us. They even dream. But their *within* is not as all-encompassing as that of ours. Birds, reptiles, and fish manifest an inner life less rich than that of our pets. Research has shown that plants have an inner response to certain sensations. For example, they seem to have clear preferences in music. Certain music styles apparently trigger healthy plant growth, while other styles seem to stunt growth. As we go down the scale of existence—from compounds, molecules, and atoms—signs of a *within* grow more and more amorphous.

Teilhard here formulates another basic evolutionary principle: *In every new or higher synthesis, its end point is somehow already implied in its beginnings* (54, 23). Thus, properties of an atom of iron must be somehow implied in the structure of its subatomic elements. The properties of a certain molecule must be implied in the structure of its component atoms. And so on up through cells, plants, animals, and humans. This becomes another principle in Teilhard's science of anthropogenesis.

You may never have given a thought to this principle of genesis and gestation, but a few examples will reveal its usefulness.

This principle holds true in the physical realm. For example, today you may qualify as an electrical engineer or a professor of psychology. Nevertheless, you began life as the synthesis of an egg from your mother and a sperm from your father. Your self-reflective consciousness and your abilities had to be already implied in your apparently unconscious egg-and-sperm beginnings. We know that your intelligence quotient (IQ) is influenced by your genes. High IQ parents tend to give birth to very intelligent children.

This principle of a higher synthesis implied in its beginnings also holds true in the chemical world. When you synthesize sodium and chlorine, you get table salt. The qualities of each new molecule of table salt were already implied in the molecule's beginnings in the joining of atoms of sodium and chlorine. Otherwise, how can we imagine that table salt's wonderful ability to flavor food comes from a mixture of atoms of a corrosive acid (sodium) and a poisonous gas (chlorine)?

Teilhard argues that even though salt may not enjoy consciousness as we humans understand the experience, it does manifest inner activity (in its atoms) since it possesses a unique ability to evoke flavor in meats, vegetables, and soups.

Teilhard suggests that some of the earliest manifestations of consciousness include *movement, reactions,* and *energy.* Although some of the most elemental chemical atoms seem fixed and unchangeable, the discovery of radioactive elements shows not only that atoms can change their inner state but that they also possess tremendous reserves of energy in their nucleus. Many of the seemingly unchangeable basic elements, such as hydrogen, carbon, and oxygen, can morph into various isotopes, each isotope possessing different properties. A good example is radiocarbon dating, a standard tool of archeologists for determining the age of an object containing organic material. Teilhard would say that this dating method uses the *within* properties of a radioactive isotope of carbon.

Rather than assuming that human self-reflective consciousness is an aberration or an exception, the challenge, says Teilhard, is to *find the universal in the exceptional.* In other words, if humans have a *within,* then a *within* must be latent, somehow, in everything.

Early in the twentieth century, experts were declaring certain achievements impossible: "No human can run one mile in less than four minutes." "No vehicle can go faster than the speed of sound." "Humans can never fly to the moon." "Only a handful of people would ever need a personal computer." "Everything that could be invented has already been invented, so there is no further need for a government patent office."

Each of these "exceptional" cases has now become commonplace. A number of runners have run a mile in less than four minutes. Many planes fly faster than the speed of sound. We've walked on the moon and are planning a human community there. Billions of people have a personal computer. Daily, the patent office is continually inundated with new inventions.

Teilhard's point is that whenever an exceptional quality is manifested in an individual human being, that quality or ability must be diffused throughout the universe. That quality's roots must reach back in anthropogenesis *by reason of the fundamental unity of the world.*

Teilhard further reasons that "since the stuff of the universe [matter] has an inner aspect at one point of itself [e.g., self-reflective consciousness in the human], there is necessarily a *double aspect to the structure* [of all stuff]...in every region of space and time" (56, 24). If humans have a *within*, then everything must have a *within* of some kind. He asserts, *"Co-extensive with their Without, there is a Within to things"* (Teilhard's emphasis; 56, 24).

This idea that every grain of sand must have some basic *within* boggles our imagination. Yet, Teilhard says, it remains the only acceptable conclusion to our reasoning. He acknowledges that a grain of sand's *within* is most likely in a state that eludes our ability to recognize its presence.

To grasp Teilhard's principle that all things have a *within*, we must begin to think in a new way. As we begin to imagine the material nature of the earliest particles of nature, we also must try to envision their hidden, unawakened biological capacity. For instance, when we look at Earth's crust made up of metals and minerals, we see its apparent lifelessness, yet we can imagine its *within* desiring to emerge and be observed. "We must think of a 'biological' layer that is attenuated to its uttermost, but yet [a *within*'s presence there in the beginning] is absolutely necessary to explain the cosmos in succeeding ages" (56–57, 24–25). If you have an artistic talent—or any other innate skill—as an adult, it must have been present somehow in the first moment of your conception. If the universe has coherence, then "life inevitably assumes a 'pre-life' for as far back before it as the eye can see" (57, 25).

How else can we explain the obvious daily experience of three phenomena all around us: the *within, Consciousness,* and *spontaneity?* The potential for these three qualities must be present from the earliest moments of the universe, just as our intelligence potential must be present, though well hidden, in the first moment of our conception in the womb. Each of these three qualities must have a "cosmic extension" going back to the earliest times, even though it remains impossible to assign a certain moment before an "absolute beginning" of a *within.*

In the following section, Teilhard begins to explore the existence and nature of the *within* in these early material stages. He does it by identifying the *qualitative* laws that govern the growth, variation, and expansion of the *within* of things.

SUMMARY

Teilhard shows that if humans have a *within*, then everything must have a *within of some kind*. He wants to show that human self-reflective consciousness is not an evolutionary aberration or an exception to the rule. To make this assertion he began searching to *observe* some consistent pattern or law. He stipulates,

- By reason of the fundamental unity of the world, the roots of consciousness must reach back into the universe's beginnings.
- Even though something seemingly impossible appears only once, its appearance implies that such a quality or ability must be diffused throughout the universe.
- The challenge is to find the universal in the exceptional.
- The basic principle is that *in every new or higher synthesis, its end point is somehow already implied in its beginnings.*
- Movement, reactions, interactions, and energy provide some of the earliest manifestations of consciousness.

2. The Qualitative Laws of Growth (58–60, 25–28)

Here, Teilhard identifies *qualitative* laws of growth. He shows how they explain the stages of advancement and development in the various spheres of the world: from the Earth's crust, to the ocean's waters, to the atmosphere, to sea life, insects, plants, animals, and humans.

Like a good scientist, Teilhard insists in *Phenomenon* that he is merely making observations of qualitative changes and identifying their characteristics. He is not assigning causes to these changes. For example, he observes changes and differences between prelife-forms and living matter, but he does not claim to say what *caused* the shift from prelife to life. As a scientist, he chooses to remain strictly in the realm of observation, not venturing into causality. His book is carefully titled *The Phenomenon of Man*, not *What Caused the Appearance of Man?*

However, he seeks to *observe some consistent patterns or laws*. He wants to account for when and how the *within* of things appear in different regions of our experience. He offers three observations, which when taken together, he says, will clearly reveal the law for which he searches.

THREE OBSERVATIONS

Observation 1. All material things appear to us in their *without* as separate and individuated. Likewise, each *within* appears as separated and individuated. (58–59, 26)

Each person's, animal's, or plant's *within* (consciousness) appears as separate and individuated. Your *within* is not mine. My consciousness is mine. Yours is yours. Your cat's experience of consciousness is not the same as your dog's. Creatures experience their *within* as their own, separate from everyone else's. The same is true for every cell in your body; each cell has its unique inner life. The same is true for every atom of oxygen or iron; its *within* is uniquely its own, as is its history.

For instance, one atom of iron may have lived for years in the steel head of a carpenter's hammer, while another atom of iron has been living in hemoglobin in the carpenter's blood stream. As Teilhard expresses this observation, "Atomicity [separateness] is a common property of the *within* and *without* of things" (59, 26). Yet, all of these apparently separate and individuated inner stories seem connected to each other.

Observation 2. All these *withins* develop complexity and become differentiated only with the passage of time (duration). (59–60, 26–27)

At the Big Bang, subatomic particles appear to be individuated, yet alike. In time, they join spontaneously in various ways as atoms and molecules. Eventually, billions of individual cells join in myriad ways to become the incredible variety of living species we know today. Consider those original 14-billion-year-old particles. Some now live in lakes, others in peacock feathers, others in our fingernails, others in colorful neon bulbs, others in satellites orbiting Earth, others in distant galaxies.

Teilhard says that the gradual manifestation of the *within* of things appears quite clearly when we look at the process *coming forward* in time from the Big Bang through early life stages up to humans. But he asks us also to shift perspective and look at the evolutionary process *going backward in time.*

As we look at evolution backward in time, as in a car's rearview mirror, things gradually appear less complex and less differentiated. Or, as Teilhard poetically puts it, "Refracted rearwards along the course of evolution, consciousness displays itself qualitatively as a spectrum of shifting shades whose lower terms are lost in the night" (60, 27).

But what we discover in looking at the process both forward and backward, he says, is an *identifiable parameter or measurement that we can use to describe and monitor the evolution of matter.* That measuring device is *Complexity.* Earlier in his text he discussed complexity as part of his evolutionary law of Complexity-Consciousness.

Here, he gives complexity a new purpose. It becomes a *scientific measuring tool.*

Complexity is a new form of measurement that Teilhard introduces to science. No one before him recognized the significance of complexity as a useful scientific measuring device. "Level of Complexity" provides a consistent way to describe any system that has parts that interact. "Level of Complexity" also enables us to follow any system's development and evolution. Complexity as a measurement may be applied to any system—mechanical, biological, social, or intellectual.

Once we accept complexity as a valid form of measurement, we can more easily observe and rank evolutionary advances. For example, we can assert that a microwave oven is more complex than a toaster, a computer is more complex than a typewriter, a fish is more complex than a flower, and a sports team is more complex than a single athlete.

A single living cell is already amazingly complex—probably more complex than an automobile. A flower or a tree is a living system made up of trillions of living cells, each cell acting within itself and interacting in concert with many other cells.

Observation 3. Every time a richer or better-organized structure (or system) appears that is higher in complexity, it will express a more developed consciousness. (60–62, 27–28)

This phenomenon is of course more easily observed by comparing the consciousness of an orchid or an ivy vine to that of a dog or a cat, or by comparing a chimpanzee's level of consciousness to that of a human. Teilhard points out that "the simplest form of protoplasm is already a substance of unheard-of complexity" (60, 27). Growth in complexity of structure is dramatically evident as life progresses up the scale of consciousness. *Consciousness grows alongside and parallel to complexity.* This principle is so central that it would provide material for an entire "chapter" in an anthropogenesis textbook.

In Teilhard's day, science did not realize the important relationship between complexity and consciousness as evidence in formulating evolutionary laws. Many scientists were still attributing evolutionary mutations in biology exclusively to random events. They failed to recognize the pattern or trajectory of the gradual growth of Complexity-Consciousness that Teilhard sees happening so clearly over eons of time.

Here is a simpler way to restate Teilhard's third observation.

> *Consciousness develops in proportion to complexity of structure.* Development of Consciousness (the *within*, the inner self) and growth in Complexity (the *without*, the material structure) "are but two aspects or connected parts of one and the same phenomenon" (61, 27). In other words, Teilhard observes, you cannot have development of *immaterial consciousness* without a corresponding growth in *material complexity*, represented in animals and humans by an increase in neural interactions in the physical brain.

Given these three observations, Teilhard believes he can state two qualitative laws relating to the *within* and *without* of things.

Two Qualitative Laws

The first qualitative law says,

- *Higher Complexity of material structure [the* without*] leads to higher levels of Consciousness [the* within*].*

In this and his many other writings, Teilhard simply refers to it as the law of *Complexity-Consciousness*. And, when we observe this law operating over eons of time, it reveals another qualitative law. The second qualitative law says,

- *The* within *is gradually assuming dominance throughout the world in comparison to the* without. (61, 27)

The early days of the universe are characterized by the dominance of the *without*. The cosmos is made up of countless simple material elements *each with a dominant* without *and a very weak* within. As creatures continue to grow in complexity, dominance begins to shift to the *within*. Natural history itself reveals clear evidence of the gradual change in dominance from the *without* to the *within*.

Certain species have fewer members. For example, there are far fewer four-footed animals and human beings on the planet than there are, say, fish or cockroaches. Teilhard noticed an interesting phenomenon in species with fewer members. Such species begin to form more complex groupings—from pairs to families to colonies. Among humans, the groupings continue to grow even more complex—towns, states, nations, and multinational organizations. Teilhard makes another general observation:

- As *each new more complex grouping emerges, its members seem to live with a richer* within.

For example, each member of the human species is made up of a complex, well-structured system of trillions of individual cells. The cells in our neural network allow us not only to manage our physical body's health, they also enable us to plan vacations, organize sports teams, go shopping, tell stories, and create food recipes. All these activities are signs of a rich *within*.

From a qualitative viewpoint, two aspects of the world that were previously seen to be separate and distinct—the *without* and the *within*—Teilhard sees as clearly united. Intellectual and spiritual growth (the centering of consciousness upon itself) and material synthesis (increasing neural complexity) "are but two aspects or connected parts of one and the same phenomenon" (61, 27).

Just as Einstein found a mathematical formula to connect matter and energy, Teilhard has found a way to show that spirit and matter are tied together, that body and mind are one inseparable phenomenon. Across the spectrum of life, as neural networks in the brain (matter) become more complex, consciousness (spirit) continues to broaden and deepen. The *within* and the *without* reflect two sides of the same law—Complexity-Consciousness.

SUMMARY

Teilhard introduces to science the concept of Complexity as a *scientific measuring tool*. When we look at the evolutionary process going both forward and backward in time, complexity emerges as a new parameter or measurement that effectively describes and monitors the evolution of matter. Teilhard notes some logical implications of his "Complexity" insight.

- Level of Complexity enables us to trace and measure any system's development and evolution.
- Consciousness grows alongside and parallel to complexity.
- Immaterial Consciousness (*within*) cannot develop without a corresponding growth in material Complexity (*without*).
- A richer or better-organized neural structure signals a more developed consciousness.
- As we observe the progress of cosmogenesis over time, we recognize that the *within* is gradually assuming dominance over the *without*.
- As *each new more complex grouping emerges, its members seem to live with a richer* within.

3. Spiritual Energy (63–66, 28–32)

Teilhard does not use the term *spiritual energy* in an exclusively religious sense. He describes spiritual energy much more broadly as *qualities or abilities of the human spirit*. Many *within* qualities are related to the intellect, but many others go clearly beyond it. Among specifically spiritual abilities (or energies), we can list *creativity, discernment, courage, commitment, compassion, forgiveness, self-expression, self-determination, moral and ethical choices,* and *the ability to transmit life* (through humor, art, story, therapy, medicine, etc.). Such qualities of the human spirit are familiar and undeniable parts of our personal *within* experience. They are energies of the *within*.

Since the physical sciences deal primarily with energies of the *without*, they find these "inner powers" impossible to make sense of in physical, mechanical terms.

To comprehend the "phenomenon," Teilhard's challenge to us is to "to connect the two energies, of the body and the soul, in a coherent manner" (62, 29). As a scientist, he wants to show that the human body and the human spirit are "mutually enlivened." Notice that Teilhard integrates *without* energy and *within* energy by scientific *observation*.

THE PROBLEM OF THE TWO ENERGIES (63–64, 29–30)

Teilhard admits that the body has its own ways of expressing energy, as does the spirit. People tend to see physical energy and mental energy as two separate kinds of energies. His challenge is to find a way to unite them. Teilhard has already described the *mutual development* of body and spirit using the law of Complexity-Consciousness.

But the problem remains: to unify the body's distinct *expressions* of energy with the spirit's distinctively different *expressions* of energy. He begins by showing that the two energies are interdependent.

Let's state Teilhard's problem concretely. The activity of thinking appears very different from the activity of eating. Yet, to think, we must eat. "But what a variety of thoughts we get out of one slice of bread!" says Teilhard. With that offhand comment, he makes a first observation: between the *within* and *without* of things, the *interdependence* of energy is incontestable. We need physical nourishment (*without*) to be able to think and plan (*within*). Conversely, we need physical energy (*without*) to carry out any of our decisions or plans (*within*). We cannot deny the interdependence of these different expressions of energy.

Establishing their interdependence marks Teilhard's first step, his starting point. Now, he must deal with their different *expressions*. Clearly, making a decision and chewing on a caramel are two different *expressions* of energy. How to see them as one? To show that they both come from the same energy source appears to be an unsolvable problem.

According to Albert Einstein, "You cannot solve an unsolvable problem on the same level of consciousness that created it." That's precisely the reason most problems seem unsolvable. You can't solve a problem in multiplication if you only know how to add and subtract. You must first expand your consciousness to a new level by developing skill in using the concepts of multiplication. That is, you must transcend the simpler level of consciousness that created the problem.

Moving to a more encompassing level of consciousness is exactly what Teilhard does to solve his problem. An apparent dualism on one level can be resolved only by establishing unity at a higher level. He says that there must be something through which material and spiritual energies hold together and are complementary. "In last analysis, *somehow or other*, there must be a single energy operating in the world" (Teilhard's emphasis; 63, 29). Otherwise, we must accept a fundamental dualism between the *within* and the *without* of things.

Teilhard proposes a "line of solution" (64–66, 30–32). Here is his reasoning.

He begins by asserting, without explanation, that "essentially, all energy is psychic in nature" (64, 30). To accept this assertion, Teilhard presumes we have been following his train of thought thus far in the book, and that we agree with him about the growing predominance of the *within* over the *without* (62, 29). He explains the steps of his thought process.

The clearest observable pattern of energy throughout the multibillion-year process of cosmogenesis shows a consistent movement (1) from lower to higher levels of Complexity and (2) from lower to higher and more comprehensive levels of Consciousness. Complexity and Consciousness seem to move forward side by side.

By the law of evolution, the universe is destined to become evermore conscious of itself, thereby revealing what the universe's true nature is and always has been from its first moments—*psychic*, that is, mental and spiritual. This is a logical step that most scientists may have a hard time taking. It is what Teilhard will try to show and explain to them in the rest of his *Phenomenon*.

ONE FUNDAMENTAL ENERGY, TWO EXPRESSIONS

Let us accept Teilhard's assumption that, fundamentally, all energy is psychic, that is, all energy is related to mind, spirit, and consciousness. He then acknowledges, "in each particular element [of matter] this fundamental [psychic] energy is divided into two distinct components" (64, 30):

- *tangential energy*, energy that can get used up like spent fuel, and
- *radial energy*, energy that keeps driving elements toward unions of greater Complexity.

The first type, *tangential energy*, is energy that can get used up or burned out. (In geometry, a tangent is a line that moves away from center and *disappears*.) Consider atoms of iron. In *tangential energy*, iron atoms may link themselves to other atoms of iron, as in a steel beam. In this form the iron will eventually rust and crumble.

The second type, *radial energy*, is energy that drives atoms toward higher unions and greater complexity. (In geometry, a radius is a moving line that never leaves the circle and constantly re-energizes its center.) In *radial energy*, iron atoms may be attracted to form unions with a variety of different atoms. This creates molecules and compounds of ever-greater Complexity with new, more complex centers. Compounds of iron, such as iron sulfate and iron chloride, are widely used in industry. Digestible iron may be found in much more complex forms in fruits and vegetables. Iron is part of blood's hemoglobin and myoglobin. Iron is an integral part of human skin tissue, muscles, bone marrow, blood proteins, and many enzymes. The iron in my brain is still identifiably iron, yet it is an essential component participating in my ability to think. This is an expression of iron's capacity to produce *radial* energy.

To most people, even scientists, these two new energy concepts—*tangential* and *radial*—need some explanation. Since Teilhard will use these two terms again and again throughout his book, it is important to grasp their distinction clearly.

Teilhard notes that while the amount of available *tangential energy* in matter keeps decreasing with use, the overall amount of energy in the cosmos keeps increasing because it is the nature of *radial energy* to produce ever-higher amounts of psychic energy. Tangential energy dissipates with use, while radial energy continually increases with use, as Complexity and Consciousness continue to increase.

If we look at the phenomenon of humanity merely in terms of tangential energy, we see only individual human bodies growing old, weak, and dying. When we look at humanity as a species today, it is generating tremendous amounts of energy in the sphere of the human mind and heart. Humans are accomplishing things that were unimaginable a century ago.

To take a simple example, as you eat a meal, your body breaks down food into fuel in the form of calories, proteins, carbohydrates, and other substances that help keep you alive and healthy. To move around and do your daily tasks, you burn up those nutrients in physical movements until their energy is spent, lost forever. You must keep renourishing your body every day. That describes *tangential energy*. It is mostly related to your *without*.

At the same time, some of that meal is transformed into sources of *radial energy*, so that you can think, plan, converse, imagine, organize, use a computer, maneuver a car, or read a novel. These are actions of your *within* that enable you to act on behalf of your "center," or your "self."

Using your personal centeredness (your *within*), you can join with others to create larger and larger circles of humans, groups that possess more complex centers—families, sports teams, research groups, a community of faith, or local, national, and world governments. Each group possesses its own life and personality, expressing its own *within* and *without*. *Each group is a center of centers.*

Using food or fossil fuels, tangential energy generates physical movement and activity. Its focus is the *without* of things. It is subject to entropy. Once fuel is used up, it cannot be recycled and used again as fuel. If tangential energy were the only kind of energy available, there would come a time when Earth would have used up all its energy.

However, humans have also learned to use food and other resources to produce radial energy. Radial energy builds and grows. It complexifies structures and systems and produces consciousness, fueling thought, imagination, planning, organization, creativity. Its function is to nurture the *within* of things. Although radial energy requires the consumption of biological fuels to operate, it takes very little biological fuel to generate a lot of *within* energy.

In complexifying and expanding consciousness, radial energy far outproduces the output of tangential energy. While tangential energy is being consumed and used up, radial energy continues to generate higher and more complex systems, richer connections, and greater consciousness.

In training a sports team among humans, *tangential* (physical) energy is expended to assemble the members into a team and have them practice physical movements together to learn to interact as a team. Science is quite familiar with this kind of tangential energy. But science can measure only the physical output spent by each team member. But the team *as a new whole* or new self (beyond the selves of the individual players) acts with a new kind of fuel. It generates additional new *tangential* (physical) energy in the individual players and in the audience that, according to Teilhard, would not exist without the team self. That new tangential energy may be expressed in the form of shouts, clapping, and other physical expressions of excitement, enthusiasm, and support. Teilhard suggests that, because of these higher unions, *tangential energy in the world keeps being regenerated.* Thus, the world will not end up dying as an exhausted whimper but will be continually re-energized.

Suppose this logic is carried to its conclusion? In time, of course, Earth's tangential energy would be exhausted, yet its radial energy would continue to multiply until it was the only energy remaining. In the end, *anthropogenesis would culminate in an expression of pure psychic energy.*

Reasoning in this way, Teilhard believes he can assert that "essentially, all energy is psychic in nature" (64, 30). If anthropogenesis will end up as essentially psychic or spiritual energy (as its *within*), then the first subatomic particles at the Big Bang (anthropogenesis's original *without*) had to possess the potential to become—evolve into—a single union of selves with a single center (totally a *within*). In other words, the universe started off as a single center (a "singularity" at the Big Bang), and it will ultimately evolve into a single center in the end.

SUMMARY

To unify the mutual development of body and spirit, Teilhard shows how to unify their apparently separate and distinct expressions of energy. He makes certain observations.

- Making a decision and chewing on a caramel are two different expressions of energy, creating an apparent dualism between the *within* and the *without* of things.
- The interactive connection between the *within* and *without* of things is incontestable. To think, we must eat.
- In every element, from atoms to molecules to compounds to cells to organisms, we are working with *a single energy that has two expressions—tangential and radial.*
- Tangential energy dissipates with use, while radial energy continually increases with use, as Complexity and Consciousness continue to increase.
- Ultimately, the universe would culminate in an expression of pure psychic energy.
- This means there must be a single energy operating in the world and that "essentially, all energy is psychic in nature."
- The first subatomic particles at the Big Bang had to be holding within them the potential to become a single union of selves with a single center.

Spiritual Implications

What a tremendous challenge Teilhard poses to the scientist: to learn to see the *within* of nonliving things. If scientists are expected to grasp the *within* of physical things, how much more important is it that people of faith grasp this reality?

For Teilhard, the *within* reveals not only the "inside story" of evolution, but also the "inside story" of God's creation and its purpose. The story of the human *within*—and every other *within*—began with the Big Bang. If humans have a *within*, then God must have put a *within* of some kind into everything, even into the elementary particles. Otherwise, those particles would never have felt the pull of attraction and the drive to connect.

If religious people wish to spend a future life in the presence of God, exploring the *within* of God, Teilhard is presenting a way for us to learn some very basic things that God has revealed about the divine inner life. God is revealing to us God's Self in the magnificent evolutionary project God initiated at the Big Bang.

Based on their belief in a static and cyclical cosmos, the ancients expressed their own limited ideas of God. But modern science can decipher more accurately the evolutionary cosmic experiment God has set in motion and how God is helping it succeed.

Consider how, in the major world religions, God's nature is consistently seen as loving, compassionate, and just. The divine nature is almost universally characterized by oneness, truth, goodness, and beauty. These are all *within* qualities.

After presenting his observations about the development of the *within* of things, Teilhard can safely assert, *Every time a better-organized structure appears that is higher in Complexity, it will express a more developed Consciousness and a richer within.*

Embedded in that assertion is a fundamental moral principle for people living in an evolving world. It might be stated as this: if the evolutionary purpose of creation is to continue to develop consciousness, then to fulfill God's project we must continue to expand our consciousness and make it more and more all-inclusive and all-embracing.

If we wonder how to go about doing this, Teilhard says that the way is very clear since *Consciousness develops in proportion to Complexity of structure.* Usually, when more complexity comes into our lives, we resist it. Instead of welcoming and integrating it, we tend to compartmentalize whatever does not "fit" with our current thinking. We put it into a separate place in our minds.

Teilhard would say that the challenge of spirituality is *to integrate what does not seem to fit.* To make it fit requires expanding one's consciousness to new levels. As people add more and more complexity to their lives and integrate it, they continue to expand and further develop their consciousness.

One of the things we can be sure of regarding the direction of God's evolutionary project is that *the* within *is gradually assuming dominance throughout the world in comparison to the* without. Thus, again, the moral imperative is to develop one's own *within* and to foster the development of the *within* of others. This imperative calls for engagement with the world, not avoidance of it as recommended in much traditional spirituality.

For Teilhard, avoiding sin is merely keeping away from that which would hinder the development of one's *within.* One can mistakenly spend all one's energy in *avoidance.* For Teilhard, the major amount of one's energy is meant to be spent in developing and expanding one's *within*. Since sin and evil are inevitable in an evolving world, the challenge is to use these unwelcome events as learning experiences, to grow in consciousness because of them.

Teilhard would tell us to be proactive. Acquire new education. Do some challenging reading. Use your life experiences and that of others to increase and enlarge your *within*. Psychologists and counselors help their clients explore, organize, and clarify their *withins*. Doing research, engaging in creative activity, and getting to know people from different cultures stretches our consciousness. Exploring various belief systems and cultures also challenge one's *within* to enlarge. Much enrichment comes from personal engagement with the homeless, migrants, the poor, the sick, the elderly, the disenfranchised, and the mentally ill. Such engagement challenges us to decipher how suffering may be turned into radial energy to further God's project.

Chapter 3

The Earth in Its Early Stages

(67–74, 33–38)

Layers of Earth

USING THE BEST scientific knowledge of his day (1939), Teilhard offers a description of Earth's formation and its various layers. I follow his explanation of our planet's evolution only in outline form, since he had no access to the many scientific discoveries about Earth's origins that have been made in the almost century that has passed since he wrote *Phenomenon*. For example, Teilhard had no knowledge of plate tectonics, continental drift, or ways to detect chemical components on other planets in our solar system.

Teilhard likes to talk about Earth in terms of "layers" or "spheres" (since Earth is essentially spherically shaped). He uses geophysical terminology, still acceptable today, to identify five layers. He begins with Earth's inner core and moves outward.

- The *barysphere* (from the Greek *baros*, meaning "heavy") is the term used to describe Earth's core and mantle. Its inner core is solid metal, mostly iron; its outer core is liquid metal, mostly iron. Radioactive elements in the outer core create Earth's magnetic fields.

- The *lithosphere* (from the Greek *lithos*, meaning "rock") describes Earth's surface, a solid crust of metals and minerals.
- The *hydrosphere* (the Greek *hydor*, meaning "water") forms a layer of water and acids upon Earth's surface.
- The *atmosphere* (from the Greek *atmos*, meaning "vapor") rises above the water and encircles Earth.
- The *stratosphere* (from the Latin *stratum*, meaning "covering or blanket") stretches out over and covers the atmosphere.

These are five *nonliving layers* of Earth and the focus of Teilhard's discussion in book 1. In book 2 and beyond, Teilhard will explore two more spheres, the *living layers* of Earth.

- The *biosphere* (from the Greek *bios*, meaning "life") includes the entire layer of living things in the air, the sea, and on the land—bacteria, plants, insects, fish, birds, animals, and humans.
- The *noosphere* (from the Greek *nous*, meaning "mind") includes the layers of mind and thought that increasingly permeate and influence all the other spheres.

In this chapter, Teilhard focuses first on the *without* of the nonliving layers of Earth and then on their *within*.

1. The *Without* (68–71, 33–36)

THE CRYSTALLIZING WORLD (68–69, 34–35)

Teilhard's first task in describing the *without* of the lithosphere and the hydrosphere is to show the qualitative difference between *aggregating molecules* (groups or networks of the same molecule) and additive or *complexifying molecules* (larger molecules made up of unions of two or more different molecules, i.e., *compounds*).

- A *molecule* is formed when two or more of the same elements join chemically, for example, O_2 (two oxygen atoms form an oxygen molecule) or Cl_2 (two chlorine atoms form a chlorine molecule).

- A *compound* is a *molecule* that contains atoms of at least two *different* elements, such as CO_2 (carbon dioxide, C = carbon, O = oxygen) or NaCl (table salt, Na = sodium, Cl = chlorine).

- All *compounds* are *molecules* but not all *molecules* are *compounds*.

- *Aggregating molecules* form a special class. They have "chosen a road which closed them prematurely upon themselves" (69, 34). This means that they are molecules incapable of forming unions with different molecules. Diamond is a familiar example. A diamond is merely a large aggregate of carbon atoms formed under intense pressure. It is incapable of greater complexification as a molecule.

- *Association*. The only way aggregating molecules like carbon atoms in a diamond can develop or grow—or get beyond themselves—is by "association." That is, these molecules become linked or attached or gathered together, but *without true union*. The commonest examples are drops of water that form a lake or grains of sand that form a beach. The lake or beach appear to form a whole, but the water molecules and grains of sand remain separate. They have simply aggregated or gathered together to form a lake or a beach. Thus, lakes or beaches do not qualify as a true union. Teilhard would say that they have no "center."

Carbon atoms in a diamond are just atoms pressed together, but without a center, like the sands on a beach. That is why a diamond can be cut without losing its diamond-ness or a truckload of sand can be carted away without the beach losing its beach-ness.

Many other simple atoms or molecules merely aggregate, as diamonds do, to form a crystalline structure (68–69, 34), as in certain jewels such as jade, garnet, or mica. These jewels have no true "center" but form "an indefinitely extended mosaic of similar elements."

Much of Earth's molecular surface is made up of either

1. *aggregating atoms of simple metals and minerals* (iron, copper, zinc, nickel, gold, silver, platinum, mercury, uranium, aluminum, sodium, calcium), or
2. *simple and stable aggregating molecules in various crystalline forms* (diamonds, silicon, sapphire, fluorite, amethyst, quartz, tourmaline, lapis lazuli, turquoise, carnelian).

Both kinds of molecules are *inorganic*.

THE POLYMERIZING WORLD (70–71, 35–36)

The planet is not made up entirely of inorganic molecules. Much of our world today is filled with *organic* molecules. These are what Teilhard called molecules that achieve new observable critical thresholds of existence. Teilhard names two types of organic molecules:

- *complexifying molecules*
- *macromolecules*

The first type of organic molecules to reach a new threshold of complexity he calls *complexifying molecules*. These molecules make up what Teilhard calls the "polymerizing world." He is not talking about the well-defined polymerizing process of today's chemists, such as nylon, polyester, Teflon, or epoxy. In his day, biology knew very little about today's polymers. Teilhard uses the term in a more general way. For him, polymers are any molecules made up of more flexible and adaptable atoms that unite to form true unions. Some natural polymers include silk, wool, and cellulose. Their complexity is measured by the number of the molecule's interdependent parts plus the number of their interactions.

Teilhard calls the second group of molecules that reach a higher threshold of complexity *macromolecules*. Macromolecules are composed of different complexifying molecules that unite to form new unions that are far larger and more complex. These larger and more complex molecules make up the world of *organic compounds*. They manifest another new observable critical threshold of existence.

We humans live among these organic compounds and are made up of some of them. Here are some that we use frequently:

- *Acetaminophen:* the active ingredient in Tylenol.
- *Aspartame:* a common artificial sweetener.
- *Caffeine:* a stimulant found in drinks and pharmaceuticals.
- *Aluminum fluoride:* used as coating material for mirrors and lasers.

Complexifying molecules also make up much of our physical bodies. The most common of these are *proteins*. Proteins are essential parts of organisms. They participate dynamically in virtually every process within the cells of living things. Some proteins are important in cell signaling, immune responses, cell adhesion, digestion, and the cell cycle. In a human body, there can be as many as two million distinct types of proteins. Strictly speaking, *proteins by themselves are nonliving*. They are merely complex organic molecules.

The billions of *nonliving* molecules we call proteins that function to keep our bodies working effectively might be compared to the many different vehicles that function to keep a city working effectively. Note that cars and trucks, like proteins, are nonliving things, yet they fulfill essential functions in a city. Other than their drivers, these vehicles are made up of chemicals, metals, minerals, and synthetics. The number and importance of nonliving things in our bodies, in our cities, and in our world are huge.

For Teilhard, both inorganic chemicals (aggregating molecules) and organic chemicals (complexifying molecules) are two inseparable facets of Earth's development. All organic molecules are made up of combinations of inorganic atoms.

Although organic molecules are more complex than inorganic molecules, and appear to reveal a new threshold of existence, they both are "already underway in the infancy of the earth" (71, 36). They began appearing in the seas and on land.

Teilhard keeps reminding us that, so far, everything that enjoys complexity is a union made up of less complex parts. The chemical makeup of any element can be broken down into elementary atoms, and those elementary atoms can be broken down into the subatomic particles that we call protons, neutrons, and electrons. Everything that exists finds its "infancy"—more accurately, its "conception"—in these original subatomic particles.

Teilhard can claim that any new observable critical threshold of existence (such as the organic molecule) *had to already exist* "in an obscure and primordial way" in those original subatomic particles (71, 36). Thus, each organic molecule had to exist *potentially* in the inorganic atoms in its makeup. And the inorganic atoms also had to exist *potentially* in the subatomic particles in their makeup.

In the development of every animal and human, the heart, lungs, eyes, and the other organs *had to already exist* "in an obscure and primordial way" in the fertilized egg carried by the mother.

2. The *Within* (of Nonliving Things) (71–74, 36–38)

This section on the *within* of things may prove to be the most difficult part of Teilhard's book to grasp, but it is of the utmost importance to do so. *We need to learn to "see" the* within *of nonliving things.* Until we can do that, we miss the power and purpose of *Phenomenon.*

The incontrovertible fact is that we spend much of our lives interacting with nonliving things. Just picture yourself in your home. Some of the functional nonliving things in your house are fixed and immovable, like floors, walls, ceilings, and stairs. You can't survive without them, since they provide the structure, safety, and comfort for much of your life. Other familiar nonliving things that have minimal movement include beds, tables, and chairs. Some nonliving things have fixed movements, like clocks, doors, drawers. Some nonliving things have start and stop movements, like faucets, thermostats, hair dryers, alarm clocks. Nonliving things of complex makeup provide many interactive functions, such as cell phones, computers, automobiles. We spend our lives interacting with all these nonliving things.

Teilhard wants you to begin to describe the *within* of each of these nonliving things in your home. While he acknowledges that it is relatively easy to see the *within* of *living things,* his purpose in this chapter is to help you to develop the more difficult skill of recognizing the within of *nonliving things.*

For Teilhard, each of these nonliving things has a *within* independent of any human participant using it. As Teilhard puts it, "The exterior world must inevitably be lined at every point with an interior one" (72, 36). Metaphorically, he is reminding us that the fabric of an expensive jacket or suit coat (a *without*) often contains a smooth inner lining (a *within*) that serves an important purpose. People usually focus on the quality, color, and weave of the jacket's outer material, but Teilhard wants us to "look for the satin lining," to develop the ability to see the *within* of things.

Recall the evolutionary law that Teilhard recognized: *Attraction leads to Connection, which builds Complexity and expands Consciousness.* If Attraction is happening and Connections are being made among things, it is a sign that the evolutionary law is at work. Even the most inorganic elements are attracted to each other to aggregate or congregate together, as happens in diamonds, agates, salts, iron, silver, gold, magnesium and other metals and minerals. Even though these atoms don't interact with each other but just stick together to form one large clump, they are still examples of Attraction and Connection at work.

Organic compounds contain many parts that can interact with each other and with things around them. Think of organic compounds like aspirin, vitamin C, and caffeine and how they interact within your body. They are adding Complexity to Attraction and Connection.

INVOLUTION

Involution describes the process of continually increasing complexity within a limited physical space.

Instead of things individually spreading out more and more, notice how the evolutionary law tends to bring things together more and more closely. On a sidereal scale, the universe did not remain an expanding sea of subatomic particles. It tended to form connections and unions that were finite and enclosed in upon themselves. Some of the first "greater unions" in the cosmos are the stars and planets.

Our Earth is a spherical planet operating within a closed volume. Its surface area is essentially fixed. Interactions that happen on Earth must happen within its limited space. As complexity continues to grow on the planet, that complexity must remain essentially contained on the planet's surface. More people must find living space on our finite planet. As human population continues to increase yet remains confined to and concentrated in a limited physical space, we are forced to complexify relationships and interactions. This is the experience of *involution*.

Familiar examples of involution also happen in limited spaces such as your home and your body. You may bring more and more complexity into your home, but it must remain contained within your home.

Today's homes are far more complex than they were two hundred years ago. Though a two-hundred-year-old brick home may look reasonably similar on the outside (its *without*) to a brick home today, the *within* of a home today is remarkably more complex in its operation. In that older home, there would be no electrical wiring, no central heating and air conditioning, no electric ranges, refrigerators, dishwashers, microwaves, coffeemakers, and so on. There would be no running water, flush toilets, or showers; no radios, television sets, or computers. In your closet there would be no synthetic fiber clothing, no shoes of manmade materials, no electric blankets or fiber-stuffed pillows. Yet all of today's material complexities need to fit into a house of the same size—or smaller—than the two-hundred-year-old house. This is *involution* happening.

Again, remember that all these nonliving items are part of the human phenomenon. They are not "separate" from us, but part of us and integral to our lives, allowing us to express thought and ingenuity in innumerable ways.

Teilhard's point is that home involution is happening not merely to kitchens and bathrooms, but to each home *as a whole, as a system.* Just as he asserts that each individual thing in our home has its own *within*, our home as a single operating system has its own *within*. Every new union of things has its own *within*.

In a similar way, just as each of our physical body's parts (heart, lungs, liver, kidneys, etc.) has its own *within*, our body as a single operating system has its own *within*. And, as we mature into adulthood, our interpersonal system is undergoing *involution*. Our daily operations are growing more and more complex. As we grow, our relationships increase and multiply. Our abilities develop. Our financial dealings become more complex. Our responsibilities expand. Our vocabulary multiplies. Our intellect widens. Our social skills mature. Our *within* becomes huge and complex. Yet, it is all happening in our finite body. Teilhard would describe this personal involution by saying that all those elements are coiling up upon themselves within us. Our *within* is growing evermore complex.

In a similar way, Earth itself as a single operating system must have its own huge *within*. And that huge *within* is growing evermore complex and more conscious every year. Earth itself is undergoing continual *involution*. Life and consciousness on Earth intensifies and is carried forward in this involution process.

The planet is involuting. To remain a functioning whole, Earth must continually reorganize itself. It must continue to welcome new interacting parts and find a fitting place for them. This continual process of synthesis and resynthesis is another way of describing what Teilhard means by *involution*.

Involution can occur only in a closed space. In fact, as Teilhard points out, the synthesis of complexity into consciousness cannot happen unless our planet as a whole is enfolded within a closed space. Consider the island we call Manhattan. When settlers first came to New York, there were perhaps a thousand people living on the island. Today, though the island has not physically expanded, several million people live and work there. Involution.

INVOLUTION AND RADIAL ENERGY

Because involution occurs only in a closed space, involution also increases *radial energy* (or spiritual energy), that is, energy driving the system toward expanded consciousness. In a contained space, says Teilhard, "spiritual energy by its very nature increases in 'radial' value, positively, absolutely, and without determinable limits, in step with the increasing chemical complexity of the elements which represent its inner lining" (72, 37).

All nonliving particles burst into existence at the Big Bang. If you look at these original elements of prelife drifting around as individual particles in outer space, they seem to have little energy to connect or, at best, they appear to connect only slowly. However, as soon as they are confined, as in and on planet Earth, the forces of synthesis (Attraction-Connection-Complexity-Consciousness) become awakened and their *withins* begin to grow at an increasing rate.

A protean force—radial energy—is at work. Early in our planet's history, complex chemical atoms began to emerge; these atoms formed molecules, then megamolecules, then evermore complex organic compounds. Evolutionary laws eventually produced nonliving acids, enzymes, and proteins that filled the oceans, the air, and muddy deposits. Teilhard observes how "ultra-microscopic grains of protein were thickly strewn over the surface of the earth" (73, 37). These nonliving things, these myriads of large molecules, are the precursors of life. A continuation of this involution process is precisely what the evolutionary laws of Complexity and energy predict must happen.

Teilhard summarizes this chapter by describing the planet at this point as "a correlated mass of infinitesimal centers structurally bound together" (74, 38). It is a unity of plurality. Over millions and millions of years, as the *within* of Earth becomes more and more concentrated and deepened, Earth becomes a single organism. It "forms an organic whole in which no element can any longer be separated from those surrounding it" (74, 38).

At this point in the universe's history, the nonliving Earth has become what Teilhard calls a *prebiosphere*. Even as a nonliving thing, Earth has been increasing in intensity and complexity. Soon, something is going to burst out upon early Earth. That something is *Life*.

SUMMARY

Teilhard wants us to become adept at recognizing and acknowledging the *within* of every nonliving thing, whether it is as small as a molecule or as large as a mountain. According to him,

- Each nonliving thing has a *within*, even though it has never been identified or comprehended by a human.
- *Involution* describes the process of continually increasing complexity within a limited physical space.
- Just as each individual part of any system has its own *within*, the system itself has its own *within*.
- Every new true union of things has its own *within*.
- Because involution occurs only in a closed space, it increases *radial energy*, that is, energy driving the system toward expanded consciousness.

Spiritual Implications

Here are a few observations for those wanting to explore spiritual connections to Teilhard's scientific text.

Beds and buttons, credit cards and computers, dishes and desks, pianos and printers, raincoats and robots, taxis and toothpaste, and on and on.

These are only a fraction of the nonliving things that fill our lives and form part of the human phenomenon.

It is amazing to realize how many nonliving things contribute to the richness of our daily experience—to our sickness and health, to our minds and spirits, to our expressions of love and devotion. Matter matters to God. For, love needs to be incarnated (enfleshed) in order to be expressed in ways that it can be recognized. C. S. Lewis puts it this way:

> There is no good trying to be more spiritual than God. God never meant us to be purely spiritual creatures. That is why He uses material things like bread and wine to put the new life into us. We may think this rather crude and unspiritual. God does not: He invented eating. He likes matter. He invented it.[1]

Our entire life is a process of involution. To remain a functioning whole, we must continually reorganize ourselves in order to welcome the flood of new interacting elements into our life and find a fitting place for them in our consciousness. These elements may be material things like drones, autonomous cars, or armed police patrolling school corridors. And they may be intangible, like attitudes, creeds, deception, rejection, love. All of them must find a place in our life and our consciousness.

In moral and ethical life today, people must integrate issues like invasion of privacy, women publicly revolting against sexual harassment, cell phone obsession, body piercing, gay marriage, gender fluidity, an opioid addicted population, global warming, polarized government, mass exodus from organized religion, genocide, subtle forms of racism, destruction of forests, oil pipelines through sacred lands, and so on.

How are we integrating these issues into our consciousness? Do we simply refuse to deal with some of them? Have we been forced to deal with one or more of them? Perhaps our child wants a tattoo. A dear friend is transitioning to a different gender. A spouse is addicted to pornography.

If we wish to evolve spiritually and fulfill our earthly purpose, one way would be to utilize the great law of evolution, the law of *Complexity-Consciousness*. If Teilhard's formulation of this law is indeed central to life, then that law must be central to the spiritual life.

Perhaps you are hesitant to acknowledge that this great law of evolution has any relevance to your spiritual life. Teilhard says that the universal drive is revealing to us something about the mind and heart of God.

In this chapter, Teilhard is also indirectly laying the foundation for new approaches to fundamental moral principles. He is pointing out the new sense of responsibility in caring for the entire system of creation that has evolved through billions of years for our use. Unexplored sources of radial energy are waiting for us to discover and use in our contribution to keep anthropogenesis and geogenesis moving forward.

For many centuries, spiritual growth has been considered an individual activity. Traditionally, our main responsibility was our own personal spiritual growth. Teilhard is suggesting that spirituality today should also include a responsibility for the life of all humanity and, of course, for our earthly habitat.

In the "duration" in which we live today, it is the whole Earth, moving the *totum* forward, that has become our species' special responsibility. We are the stewards of creation. We have only recently consciously realized the urgency of this global responsibility. In many ways, the need to care for the Earth, our true home, demands an evolution of the very idea of spirituality and spiritual practice.

BOOK TWO

LIFE

Chapter 1

The Advent of Life

(77–102, 41–60)

A Reminder

TEILHARD BEGINS BOOK 2 by reminding us that he is focused on *embriogenesis*, that is, *searching for a thing's earliest manifestation* deeper in time.

As Teilhard looks at the earliest manifestations of the two major sets of phenomena, *nonliving* and *living,* he focuses on their shared genesis that reaches back eons. Seen from their earliest beginnings, these "two antithetical creations" seem far less antithetical.

Suppose, hypothetically, you and I had been around during those earliest stages of the universe yet knew nothing of the future. Suppose we were shown that the atoms and molecules from the Big Bang spinning around us would eventually become—pineapples, panda bears, pine trees, pigs, and ponies. These living things so familiar to us today would have been unimaginable to us at that time. Yet, over time all those different living forms eventually emerged. Each living thing we see today is physically composed of some of the first amorphous swirling mass of particles.

Teilhard notes that a debate was going on among biologists of his day. They were searching for the earliest manifestation of life. Biologists agreed that animals clearly differed from plants. As they pushed their analysis back to the very first signs of life—creatures of only a single cell—they faced the question, Was that single-celled living thing a plant or an animal? Some of those original cells multiplied and eventually became plants, while others multiplied and became animals. Yet, from those first single-celled creatures, *which were neither plant nor animal*, there emerged the myriad species both of plants and animals as well as of all the varieties of nonhuman and human life that we see today.

Teilhard points out another irrefutable fact. Despite the complexity and capacity for life of those first single cells, every single living cell was made up completely of *nonliving* atoms and molecules—"dead" acids, enzymes, proteins, and so forth.

He acknowledges that these first living cells had a *historic birth* on Earth, a birth date. But he wants to emphasize a different point, namely, that these first cells must also have had an *embriogenesis*. They had a "conception" and "gestation" period that began with subatomic particles at the Big Bang.

In other words, you can't say that a thing had a birth, but had no embriogenesis. If it was born, it had an embriogenesis. In fact, everything that exists in the universe today has the same beginning. Everything that exists today has in some very real sense existed, potentially, from those first moments. And because you and I enjoy a self-reflective consciousness (a *within*), it is only logical that our consciousness (our *within*) began its embriogenesis then, too.

Teilhard does not want to deny that, as the universe evolves, there are major *historic "births"* happening again and again—critical points, changes of state, developmental jumps. His text acknowledges these historic "births." Hydrogen had a birth date. Helium had a birth date. Carbon had a birth date. Water had a birth date. The first cells had a birth date. But his focus here is on their embriogenesis—their true beginning.

Teilhard notes that some scientists in his day claimed that the only way to explain the appearance of life on Earth was to look to outer space. To their suggestion that the first living cells had to be transported to Earth from somewhere else in our galaxy, he replies that there is no need to look to outer space for life's origins. But, even if life had been deposited on Earth from outer space and had experienced a different *historic birth*, it would still have had the same embriogenesis (78, 41).

For him, the emergence of living cells is already present—and waiting—in the *within* of nonliving things everywhere in the universe. The only things needed are the right conditions for their emergence. Today, we know that, when the time was right, single-celled living creatures emerged simultaneously all over our planet. Life on Earth did not spring from a single solitary cell but from a multitude of them.

Multiple simultaneous emergence is a consistent pattern in the universe. Simultaneous emergence happened with the appearance of atoms. It happened with the appearance of molecules. It happened with the appearance of chemical compounds. And it happens with the appearance of the living cell. The simultaneous emergence process remains consistent with the appearance of any new species.

Book 1 showed how each evolutionary change of state of nonliving matter manifested the same three qualities: *plurality, union (unity)*, and *energy*. Countless individual subatomic particles (*plurality*) joined to form a variety of atoms (*unity*); countless individual atoms (*plurality*) joined to form a variety of molecules (*unity*); countless individual molecules (*plurality*) joined to form a variety of compounds and megamolecules (*unity*). In each of these new unities emerged new abilities to act and interact (*energy*).

It's no surprise that with the emergence of life the pattern remains the same.

- *First, a great multitude of individual living cells appear (plurality).*
- *Next, these individual cells are attracted to form more complex connections (unity or union).*
- *Each of these new unions reveals new potential (energy).*

In book 2, Teilhard shows that among living things this three-stage process is driven by the same basic evolutionary force—Attraction-to-Connection—that operates in the nonliving world.

Teilhard offers his personal imaginal description of the first emergence of life on Earth billions of years ago. He pictures various chemicals floating in seawater warmed by the sun in many places worldwide. Life begins in the seas. Deep waters offer our first glimpse of the living *within* on Earth and where life first emerges (71, 36). "Then at a given moment, after a sufficient lapse of time, those same waters here and there must unquestionably have begun writhing with minute creatures" (78, 42). Their proliferation marks the historical birth of the *biosphere*. The form of these primordial microbes would have been similar to modern bacteria living at the bottom of the sea near iron-rich hydrothermal vents.

Such a striking change that happens with the appearance of life cannot be the result of a simple continuous process, Teilhard says, but has to be a "particular moment of terrestrial evolution coming to maturity, a threshold, a crisis of the first magnitude, the beginning of a new order" (79, 42). A birth date.

SUMMARY

To summarize principles we have learned so far in this chapter:

- Focus on embriogenesis, searching for a thing's earliest manifestation.
- As the universe evolves, there are many *historic "births."*
- You can't say that a thing had a birth but had no embriogenesis.
- If it was born, it had an embriogenesis.
- Every living or nonliving thing in the universe today began its embriogenesis at the Big Bang.
- The first *living* cells, every one of them, was made up completely of *nonliving* atoms and molecules.
- The potential for living cells must already have been present in the *within* of nonliving things everywhere in the universe.
- All that is needed for new historic births are the right conditions for their emergence.
- The evolutionary pattern remains the same: *Attraction-Connection-Complexity-Consciousness.*
- Everything that emerges at a new level has the same three observable qualities: *plurality*, *unity*, and *energy*.

The rest of this chapter explores the nature of the transformation from prelife to life as well as the time and place of it.

1. The Transit to Life (79–90, 42–45)

Life begins with the cell.

Clearly, "the cell is the natural granule of life in the same way as the atom is the natural granule of simple, elemental matter" (79, 43). To understand the transit to life, we must understand the cell.

Hundreds of books as well as thousands of research papers have been written on the cell. It would seem that, with all this study—*biological, histological* (study of microanatomy), and *physiological* research applied to *cytology* (the study of the cell)—we have exhausted our understanding of our most primitive living ancestor.

Teilhard observes that cytology studies the cell only from its *historic birth* on Earth forward in time. Cytologists trace cellular development from the simplest cells to the highest forms of life, but they do not bother to search the cell's prelife layers. Science has been treating the cell as if it had no antecedents (80, 43).

Teilhard chooses to look backward at the cell's prelife layers, its embriogenesis. He explores the roots of the cell's origins in the inorganic world. From what did the cell emerge?

For Teilhard, treating the cell as the "outcome of long preparation" is the only way we can ever truly grasp "the essence of its novelty" as a thing that was born on Earth (80, 43).

In this chapter, Teilhard carries out his genesis exploration in three stages. He looks at

1. the cell's preparatory process in organic compounds and megamolecules
2. the milieu in which the transformation happened
3. the emergence of the cell's *within*

MICROORGANISMS AND MEGAMOLECULES (81–83, 44–45)

Teilhard notes the debates and struggles biologists of his day were having as they tried to integrate the evolutionary theories of Darwin with the discoveries of Lamarck and Mendel. A blend of the insights of these three biology pioneers eventually became known as neo-Darwinism. Teilhard points out that his focus on embriogenesis transcends this debate.

Teilhard is looking *backward* into precursors of the cell, those metals and gases and various megamolecules that make up the cell's structure. He is interested in how organic compounds evolved into the first cell.

To grasp the difference in Teilhard's perspective, consider the automobile. Most auto buffs focus their attention on the historic birth of the motorcar and its evolution to contemporary makes and models.

In contrast, Teilhard would explore the motorcar's progenitors, its embriogenesis. What came before the motorcar, the basic elements that enabled it to be created? Who invented the wheel, the axle, the steering mechanism, the brake, the gearshift, the engine, and the fuel used to propel cars? Who finally assembled the parts to produce the first motorcar? Teilhard is interested in molecules and megamolecules because, to him, they are the basic elements that assembled themselves into the first cell.

The chariot, the farmer's wagon, the stagecoach, and the steam locomotive are precursors of the gasoline-driven automobile. Similarly, many different molecules and their interactions are the progenitors of cells.

Teilhard writes excitedly about the recently developed electron microscope. For the first time in the mid-1930s, biologists and chemists can observe these microorganisms and megamolecules. For him, this means scientists can begin to take a closer look at the many molecules and compounds that supply a cell's building blocks. Today's basic high school biology textbooks present vivid photos of various cell samples, even of various elements operating inside the cell's membrane. Teilhard had no such photos to study as he was writing *Phenomenon*.

A Forgotten Era (83–86, 45–48)

Teilhard emphasizes the period in Earth's development that marks the evolution of the megamolecules. Scientists like to give names to specific eras in Earth's history, such as the 165-million-year era of the dinosaurs, or the Mesozoic Era.

Teilhard says there was a similar period (duration) when megamolecules dominated Earth, preparing the necessary evolutionary layer from which the cell could emerge. The era of the megamolecule is a forgotten era, a distinct evolutionary period, lasting many millions of years. It is situated between the era of the ordinary molecule and the era of the cell.

To be fair, chemists in Teilhard's day had just discovered megamolecules and so possessed a very rudimentary knowledge of—or interest in—their structure. Today, we know much more about these giant molecules. They might be microscopic in size, but macromolecules are absolutely *gigantic* in the complex structure of their elements.[1]

THE CELL'S MILIEU (86, 48)

Teilhard recognizes that these huge molecules have a vital role to play in the emergence of life on Earth—and possibly elsewhere in the cosmos.[2] He is perhaps the first to give megamolecules their rightful place and importance in evolutionary history.

Today, megamolecules pervade our daily life. Wood and many stones consist of macromolecules, so they become parts of our homes' walls, floors, and furniture. Megamolecules fill our closets since all cloth fibers are made from them. Without macromolecules, there would be no photographic films, no electronic equipment, no television sets, no computers, no smartphones. Humans, animals, and plants would cease to exist without these highly structured molecules since they are essential components of meats, eggs, cereals, vegetables, and fruits. More importantly, the DNA and RNA molecules that uniquely identify each person and animal are megamolecules. The appearance of megamolecules marks an evolutionary breakthrough and their dispersion throughout the natural world proves prodigiously successful. Although megamolecules are nonliving, they make possible the appearance of all future living cells.

What mark the cell as a critical point of transformation are its *emergent properties*. Emergent properties are new capacities or functions of an evolved object that are not possessed by any of its predecessors or its parts. The motorcar is a critical advance over the stagecoach. Its advance is shown in its emergent properties—capacities that it possesses that a stagecoach does not possess.

Similarly, cells possess emergent properties that megamolecules don't have. For instance, living cells develop "a new method for agglomerating a larger amount of matter in a single unit" (86, 48). Each cell also has an outer protective covering and an inner energy source (mitochondria). Cells also possess capacities of movement, nutrition, elimination, reproduction, and so on. More importantly for Teilhard, each cell possesses a nucleus that governs its own inner life (its *within*).

Everyone acknowledges that cells manifest an evolutionary leap. For Teilhard, more significant is the fact that, from the beginning, *cellular inner structure becomes established and predictable*. Over time, even though cells continue to grow more complex and evolve into many distinct species of plants, fish, birds, and animals, *all cells everywhere remain true to their shared basic structure*. Basic structure and

91

components, essentially established among early cells, remains the same throughout eons of time and evolution.

THE CELLULAR REVOLUTION (THE CELL'S *WITHIN*) (86–90, 48–51)

Teilhard calls the cell's structure "a new type of material for a new stage of the universe" (87, 49). In the cell, evolution achieves a higher rung of complexity. By the law of Complexity-Consciousness, it advances still further in interiority, that is, in consciousness (87, 49). For Teilhard, the cell marks "a decisive step in the progress of consciousness on earth" (88, 49).

But what does it mean for a cell to have consciousness or a *within*? The cell is the first physical expression of evolution on Earth that has a *covering* and a *nucleus*. Think of a cell's covering like the circumference of a circle and its nucleus like the circle's center. Outwardly, the cell expends its (*tangential*) energy in activities—movement, feeding, eliminating waste, and reproducing. Inwardly, it continues to generate (*radial*) energy within itself through its nucleus, or center.

According to Teilhard, the cell's super-organization of matter plus its explosion of internal energy "is precisely the event which our theory [of Complexity-Consciousness] could have led us to expect" (89, 50).

In book 3, Teilhard will show how evolution uses this same pattern to move life to the next level—to thought and reflection. Just as the cell's structure provides "a new type of material for a new stage of the universe," our human structure provides "a new type of material for a new stage of the universe." Although human activities—walking, talking, lifting, gesturing, ectcetera—expend a person's (tangential) energy, each human is capable of continually generating new internal (radial) energy through thought, learning, and relationships.

Next in this chapter, Teilhard wants to look at the cell and its historical appearance, in *space* and, then, in *time*. But first, here is a summary of what we have learned so far.

SUMMARY

- The cell is the natural granule of life in the same way as the atom is the natural granule of simple, elemental matter.

- The age of the megamolecule is a distinct evolutionary period, lasting many millions of years.
- Living cells devise new methods for gathering and integrating larger amounts of matter into a single unit.
- Emergent properties are new capacities or functions of an evolved object that are not possessed by any of its predecessors or its parts.
- Cellular structure is essentially fixed among early cells, and the same basic structure is maintained through time and evolution.
- The cell's structure presents "a new type of material for a new stage of the universe."
- The cell continues to generate (radial) energy within itself through its center.

2. The Initial Manifestations of Life (90–96, 51–56)

There is no chance of ever finding a living example of the original cells that appeared in Earth's oceans more than three billion years ago. We can hope to discover fossilized remains, of course, but all *living* evidence has vanished. The disappearance of a thing's historical beginnings is a common phenomenon on Earth. We could never resurrect the first fish, the first turtle, the first monkey, the first chimp, the first Neanderthal, the first *Homo sapiens*. Finding living examples of any of these "firsts" remains "materially out of our grasp," says Teilhard. This is a phenomenon that runs through Earth's history. He calls it "the automatic suppression of evolutionary peduncles" (90, 51).

Teilhard uses this word *peduncle* (pronounced *puh-DUNK-el*) many times in his text, often metaphorically, so it is wise to grasp what he means by it and how he uses the term.

In botany, *a peduncle is the main stalk or stem of a flower or a fruit.* It is the stalk (or peduncle) that gives birth to the flower. Yet, if you show a person only the stalk, they cannot envision the flower or fruit to which it will give birth. Conversely, if you look at a violet or a lily blossom, you cannot easily envision the peduncle (stalk or stem) from which it came. The blossom does not look at all like the stem from which it came, yet the blossom emerges from the stem.

Today, metaphorically, we see only "blossoms" of dog life—such as the Dachshund, Dalmatian, and Poodle among hundreds of breeds—but we have no living examples of their stem (peduncle)—the mammal from which they historically emerged many millions of years ago. The same is true of the first cells.

THE CELL'S PEDUNCLE

Although we cannot directly envision the "stem" (peduncle) of the first cells, Teilhard says, we can get a sense of the cell's peduncle by looking at four contexts. He calls these contexts

1. their milieu,
2. their small size and countless number,
3. their multiple locations of origin, and
4. their interrelationships and shape.

1. *The ocean provides the milieu of the first cells.* It was "perhaps a thousand million years ago...in a heavy liquid environment that the first cells must have formed" (90–91, 51–52).[3] Teilhard envisions "tiny granules of protoplasm, with or without an individually differentiated nucleus" (91, 51). Teilhard uses "protoplasm" generally to include all living parts of a cell, such as its *cytoplasm* (a gel-like substance that fills the cells membrane) or its *organelles* (the functional parts interacting within a cell). He pictures the seas teeming with molecules and mega-molecules attracting each other and joining together.

2. *Early cells are small in size and countless in number.* As Teilhard envisions these granules of protoplasm, or cells, they are extremely small and countless, microscopic and innumerable. Multitudes of them is what we should expect, since that is evolution's consistent developmental pattern: *first, a great multitude of individual units appear (plurality), then these individual units are attracted to form connections or unions (unity).* A union is structurally more complex than any of its individual parts. *The new unities emerge with new abilities (energy).*

3. *Cells originate in a number of places.* "Life, no sooner started than it swarmed" (92, 52). "We can suppose that the transition from megamolecules to cells took place simultaneously at a great many

points," since the conditions for their emergence was widespread (92, 53). Scientists today agree.[4] Teilhard notes that the phenomenon of *simultaneous emergence* continues to happen on all levels, for example, with creative ideas among humans. A new insight or discovery often happens simultaneously in various parts of the world. Such serendipity is often attributed to the *zeitgeist*, the spirit of the times.

Teilhard's point is that these first cells are the "peduncles" of all terrestrial life. They must "have enjoyed an exceptional aptitude to branch out into new forms" (93, 53). Today we might describe these early cells as *pluripotent*, like stem cells in a human embryo that can morph into arms, legs, heart, liver, and so on.

"From whatever angle we look at the *nascent* cellular world, it shows itself to be already infinitely complex" (93, 53). Newborn cells are appearing all over the planet, rapidly adopting various outward expressions and growing in various climates and chemical environments. Like stem cells, these early cells formed "an enormous bundle of polymorphous fibers." They became organic masses or multitudes in movement (93, 54).

4. *A cell's parts and its shape are interrelated.* Interrelationship is the key distinguishing feature of the cell. Typically, forms of lifeless matter—atoms, molecules, megamolecules—either tend to float about independently or else large numbers of similar molecules get bonded together. What is distinctive about developing cells is that, in each cell, its elements tend to become *a unified functioning system.*

A cell's elements are not simply glued together like molecules in a crystal. Rather, they interrelate and interact as a single cohesive team. A cell's parts are like players on a sports team. Its parts are interactive and interdependent, not merely mechanically connected or bonded together. A cell's parts are also symbiotic, that is, "they share a life in common" (94, 54).

Because of this interrelatedness, each cell part tends to become individualized or to manifest a special uniqueness. Just as each team player has a position on the playing field and gets to perform a unique role, each cell part gets its uniqueness by its elements and position. These determine how it interacts, and the functions it performs. The cells themselves, too, become individualized and unique.

When all the early cells on Earth are viewed as a single whole, they form the beginnings of the *biosphere*, "the living film of the earth" (94, 54).

How All Cells Are Alike

Early cells and the innumerable elements composing them are not constructed haphazardly. As operating systems, all cells are alike. The inner makeup, functions, and structures of all cells are similar as are the relationships among their elements. Teilhard finds this fact amazing. He explains why.

All cells, from those in the simplest bacteria to those in a human brain, contain the same set of elements, the same types of proteins and acids. This is true, despite the fact that first cells emerging around the world could have been made up of other chemical formulas and structures. Because different cells were born in different climates and conditions, they had the opportunity to develop in a variety of ways. *Yet, variation did not happen.* The liquid bath in which a cell's parts move around has the *same chemical makeup in all cells on Earth today.*

Because such a universal similarity in makeup does not appear logically necessary, it suggests nature made an early choice. The similarity of liquid bath in all cells worldwide "has been taken as proof that all existing organisms descended from a single ancestral group [of cells]" (95, 55).

Teilhard notes that, whatever the initial impetus for cell formation and reproduction was, "it exhausts only a part of what might have been" (96, 55). By that, Teilhard means that there might have been dozens of ways chemicals could have come together to form the first units of life. He suggests that, perhaps, on other planets different combinations of chemical elements may have come together to form life. But, on Earth the combination of chemicals that are used to form life remains consistent.

Here is another moment when Teilhard is awed by the workings of evolution. He stands in wonder at the fact that the basic inner structure of every atom in the table of chemical elements (prelife) remains the same despite their growing complexity. The basic makeup of every cell (life) remains consistent despite their growing complexity. How can this be?

All forms of life on Earth originate from this one basic stem structure, or peduncle—the original group of cells. From this stem, manifestations of life branch out in myriad forms of fish, plants, reptiles, birds, and the rest of the animal world. Rooted in this basic stem, life

96

on Earth branched out and will continue to do so indefinitely in a continual emergence of new species.

All cells on our planet share an "inherent kinship" (100, 58) manifested in the absolute and universal *uniformity of the basic cellular structure* found in all living things on Earth.

Moreover, even as organisms become more complex and more conscious, *they find identical solutions* to the basic problems of perception, nutrition, and reproduction. For example, all animals are similar in their vascular and nervous systems, in the formation of blood, organs, gonads, and eyes. This similarity is why scientists can reliably prepare new medicines for humans by testing them beforehand in animal trials. Current research in DNA confirms Teilhard's statements in this section even though DNA hadn't been described or mapped when he was writing *Phenomenon.*

Among conscious creatures, different species also consistently develop similar forms of gathering and socializing for work, play, and family life. This includes humans. Each of us is unique, yet basically we are all alike. We can contribute blood, kidneys, and hearts to one another. We all want to be loved and valued. We all want to form friendships and families. We all are curious and want to learn about ourselves and each other. The development of our *withouts* and *withins* seems to be guided.

From his planetary vantage point, Teilhard makes another observation: "Elementary life looks like a variegated multitude of microscopic elements, a multitude great enough to envelope the earth" (plurality). Yet, this multitude is "sufficiently interrelated and elected so as to form a structural whole of genetic solidarity" (unity) (96, 55). This unity is the *biosphere.* We are all linked together by our genes.

AUTOPOIESIS

In 1973, decades after Teilhard's death, two Chilean biologists introduced a new term into the scientific lexicon called *autopoiesis* (pronounced *auto-poy-AY-sis*). It means, literally, "self-making and self-maintaining."[5] The Greek verb *poiein* means "to make or create." Biologists first used the term to describe the self-maintenance and self-reproducing abilities of living cells. Autopoiesis emphasizes, not merely the cell's makeup or its ability to repair itself and adapt, but also its ability to reproduce and guarantee its ongoing life.

Using nutrition and fuel absorbed from the environment, a cell repairs itself and produces the components needed to maintain its organic health and even to reproduce. Cells are autonomous in the sense that the construction of their elements and their repair is not produced by an outside agent, as is required for repair of an automobile or refrigerator. The cell repairs itself. It is self-making and self-maintaining.

Autopoiesis has come to be used to describe any system that is capable of reproducing and maintaining itself. The term may apply not only to biological entities but also to social and intellectual systems. Examples of autopoiesis on the social level might include a corporation or a nation. Those on an intellectual level might include the scientific fields of mathematics and physics. Each of these systems makes and maintains itself.

Over time, many autopoietic systems tend to grow and develop. Small businesses may grow into large complex corporations. Mathematics has evolved from its earliest elements of arithmetic and geometry to include an array of more complex elements such as calculus, number theory, matrix theory, topology, probability, and statistics. At the same time, these emergent systems are still identifiable as having developed from their earlier stems (peduncles) of arithmetic, geometry, and algebra.

Although Teilhard was not around when the term *autopoiesis* was coined, he would have liked it. And used it. I believe that Teilhard would have described our universe as an *evolving autopoietic universe* from its first moments. He would add that autopoiesis did not begin with the first living cell but began with the Big Bang. He would say that the universe has been "making and maintaining itself" for almost 14 billion years, and that Earth has been "making and maintaining itself" for over four billion, even though autopoiesis became clearly evident only with the emergence of cellular life.

Teilhard's discovery is that the universe, which began as a chaotic explosion of numberless subatomic particles, has been driven from the beginning by the evolutionary law of Attraction-Connection-Complexity-Consciousness.[6] To be precise, Teilhard calls this law that he discovered simply "Complexity-Consciousness." But he also acknowledges that "attraction" was a most fundamental force in the universe. Attraction creates Connections. Connections produce Complexity, and Complexity requires Consciousness.

Because of this inbuilt drive, the totality of subatomic particles, through countless random gropings, formed an autopoietic whole. That totality would slowly discover through trial and error—by *groping*—how to make and maintain itself while growing evermore complex and more conscious. Groping expresses a most primitive way of expressing the drive to evolve. Groping continues to operate in this way even among the most advanced human societies.

SUMMARY

To summarize the additional principles and insights we have learned so far in this chapter of *Phenomenon*:

- *A peduncle is the main stalk or stem of a flower or a fruit.* The first cells are the "peduncles" of all terrestrial life.
- Cells follow evolution's consistent developmental pattern—*plurality, unity, energy.*
- Interrelationships among a cell's parts are its key distinguishing features.
- As operating systems, all cells are structurally alike.
- The various parts of cells interrelate and interact as a single cohesive interdependent team.
- Cells are symbiotic, that is, their parts are interrelated in such a way that they share a life in common.
- All the cells on Earth, viewed as a single whole, form the beginnings of the *biosphere*, "the living film of the earth."
- The liquid bath in which a cell's parts move around has the *same chemical makeup in all cells on Earth today*.
- All cells on our planet share an "inherent kinship" in the universal *uniformity of the basic cellular structure*.
- As organisms become more complex and more conscious, *they find identical solutions* to the problems of perception, nutrition, and reproduction.
- Autopoiesis also emphasizes a cell's ability to reproduce and guarantee its ongoing life.
- Cells are autonomous in the sense that each cell repairs itself. It is self-making and self-maintaining.

3. The Season of Life
(96–102, 56–60)

In the previous section, Teilhard described the origins of the cell and the formation of the biosphere as it happens in *space*, that is, on the planet's surface. In this section, he looks at the origins of the cell and the biosphere as it happens in *time*.

Many events on Earth are cyclical and seasonal, that is, they recur periodically and predictably. Such periods may be short as in daily sunrise and tidal movements. Other cyclical periods are longer as in the moon's monthly orbit or the Earth's yearly orbit. Despite its many cyclical events, Earth—and the universe itself—are in a forward-moving evolutionary process.

Teilhard says that using *time* as a measure confirms that our planet Earth must have had its own historic birth. Most recent estimates set Earth's birth around 4.5 billion years ago. Since its birth, the planet has been going through many transformational changes. Only when it reached a certain age was it ready to bear life. The appearance of the first cells was a unique event *in time*. The subsequent historic births of fish, trees, reptiles, birds, and other animals were also unique events in time, as was the emergence of *Homo sapiens*.

What becomes clear is that Earth continues to go through its evolutionary process. Its development is both "continuous and irreversible" (101, 59). It follows an ever-ascending curve, measured by continued increases in complexity and consciousness over time. Earth has an open-ended future, not a cyclic one.

The appearance of the cell *in time* "renews our perspective of the world" as a planet in evolution (102, 60). It also implies that the living layers on our planet (the biosphere) will continue to develop "from within." Because of Earth's limited surface, any radial energy generated by life must continue to intensify. Teilhard pictures Earth nourishing itself by planet-sized deep breaths. In his words, "Life was born and propagates itself on earth as a solitary pulsation" (102, 62). Earth is always "giving birth" to new species and renewing itself, providing a magnificent example of autopoesis. With space travel and exploration, Earth is expanding its potential beyond our planet.

Summary

Time to summarize additional principles and insights we have learned so far in this chapter of *Phenomenon*:

- Earth—and the universe itself—are in a forward moving evolutionary process.
- The appearance of the first cells was a unique event *in time* that "renews our perspective of the world" as a planet in evolution.
- Earth is primarily an evolutionary process, "continuous and irreversible," measured by increases in complexity and consciousness.
- Earth is always "giving birth" to novelty and development.

Chapter 2

The Expansion of Life
(103–40, 61–90)

Perspective

IN THIS CHAPTER, Teilhard presents "a simplified but structural representation of life evolving on earth." From his perspective, his presentation represents "a vision so homogeneous and coherent that its truth is irresistible." But he is aware that he offers a perspective that his readers "may see and accept—or not see" (103, 61).

The chapter looks at the observable expansion of life on Earth in three areas:

1. The elemental movements of life
2. Life's spontaneous ramifications
3. The tree of life

Notice that in this chapter Teilhard is taking the perspective of life's *without*. The following chapter describes the same expansion from the perspective of life's *within*.

1. The Elemental Movements of Life
(104–12, 62–65)

At every advancing change of state in the nonliving world—from particle to atom to molecule to compound—Teilhard recognizes the presence of the same three characteristics: *plurality, union, energy.* He now identifies evidence for these same three characteristics in the emergence of life in the cell.

In this section, Teilhard develops the *plurality* of cellular life plus some of its *energy* potential. In the following section, he focuses on the *unity* of cellular life.

SIX EMERGENT PROPERTIES

Teilhard begins by describing *six of life's emergent properties* and their importance. He adds a corollary that he calls "the Ways of Life."

- *Reproduction.* Cellular life introduces the totally new phenomenon of reproduction. A single cell divides and gives birth to another cell similar to it. Each of these "baby" cells is capable of dividing and giving birth to new "baby" cells. The new phenomenon of reproduction emerges *because cells die.*

   Cells die in contrast to atoms and molecules that seem to have an infinite lifespan with an equivalent rigidity. Thus, an iron atom remains an unchanging iron atom forever. An undissolved salt molecule remains a salt molecule. Because living cells are finite and die, they discover a way—reproduction—to survive "in self-defense." Their ability to reproduce turns out to be "an instrument of progress and conquest" (104, 62). Cells learn to perpetuate themselves and *to improve themselves in the process.* They are self-evolving—an expression of *energy.*

- *Multiplication.* Because of the cell's ability to repeatedly divide itself and to pass on this ability to each of its descendants, it can *quickly cover the world.* This is its quantitative aspect. *Plurality.* Cellular life becomes "a force of expansion" that proves to be "invincible" (105, 63). Because the property of cell division is spontaneous, nothing from within the cell can "arrest its devouring and creative conflagration." Nor is there anything to stop its progress (105, 63).

- *Renovation.* While the energy inherent in nonliving atoms and molecules tends to get used up, the living cell reproduces itself. The cell "multiplies without crumbling" (105, 63). Reproduction not only allows the cell to go on living in its descendants, it also, little by little, transforms its offspring by "inner readjustment" (small adaptive mutations). This renewal process allows newborn cells *to take on "new appearance and direction"* (105, 63). As a self-evolving creature, the cell becomes the *locus of diversification*. For example, in our day, bacteria adapt and diversify to become immune to certain antibiotics. An expression of *energy*.

- *Conjugation*. Conjugation is a term to describe cells mating. While some cells continue to divide and reproduce themselves, other cells are attracted to join and mate (conjugate) with different cells. For example, among *bacteria, conjugation* is defined as the transfer of genetic material between bacterial cells by direct cell-to-cell contact or by a bridge-like connection between two cells. It is a mechanism called *horizontal gene transfer* that happens among protozoa and some algae and fungi.[1]

  Early in cellular history, the phenomenon of male-female sexual differences has not yet manifested. Even so, different cells begin conjugal relationships. *Offspring of these innovative unions emerge from two centers, or two nuclei*, "exchanging and varying their respective riches" (106, 63). *Cell conjugation becomes a prodigious invention*, opening the way to endless cellular variety and potential. An expression of *plurality* and *energy*.

- *Association*. Cells begin to press against each other. Some new cells may be born in clusters. Various living particles begin to group themselves into associations of complex organisms. Such groupings, says Teilhard, are "an almost inevitable consequence of their multiplication" (106, 64). We can look back on these earliest associations and realize that they marked "stages of this *still unfinished* march of nature toward the unification or synthesis" of the products of association and reproduction (107, 64).

  The drive to association and synthesis (Attraction and Connection) keeps cells growing into higher and more complex forms of union. Eventually, they result in the complex sexual identities reflected in human society today (Complexity and Consciousness).

Teilhard points out that *association* as a symbiotic phenomenon is "not sporadic or accidental." Socialization, forming groups with shared ways of growth, protection, and survival, "represents one of the most universal and constant expedients…used by life in its expansion" (107, 64). This represents *union* or *unity*.

Teilhard sees the continuous emergence of ever-larger forms of association as "ascending" and "invincible." Nature seems driven to continually find new ways to keep groups ascending the ladder of Complexity-Consciousness.

- *Controlled Additivity.* While simple multiplication and variability can cause cellular life to expand and cover the globe horizontally, such *horizontal* spread of itself does not create *vertical* movement toward higher complexity and consciousness. Controlled additivity, the continuous accumulation of properties, "intervenes and acts as a vertical component" (108, 65). Teilhard suggests a better term here might be "controlled *complexity*."

Biology's name for this "vertical" phenomenon is *orthogenesis* (literally, development moving in the right direction). Though orthogenesis is typically used to describe an individual fetus "moving in the right direction" during gestation, Teilhard applies the term *orthogenesis* to the totality of cellular life in the biosphere "moving in the right direction." For Teilhard, moving toward the development of thought in the noosphere is "moving in the right direction."

Teilhard points out that the controlled complexity process has been happening since the Big Bang. In guiding the embriogenesis of the cell, evolution continues to add complexity to the mix. Notice that in each case of increased complexity—particles to atoms to molecules to compounds to cells—we also see an increase in centeredness, which process Teilhard calls "centro-complexity" (108, 65). Each cell has its own nucleus or "center."

Despite or because of "the complication and instability" of these growing cellular systems, "instead of falling and failing, they seem to rise toward forms that are more and more improbable" (109, 65). Observing these primitive cells, for instance, who could have predicted the appearance of dinosaurs? In the time of the dinosaurs, who could have predicted *Homo sapiens*? Without the drive of orthogenesis, life would have merely spread horizontally in a homogeneous fashion. But with the orthogenesis drive "there is an ascent of life that is invincible" (109, 65).

The drive of orthogenesis in the sphere of life (biosphere) eventually gives rise to the sphere of thought (noosphere).

A COROLLARY: THE WAYS OF LIFE (109–12, 65–68)

In the next section, the "Tree of Life," Teilhard sketches the grand sweep of the growth of life over a few billion years. Before doing that, he wants to look at some key characteristics of cells, what he calls their "ways of life." He also wants to see how their typical ways correspond with basic evolutionary laws, such as the drive to complexity and consciousness.

He identifies three qualities that characterize cellular life. Life moves forward using

- *profusion*
- *ingenuity*
- *indifference*

He notes that these three qualities characterize *all* life, not just cellular life (109, 66).

- *Profusion.* "Life advances by mass effects, by dint of multitudes flung into action without apparent plan" (109, 66). Despite the prodigious waste and ferocity of living things, there is "a great deal of biological efficiency in the *struggle for life*." This struggle is more than "a series of duels." Teilhard describes it rather as "a conflict of chances"—chances to enhance *survival*, chances to ensure *progress*. Not all species survive. Among those that do, some ensure progress.

  Progress in cells is achieved by "groping." Teilhard

defines groping as *directed chance* (110, 66). He describes how cells do this. The fact that cells pervade everything everywhere, he says, allows them to try everything. And in trying different possibilities, they find out what works to their advantage. They discover—and use—those changes that increase chances of survival and opportunities for progress.

That is why *profusion* is a basic characteristic of cellular life. Profusion allows for groping. And groping enhances survival and progress. Profusion and groping over billions of years has allowed life to evolve from single-celled creatures to humans.

- *Ingenuity.* Life also continually manifests cleverness and creativity. Teilhard calls ingenuity the "indispensable condition of additivity" (see "Controlled Additivity" above). Cells and life-forms generally act like creative bioengineers. Not only does life have to continually invent the needed mechanism to foster survival and progress, it must also "so design it that it occupies the minimum space and is simple and resilient" (110, 66). Not only do life-forms need to assemble their mechanism, but the mechanism also needs to be so constructed that it may be taken apart and its parts repaired or replaced, as needed.

  Many "parts" of our lives must be recharged, repaired, or replaced from time to time, such as batteries, eyeglasses, light bulbs, and phones. All are the products of human ingenuity to foster survival and progress.

  A cell is a living whole. It is an operating system. A system is not defined simply as the sum of its parts, but as the *product of its interactions.* Each cell—and each living organism—acts as a whole, as a living system. Teilhard describes the entire future of life on Earth beginning with the cell as a "triumph of ingenuity" (111, 67).

- *Indifference.* Teilhard admits that he named this characteristic "from our human perspective." The way we see living creatures eat, assimilate, and destroy each other, it would seem that these creatures are "indifferent" to the survival of various forms of life. But Teilhard assures us that *life itself* is hardly indifferent.

Life is focused on enriching and furthering life. "By the force of orthogenesis the individual unit [of life] becomes part of a chain. From being a center [of life] it is changed into being an intermediary link—no longer existing, but transmitting; and as it has been put, life is more real than lives" (111, 67).

Teilhard clarifies what he means by life's indifference. Life shows little interest "toward whatever is not future and totality" (111, 67). Moreover, life tends to resolve the difficult situations it encounters in such a way that life may go forward and become more and more a single, centered whole (a totality).

The indifference principle is also true of humans. When someone is obsessed with negative past events, it is difficult for that person to focus on the future. But those who can let go of the past (be "indifferent" to it) can go forward and become better and more integrated.

- *Global Unity.* Teilhard adds a fourth characteristic of life, a drive toward global unity. Earth, as a single, centered whole, is the natural outcome of the other three characteristics—*profusion, ingenuity,* and *indifference* (112, 68).

  Once a certain level of solidarity is achieved, life never loses it. The planet makes continual adjustments among its physical parts (its *without*) to maintain and increase solidarity, or global wholeness. As life spreads and evolves over Earth, it is clearly aiming toward creating "one single and gigantic organism" (112, 68).

  Supporting this unifying *without* process, Earth's *within* maintains a "profound equilibrium." This is a key insight for Teilhard: *life on Earth is destined to become one single conscious organism.* It will have one nucleus, or one conscious "center," at its heart.

Teilhard cautions that if we don't keep in mind this drive of the biosphere toward global organic unity, we cannot truly understand the human phenomenon. He will show how humanity's development, while integral to the biosphere's drive, transcends it. Here in book 2, Teilhard is still primarily focused on the dynamics of the *biosphere*. He is not yet describing the dynamics and functions of the *noosphere*. That is the theme of *Phenomenon*'s book 3.

2. The Ramifications of the Living Mass (112–22, 68–75)

So far, Teilhard has been analyzing the development of the biosphere in terms of "cells or groups of cells taken in isolation." Shifting his focus from *plurality* to *union*, he now wants to look at the biosphere as a huge "living mass" of life moving forward, like an advancing army, becoming the "'front' of advancing life" (112, 68).

In the initial stages of the biosphere, global unity still appears diffuse. But with life's evolutionary ascent, the planet's organic *unity* grows ever sharper and clearer, more and more complex. Everything around us is becoming more inextricably intertwined. Earth continues to "center itself under our eyes" (112, 68). We begin to recognize it as one magnificent organism, of which we humans are a part.

In this section Teilhard describes the branching, or ramification, of life-forms. He is trying to show a path of development from the first masses of primitive cells to the tens of thousands of distinct species of fish, birds, flowers, plants, trees, and animals on Earth today.

Biologists today classify all living species under various categories, such as amphibian, reptile, insect, vertebral, four-legged, and mammal. Zoology also classifies life-forms from the most general to the more specific, arranged in tiers. Zoology's classifications, beginning with the most general, are *kingdom, class, order, family, genus,* and *species*.

Teilhard wants to show that these botanical classifications or headings are not mere abstract labels, but are actual, identifiable stages in the advancing development of life. A *kingdom* of life-forms has its own life and identity, separate from all the individual life-forms in it.

The *biological advance—from kingdom to class to order to family to genus, and species—is neither chaotic nor continuous.* Rather it is organic and divergent. "As life expands, it splits spontaneously into

109

natural, hierarchical units. It *ramifies*" (113, 68). It branches ever outward, organically, from its trunk (or peduncle) like branches and limbs
of a tree. Biology focuses, not on the trunk, but on the branches. What
biology studies are divergent *groups* of life (*unions*).

Teilhard sees the phenomenon of ramification as a key characteristic of life in large masses. Masses of the earliest winged creatures
branch out into thousands of bird species. Masses of the earliest four-
footed creatures branch out into thousands of animal species. For large
living masses, ramification serves as a new form of "reproduction."
Ramification is as essential to these masses as (mitotic division) is to
cell reproduction.

Teilhard chooses to highlight three factors in the ramification
process of huge masses of primitive cells:

A. *Aggregation*
B. *Maturity*
C. *Distance*

Aggregates of Growth (113–15, 69–70)
Aggregation and Orthogenesis

Aggregation may be described as a dispersion of individual early
cells into large groups—to form masses within masses. That this happened was a new and unexpected occurrence. Countless primitive
cells did not remain a bewildering confusion, as might be suspected.
Rather, as these cells multiplied, they were being pressed closer and
closer together in a kind of chaotic mix. Yet, says Teilhard, they defied
the laws of probability and evolved identifiably into more complex
units, or aggregates. How did this happen? How did these seemingly
amorphous messy, crushed-together masses of cells eventually resolve
themselves into a series of distinct species of life that we see today?
The odds were that this chaotic mass of cells would remain forever a
"complicated tangle" (113, 68).

Chaos theory today might predict that some kind of order was
bound to emerge from this confusion. Teilhard suggests that there was
an evolutionary force driving this process, called *orthogenesis* (literally, *proper development*). He would rather suggest that, despite the
odds, these chaotic masses of microbes and microorganisms gathered

themselves into a series of "different lines radiating orthogenetically." That is, they were developing "in the right way" into amphibian, reptile, insect, mammal. Each of these lines became recognizable by a predominance of certain characteristics. Zoology eventually identified them by different *levels of union*, as kingdoms, classes, orders, families, genera, and species.[2] These identifiable lines or "privileged axes" became a "new and unexpected fact" in Earth's history (113, 69).

Orthogenesis, or proper development, can account for the attraction and mutual adjustment of those evolving lines. Orthogenesis is the overall force or law that governs the masses of cells in their process of diversification "into a restricted number of dominant directions" (113, 69).

At first, this diversification is indistinct and indefinite. But once theses masses of cells "reach a certain degree of mutual cohesion (*union*), the lines isolate themselves in a closed sheaf [bundle] that can no longer be penetrated by neighboring sheaves" (114, 69). Thus, reptiles cannot mate with insects, nor can birds mate with chipmunks. Similarly, each major branch of the biological "tree" enjoys its own identity; members of life's different tree branches cannot "mate" with each other.

From then on, each bundle—of reptile, insect, mammal, and so forth—evolves on its own, autonomously. Each bundle becomes individualized, and the *phylum* is born.

The Phylum

In biology, a *phylum is a living bundle of bundles, a line of lines.* A phylum has three characteristics.

- First, it is a *collective reality*, a *living union.*
- Second, in its structure, a phylum is *polymorphous and elastic*; it can produce examples of itself that can differ in size or in multiple expressions.
- Third, a phylum has a *dynamic nature.* Its members interact. They begin to consolidate, pool resources, socialize, and, as a new whole, generate new abilities.

Teilhard develops these three points more fully here and in the following subheadings. He uses the image of a tree with its limbs and branches to help explain these three characteristics.

First, for Teilhard, a phylum is a *collective reality,* a *living union,* not just an artificial category named for the sake of classification. Looked at in sufficient magnification, a phylum may be seen as a clearly identifiable structured reality, just a major limb branching off from the trunk of a large tree is a clearly identifiable reality all its own. When we look at a tree, we are so used to focusing on its outer leaves or blossoms that we tend not to notice the smaller branches, larger limbs, trunk, and roots from which the blossoms spring and to which they are connected.

When we step back and look at the whole tree, we can see how the leaves and blossoms as well as the smaller branches are all subordinate lines emerging from each large limb connected to the tree's trunk. Each large limb reaching out from the trunk is a major line, the tree's lesser branches are the subordinate lines. Together, they form a collective reality, a living *union,* a phylum.

A major limb is also identifiable as an initial sectioning from the trunk and a real natural unit of the tree. A phylum is not just a category for classification. It is just as real and alive as a major tree limb.

For Teilhard, the phylum is "one of the *natural units* of the world" (115, 70). It represents an initial expression of living autonomous development. For example, dinosaurs form a phylum. A phylum, just like a major tree limb, behaves as a living thing. In its own way, *even as a limb it grows and flourishes.* A phylum evolves. The phylum of dinosaurs evolved over millions of years.

Second, a phylum as a living systemic structure is *polymorphous and elastic.* Like the branch of a tree, a phylum can change its size, shape, form, weight. It can stretch or shrink or shift direction to continue adapting and developing. Some dinosaurs evolved feathers and learned to fly.

Third, a phylum has a *dynamic nature.* A phylum discovers and creates its future by *groping.* Groping is a natural exploratory evolutionary process that Teilhard described earlier. A phylum of life learns how to survive and increase its viability. It develops into an efficient form. A bird phylum develops beaks for pecking; a mammal phylum develops four legs for movement. A phylum spends time internally modifying itself, then each time testing the result. Once a modification proves effective, it spreads and consolidates. The bird beak may modify itself with small adjustments, but the beak remains permanent. The mammal's legs may make small improvements or variations—hooves, paws, toes—but having four legs remain permanent. The phylum enters a period of stability. It multiplies, but without further major diversification.

THE FLOURISHING OF MATURITY (116–18, 71–73)

To use the tree metaphor again, when a major limb emerges from the tree trunk, it continues to thicken and give birth to diversification by sprouting smaller limbs or branches. Each branch brings a new expression to its parent limb, but the new branches have "no power or reason to eliminate each other" (117, 71). They all share life in the phylum (major limb).

The major limb keeps splitting and branching outward, subdividing qualitatively and simultaneously spreading quantitatively. Each smaller branch, or ray, keeps fanning outward in fresh lines while maintaining its identifying characteristics. The oak tree in all its branches remains an oak. The elm tree in all its branches remains an elm.

Teilhard describes a phylum in full bloom as a "verticil of consolidated forms" (117, 72). A *verticil is any branch or stem from which emerge a series of smaller branches sharing similar characteristics.* The blossoms on a tree or a flower are examples of "consolidated forms." All blossoms of a tree are like one another and form a consistent appearance. All the leaves of an oak are consistent in appearance. So are the leaves of an elm. If a tree's trunk is its *peduncle*, its branches are its *verticils*.

Maturity and Socialization

Teilhard notes that when we observe a phylum of living and moving cellular organisms, for example, trees, ants, apes, or humanoids, and follow that phylum to its final form or expression, we see "a profound inclination toward socialization" (117, 72).

Socialization, Teilhard claims, is the highest expression of the "vital power of association." Mutual adhesion, or consolidation, exemplifies socialization as one of the most essential laws of organized matter. Socialization provides resistance to destruction and a capacity for conquest. For Teilhard, to consolidate means to solidify connections or, more concretely, "to form societies" (118, 72). Consolidation is the sign of a phylum's *full maturity*.

While a tree with its trunk, limbs, branches, twigs, and leaves is a good metaphor for some aspects of a phylum, it doesn't describe everything about it. With a natural tree, the trunk, branches, and leaves are all genetically one *species*. Such a tree could not model a phylum undergoing species mutations such that each different "branch" of it could evolve into a different kind of tree species.

The imaginary trunk of the "tree phylum of life" that Teilhard describes would have multiple limbs with multiple branches, each limb spawning *a different tree species* — oak, maple, linden, cedar, pine, chestnut, and so on. Better to use animal phyla as examples, such as reptiles, birds, or mammals. The beaked bird phylum branched into sparrows, crows, wrens, and hummingbirds. The four-footed mammal phylum branched into lions, sheep, horses, cows, pigs, dogs, and cats.

As Teilhard describes it, a phylum is also a "forest of exploring antennae" (118, 73). As a living thing, a phylum *as a whole* is always groping, searching, feeling around, reaching out, trying this and that, looking for ways to further enhance and spread its life.

In some cases, Teilhard notes, that after a phylum reaches full maturity, a process of self-fertilization starts somewhere within the phylum and a new "bud" appears in the form of a mutation. From this bud, a new phylum appears, grows, and spreads out above the branch on which it is born.

More and more branches (new phyla) may germinate — "always provided the branches are on the right path [orthogenesis] and the general equilibrium of the biosphere is favorable" (118, 73). For example, although pine trees may grow in most climates, palm trees cannot. Palm trees have reached a limit, a climatic boundary beyond which they cannot spread.

THE EFFECTS OF DISTANCE (IN TIME) (119–22, 73–75)

We humans are not accustomed to comprehending distance, measured in long periods of evolutionary time. Because of this, the evidence of nature in front of our eyes today distorts the evolving phenomenon of life as it really happens over time. To use the tree metaphor again, it's as though we can see only the leaves and blossoms of the tree today. The trunk and its branches have disappeared from our vision. We can see roses, lilies, daffodils, violets, and gardenias, but we cannot see the original limb of the phylum from which they all evolved.

The point Teilhard is making here is not about life's evolutionary movement in itself, *but in our inability to see it.* All we see of an evolutionary movement is its present moment, "corrected according to its alteration [caused] by *the effects of distance* [in time]" (119, 73). If we could watch centuries of mutations in a phylum using time-lapse photography, we could observe how life has fanned out (radiated) into distinct species from each phylum. We could watch the flower phylum radiate out into roses, lilies, daffodils, violets, and gardenias. To help us see the evolving picture over time, Teilhard suggests two techniques: *exaggeration* and *suppression.*

First, Teilhard *exaggerates*, or accents, each phylum and its dispersion into several species by drawing them in something like a tree or a fan that spreads outward. What we see today are only the most recent tips of a phylum, such as the vast variety of trees or plants in the forest. What we no longer see are the originating germinating organisms that mutated into these phylum tips. To use another example, we know that life began in the sea and only millennia later did forms of animal life appear on the land. We have no image or physical evidence of the first creature that crawled out of the sea onto land. A fanlike drawing would include both the originating organisms as well as the large variety of branches.

Many gaps exist in our understanding of the branching or ramification story in the animal and vegetable kingdoms. Using the tree metaphor, it's as though many of its branches have dried up, broken off, and disappeared. This symbolizes Teilhard's second technique, *suppression.*

Teilhard calls his second technique "suppression of the peduncles" (120, 74). It is exceedingly difficult to identify or prove the birth of a species for the simple reason that *its stems or roots have been suppressed.* Sometimes nature does the suppressing, sometimes humans do it.

Here is an example of human suppression. Suppose that many thousands of years from now a geologist of transportation technology wants to explore the species of transportation called "automobile." The only vehicles he or she will find buried in earth are the latest models of cars before the motorcar became an extinct species. Elderly people living today know a lot about the "peduncle" of the motorcar in its most primitive versions such as the Model A Ford. The future geologist will find only the latest models (unless he luckily digs up an auto museum). We humans have effectively suppressed the peduncle of the motorcar. You and I know that, for someone far in the future, the stem or starting point of the automobile will be hidden from view.

Teilhard's point is that it would seem to a future geologist that our invention of the automobile had been created without any previous evolutionary groping. It would seem to him that the most sophisticated motorcar had been completed and fixed in our first attempt. His understanding of phylum of the species "automobile" would be severely distorted.

Similarly, when we try to discover the starting point or stem that evolved into a contemporary species of life, such as a rose, a chipmunk, or a trout, its peduncle is hidden from our view. Nature naturally does away with such primitive stems, much as an artist erases unnecessary lines of his earlier drawings, or a writer feeds earlier versions of his novel into a paper shredder.

To use another perspective, compare the trunk of a tree to a leaf on its outermost branch. Imagine a child who had never seen a tree, and you show that child a leaf. Then, you point to a major limb near the trunk of that tree. You insist that the limb is the parent of the leaf, that both leaf and limb, even though they look totally different, are really the same species. The child would say that's impossible. Yet, we know that the branch is the "stem" that produced the leaf.

Now, imagine that an amateur geologist digging in the earth came across a large bone that was a certain dinosaur fossil. The expert geologist looks at the bone and says to the amateur, "That's where the chicken came from. That dinosaur is the peduncle of today's chicken." The amateur might reply, "No way!"

In many cases, we would be totally surprised at—and probably not recognize—the stems or peduncles from which today's species evolved. Today, DNA evidence helps to trace the stem of a contemporary species, but Teilhard in 1939 knew little about DNA or of recent research in genetics.

3. The Tree of Life (122–40, 76–90)

Teilhard says we're now ready to look at a much more expanded picture of the Tree of Life. This long section is divided into three headings.

A. He takes up the four major branches of the Tree of Life, its quantity of units (122–27, 76–80), its layers (127–30, 80–82), and its branches (130–33, 82–83).
B. He looks at the Tree's dimensions (133–37, 84–88) in terms of their number, volume, and duration.
C. He summarizes the evidence for his findings about the Tree (137–40, 88–90).

FOUR MAJOR BRANCHES OF THE TREE OF LIFE

There is probably no reason for the ordinary reader to struggle with Teilhard's detailed analysis in this long section on the Tree of Life. Nor is there need to research the geological and botanical terminology used here. Basically, Teilhard wants to show that all living things on Earth today form a single Tree of Life.

Although there may be tens of thousands of living species visible on the outer edges of the Tree, they all may be traced back in time to four main branches that emerged from a single trunk.

- *Plants*: shrubs, trees, flowers, vines, and all other forms of vegetation
- *Lepidoptera*: creatures with four broad wings, such as butterflies and moths
- *Arthropods* (invertebrates, i.e., without spines): snails, squids, octopus, crabs, lobsters, barnacles, shrimp, insects, arachnids
- *Vertebrates*: all those with spinal cords, such as fish, reptiles, birds, and all mammals including humans

As evidence of human evolution, Teilhard uses the mammals, a subphylum of the vertebrates (*Chordata*), to trace human lineage. Earth today is teeming with mammals. We can find mammalian fossil evidence back beyond 300 million years ago.

To get a summary picture of the complex material Teilhard is working with, spend some time with his playful diagram of the Tree of Life (135, 86). Use Google to define any unfamiliar terms you find there.

THE TREE OF LIFE'S DIMENSIONS

The Tree of Life is a metaphorical concept designed to trace the branching of species. Unlike a tree in the forest or your back yard, whose blossoms are all the same species, each branch of this larger metaphorical zoological "tree" produces leaves and blossoms of millions of distinct species.

Teilhard looks for a sample phylum where he can get a clear view of that phylum's transformation, so that he can show both the emerging leaves as well as the ancient branch from which they come. He chooses the "great family of the mammals," because in this phylum (line) there is geological evidence not only of adult (most recent) forms of mammals but also of the branch (peduncle) from which they emerged.

In following metaphorically the evolution of mammals, we can recognize relatively fresh "leaves" (examples of mammals) emerging within the most recent fifty million years. And we also have fossil evidence that allows us to trace the peduncle of those examples back well over 200 million years.

In this vast geological history, it is easy to get lost and lose the purpose of Teilhard's exploration of the Tree of Life. No matter how far back in time he goes, he is always focused on his main purpose, *tracing the embriogenesis of the human phenomenon*.

Most of us have seen the familiar cartoon of a line of creatures starting with the ape walking on all fours and culminating in an erect *Homo sapiens*. The implication is that humans emerged from the apes, specifically from those belonging to the family of hominids. For Teilhard, the cartoon line does not go far enough back in history to the beginnings of humanity's embriogenesis. He wants to make up for this lack.

His intent in *Phenomenon* is to paint a complete picture of humanity. We cannot understand the human phenomenon, he says, until we follow its winding path back in time to the peduncle of *Homo sapiens*, to the deepest "stem" from which humanity emerged.

Geological Periods

Teilhard traces two paths backward in time to get to a deep branch of the Tree. First, he explores a path using *geological periods*. Second, he uses *zoology classifications*.

Geological Periods

Geologists divide the history of life on Earth into roughly fifty-million-year periods.

Permian: from 250 to 300 million years ago (mya).[3] Dominated by amphibians, fish, worms, insects.

Triassic: from 200 to 250 mya. Algae, sponge, corals, and crustaceans recover; reptiles began to get bigger.

Jurassic: from 145 to 200 mya. Dinosaurs dominate. Crocodiles evolve. The first true mammals evolve.

Cretaceous: from 66 to 145 mya. Dinosaurs still dominate, becoming increasingly common and diverse.

Cenozoic: from 2 to 66 mya. Dinosaurs disappear. Birds proliferate and diversify. Mammals diversify and dominate.

There are many more geological ages to account for in Earth's four-billion-year history, but these five ages are enough for Teilhard's purposes.[4]

To get a sense of these huge spans of time, consider that life on Earth has been going on for almost four billion years. Dinosaurs roamed the planet for close to 180 million years. Humans have been going about their daily activities for somewhat more than 200,000 years. Civilization has flourished for a mere ten thousand years or so. Civilized humans would have to keep evolving for another 800,000 years before we can claim to have been on Earth for just *one* million years. Paleogenetics, using DNA evidence, keep changing *Homo sapiens* numbers and finding more "twigs" on the Tree of Life.[5]

While geologists focus on rocks during these early periods, pale-ontologists tend to focus on the evolution of living organisms.

Taxonomy's Approach

Teilhard traces a second path backward in time to get to a deep branch of the Tree of Life. This time, he uses zoologist classification.

Taxonomy is a branch of zoology focused on classifying forms of life. The principal ranks of classification used today, from the most general to the most particular, are *kingdom, phylum, class, order, family, genus,* and *species.* Here is how we humans are classified:

Zoology's Classification of the Animals Kingdom[6]

Kingdom: *Animalia* (animals)
Phylum: *Chordata* (having vertebrae plus a brain encased in a skull). The tetrapods (four-limbed) form a subset of this phylum, which breaks down into four *classes*: amphibians, reptiles, mammals, and birds. Teilhard considers only the mammal class.
Class: *Mammalia* (having breasts for nursing, a neocortex, and three inner ear bones)
Order: *Primates* includes lemurs, lorises, tarsiers, monkeys, apes, and humans.
Family: *Hominids* includes great apes: orangutans, gorillas, chimpanzees, and homo.
Genus: *Homo* includes the past genetic tree of humanity, with Neanderthals, Denisovans, and other extinct species of the subfamily *hominin* (e.g., Australopithecus, Paranthropus, and Ardipithecus).
Species: *Homo sapiens* (the only surviving species of the genus *Homo*)

Because humans are *Chordata*, they share that major branch (or phylum)—*mammals*—that Teilhard is studying. The earliest mammals are involved in the embriogenesis of humanity and so are involved in the human phenomenon.

By the way, Teilhard knows that his readers, whether scientific or lay, consider the human being to be unique among all creatures. Many will insist that humans are so unique that they could not possibly have emerged from the order of primates or the family of hominids (great apes, orangutans, chimpanzees, and gorillas). They may even insist that *Homo sapiens* exists outside of any biological phylum.

The Bible teaches that humans have immortal souls and that our first parents were created by God as "originals." To such readers, Teilhard must show how the human body is a natural evolutionary result, that *Homo sapiens* emerged as a new "twig" on the Tree of Life. Humanity evolved from some progenitor "branches" already living on Earth.[7]

Mammals

In this section, Teilhard attempts a defense—or logical explanation—of humanity's evolutionary origins. He agrees that humans are unique but insists that their uniqueness emerges on Earth's Tree of Life—not on some other "tree." Humans came to have their special emerging qualities and capacities just as did every other species, by evolving from earlier forms. Humans share a similar reproductive process and early nurturing with all mammals, especially the *placentals*.

There are three main groups of mammals alive today.

- *Placentals* (from bats to blue whales, including humans): These carry the fetus to full term nourished by a placenta inside the mother's uterus.
- *Marsupials* (kangaroo, koala, possum): Marsupials carry their fetus for a short time (about five weeks) nourished by a placenta inside the mother's uterus.
- *Monotremes* (platypus): These very rare mammals lay eggs instead of giving birth. When hatched, babies nurse on the mother's breast.

Amniotes

Teilhard will also use the term *amniote* as a way of comparing the gestation period of a human fetus to that of other placentals. Amniotes refer to all animals that carry fetuses in the womb in a "membrane surrounding the fetus." The term derives from the "amniotic fluid" that fills the maternal placenta. Such a membrane may be found in eggs (of birds, chickens, ducks) as well as placentas.

In contrast, nonamniotes (technically, *anamniotes*), such as fish and frogs, lay their eggs in large batches in water, where, in most cases, they are then fertilized by the male, often by spraying the batch with sperm.

Phenotypes and Genotypes

Teilhard uses the best geological tools of his day. He follows a centuries-old classification method called *phenotyping—classification by appearance and physical evidence.* (*Pheno-* is also the root of *phenomenon*, meaning "something observable.") Phenotyping of mammals and reptiles involves comparing observable features, such as cranial shape and size, number and structure of teeth, nature of the spinal cord, and size and shape of feet and limbs.

Today, biologists are confirming, adjusting, and correcting phenotypes by *genotyping—classification using DNA and other genetic markers.* Even though the phenotype of a dinosaur might not look like that of a chicken, or the phenotype of a pig might not look like that of a cow, in each case genotyping will clearly verify their common roots.

SUMMARIZING THE EVIDENCE

Tracing the evolutionary path of any creature is a very complex subject. Thousands of professional geologists, paleontologists, biologists, and anthropologists plus millions of amateur collectors of ancient fossils have spent countless hours, months, and years searching the planet for evidence of life's evolutionary meanderings. To get a sense of this immense amount of work, Teilhard recommends a trip to a major geological museum. There is where much of this painstaking work is gathered together and housed. He calls the thousands of these professional and amateur evolutionary paleo-searchers "a host of travelers."

> Anyone who wishes to think in terms of evolution, or write about it, should start off by wandering through one of those great museums—there are four or five in the world—in which (at the cost of efforts whose heroism and spiritual value will one day be understood) a host of travelers has succeeded in concentrating in a handful of rooms the entire spectrum of life. (133–34, 85)

Unfortunately, anyone who might wish to trace human origins back through the major branch of the vertebrates and into the Tree of Life's trunk and roots would find scant, if any, evidence for the earliest unicellular life-forms. Before the Precambrian era (time prior to about 540 million years ago), Teilhard suggests that there are no specimens of life for geologists to examine. They can only infer the form of those deepest strands of life by using evolutionary laws in reverse. Teilhard writes,

> Below the Precambrian stage the unicellular creatures lose every kind of calcareous or siliceous skeletal form. And so the roots of the tree of life are lost to view in the unknowable world of soft tissue and the metamorphosis of primeval slime.[8] (133, 84)

None of the creatures that lived thousands of millions of years ago, Teilhard notes, would have had a preservable skeleton of bones made of minerals like calcium and silicon ("calcareous or siliceous skeletal form"). All creatures back then would have been made of soft tissue that would quickly disappear after death.[9]

In summary, Teilhard says that hundreds of years of evidence and analysis confirm the fact that evolution can no longer be considered some wild hypothesis. Evolutionary theory has become the foundation of all science. Teilhard writes,

> Evolutionary theory has long since ceased to be a hypothesis, to become a (dimensional) condition which all hypotheses of physics or biology must henceforth satisfy. (140n, 90n)

In his own thinking, Teilhard comes to realize that evolutionary theory and the laws of evolution form the underlying structure not only of the physical and life sciences—the "matter" of physics and chemistry as well as the living organisms of biology. The laws of evolution must also apply to everything happening on Earth, especially all systems of thought such as mathematics, music, law, morality, philosophy, and theology. If those evolutionary laws apply to atoms, molecules, and compounds of physical matter, and to all living organisms, why would those laws cease to operate as Earth evolves to the stage of thought and consciousness? As Teilhard realizes, it is those very laws of evolution that bring the universe up to and into the stage of thought and consciousness.

Chapter 3

Demeter

(141–60, 91–106)

Orientation

THIS CONCLUDING CHAPTER is named—unscientifically—after Demeter, a female divinity from Greek mythology. Its first section is named after Ariadne, a human woman from Greek mythology.

To the ancient Greeks, Demeter was revered as the goddess of the harvest and fertility. In the Greek pantheon of gods, she was the female divinity who sustained humanity with food and enabled women to give birth. She was also called Mother Earth and Great Mother. In an evolutionary age, Teilhard might say that Demeter was put "in charge" of geogenesis.

Because Demeter was the daughter of Chronos, the god of time, she also presided over the cycle of life and death. She was called the legislator of the sacred unwritten laws of life and death.

In *Phenomenon*, Teilhard identifies and formulates some of those "sacred unwritten laws of life and death" as they pertain to evolution. Teilhard is aware that "mother" comes from the Latin word *mater*, from which root word we also derive English words like *matter* and *material*. Thus, Demeter is the goddess of physical matter (what takes up "space"), and as the daughter of Chronos, god of time, she presides over the cycle of life and death (what takes up "time"). In evolutionary terms, Teilhard would say that Demeter is the goddess of space/time. She is "in charge" of cosmogenesis.

124

I began to realize that this chapter might be one of the most important and integrative parts of *Phenomenon*. Here is where Teilhard sketches his background for rewriting the natural history of the world, allowing him to re-envision the story of the universe from a new perspective.

1. Ariadne's Thread (142–46, 92–95)

ARIADNE AND THESEUS

Ariadne is a figure in Greek mythology associated with mazes and labyrinths. As the story goes, the monster Minotaur demanded an annual ritual sacrifice of young Greek men and maidens. This devouring creature, who lived in a labyrinth, was the only one who knew his way among the confusing network of winding paths, corridors, and dead ends of his tall-hedged, mazelike warren.

One year, a young man named Theseus was chosen to be among the sacrificial offerings to be sent into the Minotaur's labyrinth to be devoured. Theseus was determined to save his people from any further sacrifice of young people. To eliminate the Minotaur, Theseus had to enter the monster's domain, find and slay him, and hopefully find his way out again. Theseus was also in love with Ariadne.

Ariadne wanted to help Theseus succeed in his quest. On his way into the labyrinth, Ariadne handed him a sword and a ball of thread. The sword was to kill Minotaur. The thread was to help him find his way out of the maze afterward.

From the moment Theseus entered the labyrinth, he was to unwind the thread as he searched the puzzling pathways for the monster. He found the Minotaur and slew him. Then, by rewinding Ariadne's thread, Theseus was able to find his way out of the confusing labyrinth and into the loving arms of Ariadne.

To most scientists of Teilhard's time, the plethora of living species on Earth seemed much like a confusing labyrinth. Zoologists of his day struggled to make their way tracing the confusing paths of endless apparently random evolving life-forms. Like librarians cataloging an endless incoming flow of new books, zoologists cataloged an endless flow of emerging new species. However, naming and classifying evolutionary branches of life might be useful, but classification does not by itself provide meaning, purpose, or direction. Life science was a labyrinth.

Darwin found some basic patterns in the various mutations and adaptations he observed in certain birds and animals. But it did little to help biologists out of the labyrinth. The best that biologists could do was to invent new names for each new emerging species—millions of viruses, bacteria, sponges, fish, amphibians, reptiles, insects, birds, marsupials, mammals, primates, and hominin, to say nothing of plants, grains, flowers, bushes, and trees. Collecting, categorizing, classifying, and naming of all these ancient, current, and future species looked like an endless task. It appeared that biologists would spend the rest of their lives in the labyrinth.

They wandered within the labyrinth, but they couldn't get out. To find their way, they needed something like Ariadne's thread. That's where Teilhard comes in. Teilhard suggests a way biologists can use to make sense of the bewildering complexity of their Tree of Life, much as Ariadne provided a ball of thread to help Theseus find his way out of the labyrinth's bewildering pathways.

To begin his solution, Teilhard weaves together three major strands in his "Ariadne's thread":

- controlled additivity
- the *without* and the *within*
- arrangement

Controlled additivity, or the "accumulation of new properties," is an evident fact in nature's evolving species. "By a continuous accumulation of properties," Teilhard says, "life acts like a snowball [continually growing in size as it rolls down a hill]. It piles characters upon characters in its protoplasm. It becomes more and more complex" (141, 91). He calls this accumulation of properties "controlled additivity" (141, 91).

Any big snowball rolling to the bottom of the hill contains more than snow. As it rolls down, it picks up stones, grass, twigs, and other loose material in its path. Likewise, for Teilhard's cellular snowball. The living cell, as it rolls through evolutionary time, continues to pick up many new characteristics and abilities. Over time, the simple interior of primitive cells grows more and more complex—in fish, plants, and animals. Because of the continuous accumulation of properties, some of these creatures gain the ability to move, feel, hear, smell, taste, and see. As certain cells add these sensory characteristics, they begin to manifest higher and higher degrees of consciousness.

Is controlled additivity going somewhere? Does it have a clear direction?

In Teilhard's day (the 1930s), nine out of ten scientists would have answered no. They would have said that evolution was a phenomenon of continual metamorphosis, merely giving rise to "more and more improbable forms" (141, 91). Geologists and archeologists were simply discovering more and more biological fossils and forms for the taxonomists to catalog.

In contrast, Teilhard claims that evolution's evidence manifests a clear *advance*, "a precise orientation" (142, 92). He describes this advance variously as "a privileged axis," "a line of development," and "a line of progress" (142, 92). He believes that, though scientists of his day fail to recognize the clearly directional nature of evolution's advance, they will in the future.

The *without* and the *within*. These are two concepts Teilhard introduced in part 1 of *Phenomenon*. They also are important to the task at hand. The *without* deals with the *exteriority* of each species, their tangible aspects. The *within* deals with the *interiority* of each species, their intangible aspects.

Teilhard reminds us of one of his earlier assertions. "The essence of the real, I said, could well be represented by the 'interiority' contained by the universe at a given moment" (143, 93).[1] He proposes to trace evolution's structure using his Ariadne's thread by weaving together the *within* and the *without*.

In addition, he shows how the *without* and *within* woven together can also deal with the issue of *radial energy*. In his language, evolution can be more clearly defined by "the continual growth of 'psychic' or 'radial' energy in the course of duration" (143, 93). He also accounts for the measurable physical energy expended in any evolutionary process, the *tangential energy* in which scientists seem most interested.

He asks himself, What expresses observably the relationship between radial and tangential energies as species develop consciousness?

He answers both the structural and energy questions with a one-word answer. He replies, "Obviously, it is *arrangement*" (143, 93).

Arrangement. By "arrangement" he refers to a continual process of cells organizing and reorganizing their contents, which they must regularly do as complexity grows. This arrangement process accounts for the successive advances in the arrangement and rearrangement among the increasing contents of the *without* and the *within* that lead to "a continual expansion and deepening of consciousness" (143, 93).

Learning the successive basic skills of arithmetic provides an example of continual rearrangement of consciousness. A child is first taught addition. To the child's mind, learning this skill introduces many new ideas and concepts into the child's content of consciousness (*within*), especially when the sums are of more than one column. Those mental operations must also be integrated into physical cortical circuits in the brain (*without*). Next, the child learns subtraction, bringing in more new concepts and another rearrangement of the contents of the brain (*without*) and of consciousness (*within*). The skills of multiplication, division, fractions, and decimals will, in turn, require many more concepts and mental operations to be integrated in the child's brain and more rearrangements of consciousness. Imagine how many more mental operations must be mastered and rearranged in the brain and in consciousness as the student encounters geometry, algebra, and the intricacies of calculus.

Over time, different forms of life—from bacteria to spiders to puppies to first graders—must absorb and organize a continually increasing amount of information and experience that is often confusing and apparently contradictory. As a result, consciousness in these life-forms must *continually rearrange this growing content* in the neural pathways of the physical brain (*without*) as well as in consciousness (*within*) to make sense of it. Continual rearrangement of the increasing number of elements is key to Teilhard's reasoning.

These rearrangement processes happening in both the *without* and the *within* "represent the very essence of complexity, of essential metamorphosis" (143, 92). Here, Teilhard uses the term *metamorphosis* in its precise meaning as a transformation from a lower form of life to a higher or more encompassing (*meta*) form.

Following the process of continual rearrangements in nature provides additional strands to the "thread" that will lead out of the labyrinth. This "thread" also provides the sword to slay the "Minotaur," who represents evolution seen as pure randomness and confusion.

FINDING PURPOSE AND DIRECTION

When we classify organisms, not merely by their bones, fingers, and cranial size (parts of their *without*) but also by including degrees of neural complexity (also part of their *without*), the order or arrangement we are looking for becomes evident (144, 93). It becomes measurable as "degree of complexity." Degree of complexity is another characteristic of Teilhard's Ariadne's thread.

Teilhard notes that complexity's ever-increasing movement reveals a clear evolutionary direction. Observing forms consistently increasing in complexity, the evidence for evolution's direction is obvious. As an example, Teilhard points out that "nerve ganglions concentrate, become localized, grow forward in the head, instincts become more complex, and socialization appears" (146, 95). He uses the elaboration of the nervous system and its growing complexity as the thread that resolves the question of evolution's direction. This consistent accumulation of properties (controlled additivity or *controlled complexity*), he asserts, cannot be a simple result of chance or random probability. *"It provides a direction and by its consequence it proves that evolution has a direction"* (Teilhard's emphasis; 146, 95).

As a corollary, it follows that "among living creatures, the brain is the sign and measure of consciousness" (146, 95). The brain is continually refining itself over time. Mental improvement (*within*) may be measured by counting the number of nerve fibers and their interactions in the nervous system (*without*).[2] More interactive nerve fibers provide to any living creature the ability to respond appropriately to a larger horizon of experiences and events. Each human being experiences this increase in complexity of neuronal arrangement in the process of maturity from infancy to childhood to adulthood and, hopefully, even to old age.

The same process happens *at the level of species*, for instance, in the evolution of the primates. As primate species evolve, they experience an increase in complexity of neuronal arrangement.

Teilhard's principle of "controlled additivity" (or "controlled complexity") provides a way to give coherence, purpose, and direction to evolution and natural history. The next step would be for humans to actively use this same principle to move evolution forward, to give new coherence and purpose to human life and Earth's destiny.

2. The Rise of Consciousness (147–52, 95–99)

In the previous section, Teilhard established a consistent correlation between the increase in brain complexity (*without*) and a parallel increase in consciousness (*within*) over time.

In this section, he begins exploring his "Ariadne's thread" focusing on consciousness. Throughout this section, he will use interchangeably the following terms: *psychic states*, the *within*, *radial energy*, *internal energies*, and *consciousness* to describe this "thread." Each of these terms helps to more fully describe the same variable.

First, Teilhard establishes the rise of consciousness (or the "evolution of the *within* of things") as key to finding evolution's direction and purpose. As a result, certain facts become clear.

- In the development of life in Earth's history, the key variable must be *consciousness* (or substitute his other equivalent terms — *psychic states*, the *within*, *radial energy*, or *internal energies*).
- Earth, even in its general chemical makeup, is revealing certain global and irreversible laws. Remember, Demeter presided over the cycle of life and death. Teilhard's laws of evolution's direction also must explain the phenomenon of death as well as of life.
- The spontaneous generation of life on Earth happened only once. It happened in many places during the same period in the ocean's many thermal vents. All rearrangements of the *within* and *without* of living forms began with this first spontaneous emergence of the cell.
- To the traditional scientist it appears that life's countless ramifications seem to have no direction or purpose.
- Upon closer look, according to Teilhard, we can observe the tide of growth in the nervous system carrying life forward toward expanded consciousness. This tide "grows, jerkily, but ceaselessly and in a constant direction" (148, 96). It has created the biosphere, covering the planet with a layer of life.
- The appearance of life adds a new dimension to

geogenesis. "The axis of *geogenesis* [prelife] is now extended in *biogenesis* [life], which in time will express itself in *psychogenesis* [thought]" (148, 96). In this sentence, Teilhard sums up the three "books" of his *Phenomenon*. From the lithosphere, atmosphere, and hydrosphere (book 1: prelife) will emerge the biosphere (book 2: life), and from the biosphere will emerge the noosphere (book 3: thought).

Teilhard's primary intent in book 2 of *Phenomenon* is to show that "life" has surpassed "matter" in guiding the future of evolution. "We see life at the head [of Earth's evolution], with all physics subordinate to it. And at the heart of life, explaining its progression, the impetus of a rise of consciousness" (148, 96).

But that "impetus of consciousness," a major theme of book 3, requires that we first explore more deeply the earlier "impetus of life." This is what Teilhard has been doing in book 2 of *Phenomenon*.

Teilhard remarks that biologists of his day "persist in looking for the principle of vital developments in external stimuli or in statistics" (148, 96), referring to principles like "survival of the fittest" or "natural selection." But if those remain the only principles guiding evolution, the living world would never advance otherwise than "to continually remake itself" (148, 97). But life does not merely remake itself. Each time it rearranges its growing contents, it becomes more complex and more conscious.

The *drive to (continual) self-rearrangement* becomes one more way to describe the law guiding the universe's development. Teilhard calls it the law of "Complexity-Consciousness." At the Big Bang, sub-atomic particles arranged and rearranged themselves into hundreds of different atoms. In time, atoms rearranged themselves into thousands of molecules. Next, molecules rearranged themselves into millions of different compounds. Then, molecules rearranged themselves into billions of cells. Over eons of time, cells rearranged themselves into countless organs and life-forms. Even today, life-forms continue to rearrange their nervous systems and brains in the continuous accumulation of properties (additive complexity)—and into larger and larger social groupings.

131

THE PARADOX

Teilhard points out that every scientist, himself included, as a thinking human being faces a paradox: "How can life respect determinism on the *without* and yet act in freedom *within*?" (149, 97).

Scientists cannot deny the determinism evidenced in biological evolution. It is clearly a law of life. While many phyla among the insects and earlier mammals seem to have stopped growing in complexity, other phyla, such as the primates, keep emerging with more and more complex nervous systems. That growth in neural complexity is undeniably "determinism on the *without*."

Yet, as creatures, such as mammals, develop more complex physical brains (*without*) based on this "determinism," they seem to enjoy an inner life (*within*) that allows them to be free to make choices. For example, put two dogs and two cats in the same situation and the animals in each pair may respond differently. Their responses appear more "free" than "determined." These species are "determined" to become more complex on the *without* and yet they grow in freedom *within*.

Teilhard's point is that the steady rise in consciousness in mammals over time "offers a new way of explaining, over and above the mainstream of biological evolution, the progress and particular disposition of its various phyla" (149, 97). We can now measure progress as well as catalogue diversity.

From his perspective on the primacy of consciousness, Teilhard can reverse traditional interpretations of certain evolutionary factors. For example, traditional biology would say, "An animal develops its carnivorous instincts *because* its molars [fangs] become cutting and its claws sharp."

Teilhard reverses the order and suggests, "An animal elongates its fangs and sharpens its claws because, following a line of descent, it receives, develops, and hands on the soul of a carnivore." It elongates its fangs and sharpens its claws not merely for survival, but to foster and develop its true nature (150, 98). By true nature, he means the development of its *within*. The number of bones, the shape of teeth, or other ornamentation—all these visible characteristics—"form merely the outward garment around something deeper which supports it" (151, 98–99). The *within*.

While traditional science must deal with natural history as a seemingly endless series of variations revealed by the study of fossils,

Teilhard takes a radically different viewpoint. He insists that in natural history, "we are dealing with only one event, the grand orthogenesis of everything living toward a higher degree of immanent spontaneity" (151, 99). In other words, to write the true natural history of the world, we need to trace its path from within. For Teilhard, the unifying factor in *geogenesis* is the emergence of consciousness.

> Right at its base, the living world is constituted by conscious-ness clothed in flesh and bone. From the biosphere to living species is nothing but an immense ramification of conscious *within* activity seeking to discover, explore, and expand itself by means of differentiations. That is where Ariadne's thread leads us if we follow it to the end. (151, 99)

Teilhard coined the term *psychism* in his text to refer in general to acts in the realm of conscious mental and emotional activity.

Evolution represents a directed process. However, it is not a "simple advance toward complexity" (152, 99). There are successes and failures, dead ends, and no limit to pure diversification. There is no increase in complexity that can go on and on without reaching a critical point that demands a change in state (metamorphosis). To integrate such increases in complexity there must occur a corresponding enlarging or deepening of consciousness. Or, as Teilhard put it, "there must be a change not merely in quantity but in quality" (152, 99).

3. The Approach of Time (152–60, *100–106*)

In this concluding section of book 2, Teilhard wants to explain the development of consciousness in another way, not by using the approach of complexity but by using the "approach of time." Demeter is the daughter of Chronos, the god of time.

Teilhard paints a panoramic picture of life on Earth "toward the end of the Tertiary," that is, during the last few million years before humanity appeared. He describes the planet at that time as an "endless green" of plant life and forests along with millions of animal species, especially mammals, roaming around. But "nowhere is there so much as a wisp of smoke rising up from camp or village" (152, *100*). There is no sign of human life yet, but the "thermometer of consciousness" is rising. Evolution is preparing for the appearance of thought.

In another allusion to Demeter, Teilhard asks, during this geological period, what is "maturing in the womb of the universal mother?" (153, *100*). In response, he begins by comparing three groups of vertebrates—insects, mammals in general, and specifically primates. He asks what has happened to each group over time.

Insects. Teilhard recognizes the insects as "very much the elders of the higher vertebrates by the date of their fluorescence." Yet, now they seem "irredeemably stationary" (153, *101*). He explains why insects cannot keep their place at the head of evolution. Despite the precision of their movements and their physical construction, psychologically they have become "mechanized and hardened." It is precisely because of the precision of their physical structure that they lack any "appreciable margin of indetermination and choice." Their consciousness growth has stopped and become "frozen" (154, *101*). The exact opposite happens in mammals.

In *mammals*, instinct is no longer strictly channeled, "as in the spider or the bee, paralyzed to a single function." In mammals, "instinct flutters, plays, acts with curiosity and exuberance." In mammals, "an aura of freedom begins to float." In them, we recognize "a glimmer of personality" (157, *102*).

The *primates* stand out among the mammals. Teilhard calls them our "near neighbors on the tree of life" (157, *103*). Among them, he lists *Catarrhines* (narrow-nosed Old World monkeys such as baboons and macaques), *Platyrrhines* (flat-nosed South American monkeys), *Lemuroids* (lemurs), *Tarsioid* (tiny jumping animals with bulging cranium and huge eyes), and *Anthropoids* (gorillas, chimpanzees, orangutans, and gibbons) (158, *104*).[3]

The category *primates* comes from the word *primitive* and refers to the fact that the limbs of these animals *remain free to evolve*. The freedom of limbs to evolve is the true definition of the primates. Because limbs are free to evolve, life itself will be able to evolve, "to carry on."

Teilhard notes that in comparing the evolution of insects to mammals, the mammal's ability to mutate a physical characteristic—such as size and number of teeth, bone structures, limbs, and organs—provides immediate superiority. When outstanding physical characteristics are irreversible, they thereby imprison a species to a restricted path. Insects are a prime example of such restriction. Specialized creatures became "limited by what their limbs and teeth had become" (159, *105*).

Some restricted species end up as either a monstrosity or a frivolity. Think of the porcupine, the salamander, the lobster, the ostrich, or the katydid. As Teilhard puts it, "specialization paralyzes, ultra-specialization kills" the evolutionary process.

Primates represent *a phylum of pure and direct cerebralization* (159, *105*). Primates do not focus on specialization of limbs and teeth but leave their development malleable and thus unlimited. In Teilhard's technical language, "*In this singular and privileged case, the particular orthogenesis of the phylum happened to coincide exactly with the principle orthogenesis of life itself*" (Teilhard's emphasis; 160, *105*). In other words, primates happen to be at the right place at the right time. Primates provide the "strictly localized" evolutionary source—the "hot point"—from which thought can be born (160, *105*).

Spiritual Implications

In Teilhard's day, people—even cosmologists—believed the activity of the stars, planets, and galaxies were eternally *fixed and unchanging in their movements*. Today, we know that stars burn out and die, while new stars are born. We know that some stars are swallowed by dark holes. We know that the universe is expanding and that larger galaxies sometimes devour small galaxies. The universe is hardly fixed and unchanging! How is one to make theological sense of this chaotic, ever-changing cosmos?

Planet Earth's activity poses many questions as well. Earth is the scene of nature's violence in a steady sequence of comet and asteroid bombardments, earthquakes, floods, tornados, hurricanes, ice ages, mass extinctions, killing, sickness, plagues, and death.

In *Phenomenon*, Teilhard is trying to show—to people of faith who can read between the lines—a way to see how this apparently disorganized, uncontrollable, and ever-changing universe might indeed be the work of an almighty and unconditionally loving God. Teilhard believes God is, above all, a divine lover of all creation.

First, a lover does not try to control every thought and action of those that are loved. A divine lover certainly would not attempt to control every event. If God is not in total control of everything that has happened, is happening, and will happen, what is God's role in all this apparently chaotic process? How does the divine lover relate to what has been created?

God the Lover blesses, inspires, affirms, liberates, protects, leads, models, guides, consoles, cares for, sympathizes, supports, nurtures, listens, coaches, accommodates, is patient, forgives, understands, encourages, offers wisdom, and so on.[4] For Teilhard, this is who God is and how God relates to creation at all levels. God is more like a compassionate parent than a strict law enforcer, more like a coach than a micromanaging boss. God rejoices in our successes and is saddened but supportive when things fail.

This is how God has always looked at and treated creation—blessing it, imbuing every particle of it with love and the desire for union and consciousness. God set creation in motion with the inbuilt drive to attract and connect. Ever since, God has been lovingly *managing* its development and evolution—*not controlling it.*

If creation is a symphony, we are the musicians, holding and playing the instruments. God is the conductor. God manages and directs the symphony but cannot control what each musician may do at any moment.

At each day's performance, we pray to be the best instruments and musicians of God's symphony that we can be. Next season's program will contain more complex symphonic music to perform so we need to develop our skills to master the evolutionary music as it is emerging.

Teilhard sees God rejoicing at each successive successful stage of the evolutionary process—the leaps from subatomic particles to atoms, from atoms to molecules, from molecules to compounds, from compounds to megamolecules, from megamolecules to cells, from cells to organisms, from organisms to plants and animals, from animals to humans. God delights to see how nature keeps creatively rearranging itself into more and more complex forms. God is now asking us to consciously use that creative power given to us. We are to use it to move evolution forward and upward.

We are not merely spectators of evolution but the creators and shapers of it. In our lifetime, each of us has a part to play—perhaps several parts.

For Teilhard, bringing the universe to its completion in a final conscious loving oneness has always been God's project. We humans who enjoy consciousness have been privileged to begin to understand what God is doing in this grand divine project. In *Phenomenon*, Teilhard is sketching, for believers as well as for scientists, a picture of God's project as it has been unfolding since the beginning.

If we were to ask those original Big Bang particles for advice on our human future, they might say, "Do what we did."

What does that mean?

In the nonliving world, all various forms of atoms and molecules made their evolutionary leaps, not by continuing to coexist, but by coalescing, by forming new unions with more complexity. The first living things made their evolutionary leap by joining together and working together. By rearranging themselves, they formed new unities. Each new union became a new oneness, with a shared purpose—to maintain and enrich life.

Many people of a peaceful disposition today seem content simply to coexist. The first cells discovered the secret to evolution, and they passed it on to us: *don't just coexist, coalesce!* Teilhard would encourage us to join others and work together with a shared purpose to maintain and enrich life on Earth for all. Keep things moving forward and upward.

BOOK THREE
THOUGHT

Chapter 1

The Birth of Thought

(163–234, 109–63)

Prenote: A Big Shift in Perspective

BOOK 3 SHIFTS focus from the genesis of the biosphere to the genesis of the noosphere. Teilhard also makes a *shift in perspective*, but he does not point this out to the reader. Only years later, when he is writing a postscript to *Phenomenon* (300, 216) does he recognize and acknowledge the shift in perspective needed to read book 3.

Teilhard easily swings from one perspective to the other without thinking. His "eyes" automatically refocus when he shifts from the biosphere to the noosphere. We need to make the shift consciously and intentionally.

Here are a few contrasts to help our "eyes" make his shift:

- The biosphere's genesis is characterized by *evolution*, the expansion and proliferation of different biological species. The noosphere's genesis is characterized by *involution*, the continual reorganization, integration, synthesis, and systematization of human thought.[1]
- In the biosphere, advances are made mostly *unconsciously*, by groping, adapting, or trial and error. In the noosphere, advances are made mostly *consciously*, by planning, design, research, and creativity.
- In the biosphere, most of the energy expended in the evolution and proliferation of species is *tangential*

141

energy. In the noosphere, Teilhard focuses on the *radial energy* expended, which is involved in involution or integrating "mental species" and systems of thought.

- In the biosphere, characteristics of evolution are observed in a plant's or animal's *without* (shape, size, color, weight, movement, etc.). In the noosphere, his focus is the human *within* (how evolution happens in the minds of artists, musicians, scientists, philosophers, parents, teachers, governors).
- Recall the basic law of evolution—Attraction-Connection-Complexity-Consciousness. In the biosphere, this law's most essential elements are *Attraction* and *Connection* and creating new *physical* unions. In the noosphere, the law's most essential elements are *Complexity* and *Consciousness* in creating new *mental* unions.

As we study evolution in the noosphere, we are looking primarily for signs of *involution*, the process of continually reorganizing more and more complexity into a limited space.

ORIENTATION AND PERSPECTIVE

In book 1, Teilhard used the word *anthropogenesis* to describe the beginning and becoming of humanity. In book 3, he introduces a new process term, *hominization*. (*Anthropos* is the Greek word for a human being. *Homo* is the Latin word for a human being.) For Teilhard, each of these two processes has a different emphasis, thus the choice to use two different root words.

Anthropogenesis focuses on humanity's evolutionary *path*, the beginning and becoming of humanity. It describes a process starting with the Big Bang.

Hominization describes a process starting on Earth. It focuses on the later stages of anthropogenesis and describes *humanity taking shape on Earth. Hominization*—what went into making today's "phenomenon of man"—is the subject of book 3.

In clarifying the hominization process, Teilhard's task involves three steps: to explain (1) what makes any *individual* "human," (2) what makes humanity as a *species* "human," and (3) what makes *planet*

Earth "human." For Teilhard, only when all three aspects are taken together can anyone fully describe the *human phenomenon*.

More simply, Teilhard's threefold task in this chapter is to clarify the evolutionary uniqueness of the *withins* of the *individual*, the *species*, and the *planet*. Specifically, he must show the following:

1. how the *within* of an individual human being has evolved beyond the *within* of any individual animal,
2. how the *within* of the human species has evolved beyond the *within* of any individual human, and
3. how the *within* of the planet (the noosphere) has evolved beyond the *within* of the human species.

At each of these three levels, Teilhard says that an evolutionary leap forward has happened—a *discontinuity* has occurred.

What Teilhard needs to show is how each apparent *discontinuity*— for example, the leap from instinct in animals to self-reflection in humans—is really a *continuity*. He reveals continuity by using his new form of evolutionary measurement, *nature's continuous rise in complexity and consciousness over time*.

A REVIEW

Before we get deeply into book 3, it may be helpful to summarize progress so far. Teilhard describes the evolution of planet Earth as an emerging series of spheres. Listed in evolutionary order, they are the *barysphere* (source of metals), *lithosphere* (source of minerals), *atmosphere* (source of oxygen), *hydrosphere* (source of water), and *biosphere* (source of life).

In book 1, Teilhard discusses the first four spheres. All four spheres are required for the emergence of life in the biosphere. Whether we look at a rosebush, an oak tree, a lobster, or a bear, they are all made up of metals from the barysphere, minerals from the lithosphere, water from the hydrosphere, and oxygen from the atmosphere.

In book 2, Teilhard explores the evolving biosphere. There, he reviews the emergence of life, from the simplest cellular organisms to the highest evolved forms of animal life and animal intelligence. Living cells from the biosphere are essential for the emergence of the noosphere. The biosphere's evolutionary role in hominization is to shape a physical organism over time for the emergence of *Homo sapiens*.

In book 3, Teilhard focuses on the *noosphere*, the sphere of human thought, consciousness, and mental activity. *Homo sapiens* created the noosphere and each generation of humans continues to evolve it *into the future*.

HOMINIZATION AND THE NOOSPHERE[2]

In book 3, Teilhard presents a parade of the higher apes and several prehuman life-forms. Each species gradually develops new sets of increasing abilities. Animals and prehumans are capable of regeneration, proliferation, movement, sensation, perception, memory, instinct, communication, association, and socialization.

For Teilhard, *hominization's* most outstanding emergent ability is *self-reflection*. Self-reflection marks a new evolutionary stage in consciousness. It includes the unique capacity to remember one's past, act consciously in the present, and plan for the future.

Teilhard's choice of "Thought" as the title for this part of *Phenomenon* is very precise. He knows that prehuman life-forms share many abilities and characteristics with humans. What is *uncharacteristic* of these nonhuman creatures, he says, is *formal thought*. We humans constantly use formal thought. For example, we spend much of our time considering, reflecting, planning, evaluating, organizing, listing, categorizing, classifying, ranking, structuring, calculating, comparing, contrasting, fantasizing, telling stories, and talking to each other using abstract concepts.

Humans are at home in the noosphere. People use a level of interaction and learning inaccessible to animals. Only humans could have created the noosphere. Only humans can continually access, enrich, and develop it.

1. The Threshold of Reflection (164–83, *110–29*)

AN IMPORTANT EVENT

In this section, Teilhard deals with the first of his three tasks. He shows what makes a human *human*. He answers the question, *How is an individual hominized?*

Evolution in the animal kingdom produced many complex creatures such as fish, amphibians, reptiles, birds, insects, dinosaurs, and all manner of four-footed creatures. Animals and birds alike develop family life, social life, hierarchies for survival and protection. They hunt and fish. They gather food and store it. They can send signals and communicate. They possess sensation, perception, memory, instinct, and the ability to imitate, learn and teach by example. They have powerful spatial and perceptual memory skills. They have learned to fight and kill.

Animals also enjoy a rich emotional life. They express positive traits such as nurturing, caring, industriousness, protection, playfulness, joy, and sharing. They also express many less desirable traits such as anger, lust, pride, greed, jealousy, gluttony, and laziness. Animals learn from one another. They imitate. They learn by experimenting. Using trial and error—groping—they improve their skills and pass them on to others. Some, like our pets, can apparently intuit our intentions.

All the above qualities could be used to identify humans as well as animals. Why then is *Homo sapiens* classified as a distinct species? What ability presents the first unmistakable signs of evolution beyond all other animals? Teilhard answers, *self-reflective thought.*

Teilhard reminds us that in the emergence of life, the first living organisms were very simple, single microscopic cells. It took millions of years before those microscopic cells symbiotically joined to form identifiable creatures such as fungi, algae, and bacteria.

Teilhard points out that this is evolution's consistent pattern—to develop from the simple to the complex. Therefore, we should not expect the first appearance of self-reflective thought in the earliest humans to immediately manifest itself in complex abstract systems such as written language or mathematical symbolism.[3]

The first sign of self-reflection on Earth has to be something very simple. Fossil evidence of reflective thinking depends on man-made items that can survive in nature for more than tens of thousands of years. Objects made of bone and stone are the two most likely materials able to survive that long.

The earliest human tools are simple ones, but they are clearly handmade since such tools do not exist in any natural form. Animals may learn how to pick up and use nearby items, like sticks, twigs, and stones, to access food. A clever animal may spot a piece of food that it cannot reach directly with its hand because its arm is too short, so it picks up a handy twig and uses it as a "tool" to move the food within its reach.

But animals don't first imagine and mentally design the shape of a tool to do a certain task and then "manufacture" it. To envision and then shape a tool for a specific purpose requires thought and reflection. It requires the ability to picture in one's mind the desired shape or capacity of a tool, and then take the time to construct it. For example, "How can I chip away at this piece of bone to make it sharp enough to cut and scrape an animal's skin?" Handmade tools are designed to accomplish specific tasks, such as a pointed spear to kill an animal, a sharp-edged tool to skin a dead animal, or a bore-like tool to drill a hole in a shell or bone and display it as an ornament. Animals may imitate and experiment, but humans envision and create.

ANOTHER DISTINCTION: PERCEPTS AND CONCEPTS

Animals have the capacity for *perception*. Animals enjoy the ability to form a sensory percept in their mind. A *percept* is defined as a unified combination of sounds, smells, and images. For example, a pet dog holds a percept—a sensory picture—of each individual family member, as well as of its own food dish and each of its toys.

What humans can do that animals can't is to form abstract concepts and invent new ones. Human family members of course can form percepts (images) of each individual chair in their home. They can also discuss the *idea* of chair, or count the number of chairs in their house, or compare the sizes and shapes of different chairs, or name the material of which each chair is made. They can consider going to a furniture warehouse to buy a new chair. All these are conceptual activities. While an animal can form a percept of another animal, a human can not only form a percept of an animal but can also use pigment to draw a picture of that animal on a cave wall. It came as a surprise to researchers in 2018, who discovered that Neanderthals—not humans—were the first cave artists in Europe. Evidence from at least 66,000 years ago show that Neanderthal artists were painting with pigments and doing stencil work on cave walls—obvious signs of conceptual thinking.

The ability to form and combine *concepts* marks an evolutionary advance over the ability to form *percepts*. The ability to tell a story—or to make up a story, create a fable, "get" a joke, or delight in the bawdiness of a limerick—marks an advance beyond very basic communication, such as an animal's ability to sound a mating call or warn others of approaching danger. Abstract concepts facilitate complex communication. A photo of a chair in your dining room cannot represent all possible chairs, only the abstract concept "chair" can.

Categories and processes are some of the most common abstract concepts we use in everyday conversation. Examples of abstract *categories* (also called *collective nous*) include words like *furniture, vehicle, liquid, building, path,* and *reptile*. Some familiar abstract *processes* include adding and subtracting, listing, alphabetizing, and scheduling.

In this chapter, Teilhard is not studying the complex human of the twenty-first century. He is exploring the *threshold* of reflective thought, its very first expressions. Crossing the threshold into a house means you have merely taken a first step into the house. The entire *within* of the house still awaits your exploration. Just as the first emergence of a single cell signals the threshold of plant and animal life, so toolmaking signals the threshold of human life.

Following his pattern, Teilhard will now formally take us, as promised, across three separate thresholds: that of (1) the *individual* (the element), (2) the *species* (the phylum), and (3) the *noosphere* (the planet).

THE THRESHOLD OF THE ELEMENT: THE HOMINIZATION OF THE INDIVIDUAL (164–74, *110–17*)

Key to the hominization of the individual human is *thought*. Regarding thought, Teilhard asks and answers four questions:

- *What is the nature of human thought?*
- *What physical mechanism is necessary for human thought?*
- *How is hominization of the individual realized?*
- *How is it prolonged and advanced?*

147

Book Three: Thought

What is the nature of human thought? Human intelligence differs from animal intelligence as self-reflective thought differs from instinct. Animals enjoy intelligence because each species is imbued with an organized set of instincts and an organized set of behaviors. The set of instincts and behaviors found in elephants will differ from the unique sets found, respectively, in giraffes, orangutans, squirrels, owls, and wasps.

In contrast, the central phenomenon of intelligence in humans is no longer instinct but *reflection.* Humans can consciously organize a set of thoughts, impressions, and experiences, and fuse them into a unity. The human mind can be *conscious of its own organization.* Teilhard would say that humans process thought in a "self-aware center." Humans know that they know. They can watch themselves think. They can take possession of themselves "as an object endowed with its own consistence and value" (165, *110*).

Being able to reflect on one's own experience and acquired learning allows an individual to invent new designs, organize new systems, create new abstractions, and make new choices. With proper education and training, people can learn to participate in research and exploration that goes on among different kinds of teams—teams of biologists, physicists, mathematicians, physicians, and artists.

Also, new activities can build upon what is already organized in one's center. Humans can create new systems of thought that are constructed totally from reorganizing and rearranging the content already in one's mind. Just as the artist can combine two different colors on his palette to create a new color, so the astronomer and physicist can combine their systems of thought to form a new system called astrophysics. These combinations bubble up everywhere. The noosphere is bursting with new knowledge. Teilhard describes the richness of activities in human inner life (*within*) as "the effervescence of the newly formed center as it explodes onto itself" (165, *111*).

Thus, self-reflective consciousness is an evolutionary step beyond animal instincts. It operates in a domain of reality in which only humans can move about freely. With self-reflective consciousness, humans cross a new threshold of intelligence. Teilhard calls it "a change of nature resulting from a change of state" (166, *111*). Now to his second question.

What physical mechanism is necessary for human thought? A certain type of physical anatomy is required to exercise the ability to think and reflect. Although humans differ little anatomically from apes, nature needed to make some structural changes to prepare a body type that would be ready for a brain able to support self-reflection.

The leap to self-reflection requires more than a bigger brain. The necessary physical characteristics include eyes that focus forward, feet that can balance an upright body, and fingers that will eventually be able to hold a pen, twist a bottle cap, thread a needle, or type text messages on a smartphone. For speech, the body will need a tongue, a throat, and a glottal structure to be able to form a variety of sounds (168, *113*).

For over 500 million years, mammal neurology continues to grow more and more complex. Brains of mammals are being rearranged and made ready for the emergence of the human species. Creating the necessary neural complexity in brain capacity (*without*) expended only a "tiny bit of tangential energy." But, with this more complex physical brain (*without*) the "radial energy produced was turned back upon itself," multiplied and evolved, so that the animal mind was totally reorganized and consolidated upon itself (involuted) to become a center of reflection in humans.

How is hominization of the individual realized? It is realized by a change of state. Since the Big Bang, there have been many changes of state — from particle to atom, from atom to molecule, from molecule to megamolecule to cell, from cell to myriad forms of living organisms, and from instinct to self-reflection.

In the biosphere, state changes happen without interruption and, over time, move consistently in the same direction — toward higher levels of complexity and consciousness. For millions of years, a series of physiological changes were preparing for *Homo sapiens*. You will enjoy reading Teilhard's description of these changes on page 170, *114–15*.

To make a comparison, Teilhard asks, At what stage in the development of the human infant does reflective consciousness appear? How do we pinpoint the emergence of "psychical transcendence over instinct"? (171, *115*). He suggests that we could surmise that the intelligence of the first humans "might have been as little visible externally in its phyletic origins [evolution at the *species* level] as it is today to our eyes in every newborn child at the ontological stage [development at the *individual* level]" (171, *116*). We don't expect a human infant emerging from the womb to be able to speak fluent English. That happens only with years of nurturing by other humans.

How is hominization of the individual prolonged? One's first glance inside the threshold of a new house is only the beginning of the process. In the realm of thought and self-awareness, to be just inside the front door does not mean that you know everything there is to know about this new home (your *within*). Your vast new dwelling of knowledge and self-awareness must be "penetrated" and integrated around a "center" to give it "coherence and a better organized perspective of everything surrounding it" (172, *116*).

Teilhard says that in dealing with the human mind we are dealing, metaphorically, with "a vortex that grows deeper as it sucks up the fluid at the heart of which it was born." Think of a curious child constantly asking questions to better understand itself and its surroundings. The child not only sucks up the information but also tries to integrate it, organize it, and give it coherence. In Teilhard's words, "The ego persists by becoming evermore itself, in the measure in which it makes everything else itself" (172, *116*). The ego is shaping itself while it organizes and reorganizes its contents. This self-integrative process never stops. It is the way an individual becomes a person. It is the way in which hominization is prolonged and enlarged in each of us.

THE THRESHOLD OF THE PHYLUM: THE HOMINIZATION OF THE SPECIES (174–80, *117–22*)

Now to Teilhard's second task. Along with the hominization of each individual, there occurs a more striking reality, the hominization of the species *Homo sapiens*. Teilhard calls this often-unnoticed evolutionary phenomenon the "collective transformation" of the species. As humans are evolving individually as they mature, the species as a whole is also evolving.[4]

Not only must individual humans continue to welcome, integrate, and resolve new levels of complexity within themselves, but they must also interact and deal with all the other individuals that share the same challenge. Thus, a larger movement is happening beyond each individual's transformation. An entirely new species, a "collective species," is forming.

A collective species is like a relationship. A relationship (a union of individuals) has a distinct identity and life beyond the identity and lives of the individuals in it. A relationship may be born long after each of the partners was born. A relationship may die before any of the partners die. Typically, a relationship grows and develops mutually alongside the growth and development of each partner.

Teilhard's "eyes" see a relationship as a new reality that enjoys a life of its own. Likewise, a species (as a union of all its members) enjoys its own life and growth independent of the individual members of that species, even though its development may be influenced by the growth of individuals within it.

Teilhard is aware that this formative growth process is mutual. Each individual's transformation is enriched by the collective's growth because each individual is interacting as a member of the larger movement. The reverse is also true. New abilities of the collective species emerge because of the interactions among many series of individual transformations. Thus, full individual personalization (or individual hominization) is achieved only within and alongside the "hominization of the whole group" (174, 117).

For Teilhard, a species is not merely a scientific category or zoological classification. A species is a living thing with its own identity, life, and stages of development. If you keep thinking of a species as an abstraction—a mental concept, no more than a name—you will miss Teilhard's insights.

Three Peculiarities

Once evolution crosses the threshold of thought, three areas of peculiarity emerge in the hominization of the species.

- the composition of the human branches
- its general direction of growth
- certain similarities and differences

The composition of the human branches. Looking at the human species as a living whole today, we can identify a variety of races, ethnic differences, tribal affinities, diverse cultures, myriad languages, many ethical systems, countless organizational arrangements, and distinct national characteristics. We cannot explain these differences by zoology alone, that is, simply as biological changes. Such differences can be accounted for only because hominization links together the biosphere and the noosphere. In Teilhard's terms, hominization unites the body and mind, the "somatic and the psychic" (175, *118*).

In the species as a whole, the interaction between the biosphere and noosphere forms a new kind of union between the *within* and the *without*. More precisely, in humanity's development "the somatic is woven by the psychic."

As Teilhard explains, given the immense "quantity of energy liberated by reflection," the psychic (*within*) is no longer merely an aura around the physical (*without*). Rather, the *within* becomes the "principal part of the [human] phenomenon" (176, *119*). We cannot explain the "thinking phenomenon" by bodily changes alone, but only by "the interplay of two partially independent variables," individuals and species (176, *119*).

There is a third variable to consider: "social constructions." The thinking phenomenon also increases in richness and complexity as individuals unite to create social unions within the species, such as teams, organizations, communities, cultures, political groups, and so on. Each of these teams and organizations enjoys its own life and its own emergent properties. These new realities add their contributions to the evolution of the species as a whole.

These three forces—individual self-awareness, species self-awareness, and social constructions—are constantly interacting. They are destined to join in a "convergence of the spirit" (176, *119*).

The general direction of growth. Before humanity appeared on Earth, the most we could say about consciousness was that "consciousness rises through living beings" (177, *119*). Consciousness continues gradually to rise in complexity through fish, birds, reptiles, animals, and higher apes. But when humanity is "viewed as a whole," we can say much more about consciousness (177, *120*).

Self-reflective consciousness puts its primary focus on increasing complexity. For instance, millions of individuals reflect reality from many different angles. As these individuals develop psychically (or psychologically) year by year, their increasing perceptions and viewpoints make their individual human lives more complex. Each individual's growing complexity contributes toward the complexity of the species. Collective human life in general keeps evolving through the course of human history (177, *120*).

We individuals become "sensitive to the presence of something greater than ourselves moving forward within us and in our midst"

(178, *120*). This "something" is far beyond heredity or "the transmission of acquired characteristics," which is the process predominant in animal instincts where behaviors are heredity-formed (178, *121*).

In the human family's "free and ingenious effort of successive intelligence," something irreversible accumulates. This "accumulation" is not inherited via heredity, but is transmitted by means of education, including the development of *systems of thought* and *systems of action*.

Some obvious *systems of thought* include spoken and written language, grammar, mathematics, philosophy, ethics, methods of induction and deduction, mythmaking, and storytelling. Some obvious *systems of action* include cooperative activity, game rules in sports, research procedures in laboratories, assembly-line tasks in factories, rules for conducting a meeting, passing a law, performing a religious ritual, and solving a mathematical equation.

These systems of thought and action get translated into a growth in consciousness both individually and collectively. For Teilhard, "Consciousness...is nothing else than the substance and heart of life in the process of evolution" (178, *121*). Evolution is—and always has been—essentially about enlarging and enriching consciousness.

The whole is often greater than the sum of its parts. For Teilhard, a species "is greater than the simple sum of the elements of which it is formed." In other words, no individual human can contain the vital potential of the race (178, *121*).

Similarities and differences. The petals, flowers, and leaves of a plant arise from its stem. So too with the human flower. Each *individual* arises from the stem of its parents and the milieu of its family and local community. Similarly, the whole species *Homo sapiens*, as a living thing, arises from its larger stem, its phylum and its social context.

We can be sure that whatever arises in humanity as a whole will arise from its present stem. Given its stem's history, we can expect evolution of the species to continue to rise, less so in the structure of the human body and organs (*without*) and more so in new tendencies and behaviors of the human soul (*within*) (179, *121*).

Teilhard predicts some things that we can expect to see "in the whole [future] course of [human] evolution" (180, *121–22*). As examples, he mentions the evolution of love, the evolution of warfare, the evolution of research, and the evolution of the social sense.

In the generations since Teilhard's day, we have seen the evolution of love in a newfound collective concern for our planet and its ecology. In war, we have seen the emergence of cyber weapons. In research, we have seen the rise of international scientific teams converging. In society, we have seen the acceptance of same-sex marital unions and the rise of social media.

The human species "only progresses by slowly elaborating from age to age the totality of a universe deposited within it" (180, 122). Teilhard describes hominization as a process of "sublimation" (181, 122). For Teilhard, sublimation is a form of species evolution especially in transforming society spiritually and mentally. Sublimation, for Teilhard, is another way of describing hominization. It is a new form of phylogeny (evolution of a species) that gradually transforms what is primarily physical into something psychic or spiritual. In his words, sublimation describes "the progressive phyletic spiritualization in human civilization of all the forces contained in the animal world" (180, 122). He says that we are witnessing sublimation as "the forces contained in the animal world" are progressively transformed and integrated into human civilization (180, 122).

Thus, the human species possesses not only a *physical* phylogeny (or evolutionary organic developmental path), as do all the plants and animals. Thanks to the process of sublimation, the human species now also manifests a *spiritual* phylogeny (or psychological developmental path). Teilhard describes this process as "sublimation" because, in collective humanity, zoology unites and integrates with spirituality (181, 122).

THE THRESHOLD OF THE TERRESTRIAL PLANET: THE NOOSPHERE (180–84, 122–25)

Teilhard now faces his third task, to show how "the living planet itself" is humanized.

Compared to other living verticils, or evolutionary stems, the human phylum is unlike any other. At the end of book 2, Teilhard remarks that "man, appearing at the heart of the primates, flourishes on the leading shoot of zoological evolution" (181, 122). The emergence of *Homo sapiens* is more than a mere next step in physical evolution. The human species "marks a transformation affecting the state of the entire planet" (181, 122–23).

Just as a collective species has its own life and reality, so planet

154

Earth itself, as a whole, has its own life and reality. We humans, individually and as a species, are only a part of Earth's life.

To understand what Teilhard is saying here, we need to remember that in this section Teilhard is talking not about individual humans or the entire human family but about Earth itself and its own evolution as a planet, what he calls *geogenesis*. (Geo- is the Greek root for Earth, as in geology, the study of Earth.)

Planet Earth also has its verticils symbolized by its many layers or spheres. Some verticils include geo-tectonics (in the formation of the barysphere and lithosphere); geo-chemistry (in the formation of the hydrosphere and atmosphere), geo-biology (in the formation of the biosphere and, specifically, the nervous system). These verticils "turned out in the end to be leading up to psycho-genesis"—the development of consciousness (181, *123*). Psychogenesis leads to humanity, and humanity leads to noogenesis (the formation and building up of the noosphere).

The implications for humanity of this eons-long process happening to Earth are enormous. Whatever is happening on Earth or to Earth affects our human choices and responsibilities—earthquakes, tornados, hurricanes, droughts, desertification, climatic changes. These events are decisive in our understanding of Earth's life. We have come to realize that the planet is our home. We humans belong to our planet. We are an integral part of it, not independent of it. We belong to each of its layers—metals, minerals, water, air, and cellular life. The noosphere, too, belongs to our planet. It is an integral part of it. And it plays a significant role in the future of our planet.

Earth itself is evolving. This is a totally new revelation to most of us. Outside and above the biosphere, Teilhard says, a new layer of Earth continues to develop, a "thinking layer," the noosphere. It is not a dead layer, symbolized merely by libraries full of inert books resting on dusty shelves. The noosphere is vitally active. It is interactive. It is the planet thinking! Its thoughts and the actions they produce continue to shape and reshape the planet.

Compare a satellite view of Earth two million years ago and a photo of our planet today. You will see what an effect the noosphere has had upon its global surface. The noosphere created modern life as we know it.

Teilhard points out that, just as many state changes happened in the biosphere, changes of state continue to happen among systems of thought in the noosphere, and to Earth itself. Each discontinuity in thought in the noosphere is part of a larger continuity of Earth.

For example, there is a discontinuity between Euclid's geometry and non-Euclidian geometries, but all geometries are part of a larger continuity in the field of mathematics. Similar changes of state happened in mathematics in the advances from arithmetic to algebra to calculus. Biology theory, originally based on endless species expansion and static growth, evolved after Darwin into evolutionary biology. A change of state happened in chemistry in going from inorganic to organic compounds to megamolecules. In physics, Cartesian mechanics gave way to quantum mechanics but they both work well in explaining different physical systems. Each evolutionary step in a field is seen as part of a larger continuity in that field and in science as a whole. These are examples of the thinking layer of Earth evolving.

It is very limiting to consider *Homo sapiens* as just one more zoological species inhabiting the biosphere (182, 123). The human race continues to transform Earth in ways that plants and animals cannot.

Just as cells propagated the planet with plants and animals and gave Earth a new *living* skin that we call the *biosphere,* so humanity gives Earth a "new *thinking* skin," the *noosphere* (182, 124). The noosphere is Earth's own skin. This latest evolutionary leap is as important as—or more so than—the leap from nonlife to life. Just as the forms of cellular life changed Earth, humanity consciously and continuously changes Earth. Earth responds to humanity's activity. Ecology is the scientific study of Earth's response to human activity. (*Eco-* is derived from the Greek *oikos* [*ecos*] meaning "home.")

Teilhard observes that biology in his day was so accustomed to measuring every species on Earth by its "material face" (*without*) that it missed the transforming influence of the planet's *within*. Over the centuries, the planet's within (the noosphere) has produced cities, highways, literature, art, culture, science, education, mathematics, theology, communication, transportation, and space exploration. This is the "immense and growing edifice of matter and ideas" that we experience every day (183, 124). For Teilhard, the noosphere is the "crown of the cosmos" (184, 125).

The noosphere continually transforms us individually, it continually transforms the human family as a whole, and it continually transforms the planet itself.

Thus, Teilhard completes the three tasks he assigned himself at the beginning. And we have barely crossed the noosphere's threshold!

2. The Original (Human) Forms (184–90, *125–29*)

Teilhard reminds us that when humanity first emerged on our planet, it did not make any sweeping changes in the natural landscape. As he put it, "Man came silently into the world" (184, *125*). In fact, humanity in its original forms first emerged exactly like any other species. Animal forms never appear on Earth as a single, isolated specimen. They first appear as a number of individuals emerging from the environment. Likewise, forms in the *Homo* genus come from a deeper verticil, that of the anthropoids, who populated the fields and forests of Africa, China, and South Asia. These include the gorilla, chimpanzee, orangutan, and australopithecus (185, *126*).

A new species may also be recognized emerging in the "*morphology of its stem.*" Morphology refers to changes of shapes, forms, and configurations among individuals in a species. Emerging biological forms tend to look like others produced by the same stem. So, to understand the verticil of *Homo sapiens*, we can study the morphology of Pithecanthropus, Sinanthropus, and Neanderthal. All of them share a similar body shape (*without*) and an inner life moving toward an ever higher and richer consciousness (*within*).

A new species may also be recognized by the *structure of its group.* Prehuman species typically break up and disperse into several subspecies. Before our *Homo sapiens* species emerges identifiably, other subspecies in our stem are already sprawling all over the planet, from South Africa to Peking, China.[5] These prehominid species are already living in groups. They communicate in primitive languages and know how to make fire (186, *127*). *Homo sapiens* does not look much different from them at first.

Teilhard dismisses the idea that hominization began with a single unique couple, such as the biblical Adam and Eve. He calls the idea "positively ungraspable" (186n, *127n*). He says we search in vain for a photograph or painting of our first human ancestors "who crossed the threshold of reflection" (186–87, 127). The deepest verticil, or stem, of the modern human, says Teilhard, is lost in a dim, unrecoverable past.

In the next chapter, Teilhard will explore some of the past that archaeologists have been discovering. He explores the prehuman past to establish evidence for his thesis of human evolution.

Chapter 2

The Deployment of the Noosphere

(191–212, 130–47)

1. The Ramifying Phase of the Prehominids (191–97, 130–35)

THERE IS LITTLE need to explore this chapter in detail for several reasons.

- The amount of archaeological data that was available to Teilhard as he was writing *Phenomenon* in the late 1930s has grown immensely and continues to multiply with new discoveries each year.
- Many names and dates of prehominid discoveries have been changed since his day. Teilhard's two favorites names, *Pithecanthropus* (Tamil man from Java) and *Sinanthropus* (Peking Man from China) (193, 132) are now listed together under the category of *Homo erectus* (upright man). Other newer categories include *Homo habilis* (handy man), and *Homo ergaster* (working man). The classification of archaic human specimens remains under continual revision as new evidence is evaluated.
- Instead of focusing on the emergence of thought and the development of the noosphere, this chapter spends

159

much of its time with body morphology. Teilhard compares physical changes in cranial size and skull characteristics of the archaic humans compared to others in the hominid line. These factors are of little significance to most readers who are not archaeologists. You may skip most of this chapter.

In this first section Teilhard makes two key points.

First, the precursors of *Homo sapiens* were already spread across the globe, from China to the South Asian islands, from East Africa to Europe. This wide distribution of early precursors (verticil) suggests that the earliest *Homo sapiens* appeared quietly and almost simultaneously in many places around the same period.

Second, these prehominids, as Teilhard calls them, were not fully human by any means. But no longer did they look and act like apes. They were (1) walking upright, (2) industrious toolmakers, and (3) using fire.

2. The Group of the Neanderthals (197–99, 135–37)

Once we get to the Neanderthals, says Teilhard, "there is never any serious doubt but that we are studying the vestiges of our own race....We have true man, then—but man who is not yet precisely us" (198, 135). In the Neanderthals, "the network of thought has extended and consolidated" (198, 136). Here are some facts.

- Neanderthals and *Homo sapiens* shared the planet for many thousands of years, at least in Europe. Some Europeans today have at least 2 percent of Neanderthal DNA.
- Some cave drawings in Europe were drawn by Neanderthals. Perhaps *Homo sapiens* learned the art of ink making and drawing from these precursors. Perhaps Neanderthals taught humans much more than we realize. Undoubtedly, they contributed to the beginnings of the noosphere.

- Neanderthals were part of a group of *Homo* species, along with *Homo erectus, Homo habilis,* and others that were "of a dying stock" and became extinct (199, 137). All of these "successive" species of *Homo* died off before thirty thousand years ago.
- By thirty thousand years ago, the only species of *Homo* remaining on the planet is *Homo sapiens.* Because *Homo sapiens* is the only one remaining does not mean that *Homo sapiens* first appeared at that time. Recent discoveries have found *Homo sapiens* fossils three hundred thousand years old.

3. The *Homo Sapiens* Complex (200–203, 137–40)

The long succession of *Homo* species described in the previous two sections occurred during the last half-million years.[1]

By the time *Homo neanderthalensis* disappears, *Homo sapiens* is spread all over Earth in a variety of hues. Teilhard describes the "*homo sapiens* complex" at this time as preblack humans, prewhite humans, and preyellow humans. But they are all *Homo sapiens* because

- they all share the same distinctive qualities and abilities,
- they are all anatomically "fully human" (*Homo sapiens*),
- there are no profound morphological differences among them (201, 138), and
- they have all developed an ethos—customs and cultures (202, 139).

Teilhard says that they also share "similar aspirations in the depths of their souls." Even though they are still cave dwellers, "we feel a strange spiritual nearness" (202, 139). With these early humans, he says, we are no longer dealing with archaeology. We have moved into the realm of cultural anthropology.

Artistically, human cave drawings reflect "a power of observation, a love of fantasy, and a joy in creation." Intellectually and emotionally,

161

their drawings reveal a mind "not merely reflecting upon itself but rejoicing in doing so" (203, *139*).

Teilhard summarizes: "Evolution has overflowed its anatomical modalities to...transplant its main thrust into the zones of psychic spontaneity both individually and collectively" (203, *140*). Evolution has shifted its forward "thrust" from the biosphere to the noosphere. The noosphere now guides evolution.

4. The Neolithic Metamorphosis (203–6, *140–42*)

We now begin dating periods as BCE (Before the Christian Era). The Neolithic Age, also called the Stone Age, begins around 10,000 BCE and ends around 3,500 BCE, when the Bronze Age begins.

The Neolithic metamorphosis marks a "decisive period of socialization" in the hominization process. Teilhard pictures "our great-great-ancestors found *in groups* and gathered round the fire" (204, *141*). Families join to become communities. Languages first emerge mostly as simple mixtures of sounds and gestures. Communities interrelate with each other by trading in food, tools, artwork, pottery-making skills, hunting techniques, and agricultural practices. Communities collaborate for hunting as well as for security and safety. Groups begin domesticating and developing plants and animals. Forms of communal leadership and governance develop. Teilhard describes the Neolithic period as "the great cementing of human elements never thenceforward to stop" (204, *140*). This period is critical in shaping the human family, "for in it Civilization was born" (204, *140*).

Teilhard notes several factors that speed up, "favor and even force the pace of hominization" (205, *141*).

- The great increase in the number of humans on the planet.
- The diminishment of available land to share with increasing populations.
- The domestication of plants and grains slowing the likelihood of frequent migration.

- The challenge to get the most out of evermore diminishing land.

As agriculture and stockbreeding become dominant, "the husbandman and the herdsman replace mere gathering and hunting" (205, *141*).

Most importantly, group stability demands the establishment of social norms for ownership, transfer of property, inheritance, morals, marriage, communal structures, juridical procedures, and so on. Among tribes, language and pictographic writing become requirements for communication, collaboration, and trade. The challenge "to get the most" out of what is available stimulates research, investigation, invention, improvement, strategy, and conscious reflection.

At this time, Teilhard says, "mankind was of course still very much split up—a veritable mosaic of groups profoundly different both ethnically and socially" (206, *142*). Nevertheless, he notes, "exchanges increased in the commerce of objects and the transmission of ideas. Traditions became organized and a collective memory was developed." The noosphere "began to close in upon itself—and to encircle the earth" (206, *142*).

5. The Prolongation of the Neolithic Age and the Rise of the West (206–12, *142–47*)

From Neolithic times onward, in humanity "the influence of psychic factors [the growth of the noosphere] begins to outweigh—and by far—the variations of ever-dwindling somatic factors" (208, *143*). Social relationships dominate this period of development. For example,

- the emergence of political and cultural life
- the development of economic links, religious beliefs, and social institutions
- a focus on coalescence and confluence of many sources of knowledge
- the continuous "germination of human collective unities" (208, *143–44*)

Teilhard insists that "social ramification" and expansion be treated as a crucial element of natural history because it is an observable human phenomenon.

He identifies some of these observables that shape the "confluence" of social patterns.

For example, before *Homo sapiens*, settling differences among animal and prehumans usually happened by competition and conquest. This was followed by elimination or enslavement of the loser. With Neolithic humans, "simple elimination tends to become exceptional or, at all events, secondary" (209, *144*).

What happens more often is "assimilation—the vanquished reacts on the victor as to transform him" (209, *144*). Often, when assimilation of another group happens peacefully, such as by immigration, the two groups "interpenetrate slowly under prolonged tension." Ultimately, the assimilation produces "a remarkable and significant interfecundity" (209, *144*). In the process, both "somatic genes" and "cerebral genes" as well as "social genes" are blended. Teilhard stresses that this blending produces not mere entanglement but a richer unity. He observes that "over the whole domain of *homo sapiens* we have synthesis" (209, *144*). This mixing and blending produces a continuous enrichment of the noosphere.

Teilhard acknowledges that synthesis happens most favorably only in certain places, where the mixing of races, ideas, and social patterns is welcomed. When it does happen, it results in "some new and superior state for the noosphere" (209, *145*). He notes five areas of the world, each independent of the others, where this cultural synthesis or integration has happened most powerfully:

- Mayan civilization in Central America
- Polynesian civilization in the South Pacific
- (Ancient) Chinese civilization in China
- Indian civilization in India
- Egyptian-Sumerian civilization in the Nile Valley and Mesopotamia (Teilhard refers to this civilization as "the West.")

Teilhard notes the gradual demise of all but the last civilization on the list, which alone proved able "in the course of a few thousand years, to produce that happy blend, thanks to which *reason could be harnessed to facts* and *religion to action*. And this without losing any of their upward thrust" (my emphasis; 211, *146*).

When "reason is harnessed to facts," *science* flourishes. When "religion is harnessed to action," *spirituality* flourishes. In the realm of action, spiritually is concerned not only with prayer and mysticism but also with morality, social justice, and improving the welfare of the human race.

Although great cities, such as Babylon, Memphis, Athens, and Rome may crumble in time, "an ever more highly organized consciousness of the universe is passed from hand to hand, and glows steadily brighter" (212, *146*). During the last six millennia, "the principal axis of *anthropogenesis* has passed through the West." In the West, what is discovered—or rediscovered—is the "ardent soul of growth and universal recasting that goes to make man today" (212, *146*).

Teilhard sees emerging in this discovery "a neo-humanity...germinating round the Mediterranean during the last six thousand years." According to him, peoples all over the world who wish "to remain human or to become more so are inexorably led to formulate the hopes and problems of the modern earth...in the very same terms in which the West has formulated them" (212, *147*).

His point is that the West has become the primary developer of the noosphere, thus the spearhead of anthropogenesis. Teilhard is focused on the human future. His question: Will we have the courage to create our future?

Spiritual Implications

Although Teilhard doesn't talk about courage in this section, it is a spiritual energy he possessed and used throughout his life. Courage is an energy of the human spirit that all future-looking people need to recognize in themselves and to continue to develop. Courage is an essential spiritual energy to carry humanity into the future, so it is important to identify it clearly.

First, courage is not the opposite of discouragement or despair. *Courage is the ability to go forward despite feelings of discouragement, despair, fear, or failure.*

Teilhard knew discouragement. He was stationed in China for over twenty years. He begged his superiors to allow him to return home to Paris where he could share his evolutionary ideas. They consistently refused his numerous requests. We are told that in China, while he was writing in his daily journal, he often wept in discouragement and depression. Yet, courageously he carried on. During this discouraging period of "exile" he composed his two great books, a book of spirituality called *The Divine Milieu* and the scientific treatise, *The Phenomenon of Man*.

Courage—from the French *coeur*, meaning "heart"—is a source of strength that lives deep in the human spirit. It strengthens other spiritual capacities, such as love, faithfulness, and commitment. Without courage urging love forward, love may devolve into mere dependency on others. Without courage, faithfulness may become mere conformism. Without courage, commitment may become mere routine.

Teilhard might say that courage makes *genesis* (being and becoming) possible. One needs courage for the self to grow and stretch beyond what is normally expected. To keep anthropogenesis advancing, many people need to exercise courage.

Courage may be expressed physically, morally, and in social relationships.

Teilhard expressed *physical courage* when he used his "eyes" to observe and describe the full reality of anthropogenesis beginning with its conception at the Big Bang. His physical courage was not violent, brash, or foolhardy, but rather quiet and persistent. He modeled a courage that wishes to create a forward-looking future for humanity.

Teilhard expressed *moral courage* in the face of a church that he knew would refuse to listen to what he was trying to say. Yet, he continued to propose his evolutionary ideas to his religious superiors. He believed these ideas would give new life to a Christianity that was still living in the Middle Ages.

His *social courage* was expressed in trying to show the possibility of a healthy relationship between science and religion revealed in the theory of evolution. At that time, and even today, each side—science and religion—mistrusted the other side and believed that the one had nothing to offer the other. Teilhard saw that the two sides were meant to be partners in anthropogenesis. Science was offering to religion new awareness of God's workings in creation, while religion could offer science a long-range, noble purpose for continuing scientific research.

Teilhard's *Phenomenon* is an example of courage for both scientists and religious believers: He is telling believers not to be afraid of welcoming scientific discoveries or new facts about the universe. He is telling scientists not to be afraid of integrating into their research the idea of a divine purpose for the universe.

The spiritual question that surfaces from Teilhard's text is this: Will there be enough courageous scientists and believers to integrate their knowledge and wisdom to keep anthropogenesis moving forward and upward?

Chapter 3

The Modern Earth
(213–34, 148–63)

A Change of Age

PEOPLE OF EVERY age think that theirs is a turning point in history. They are right because, as Teilhard points out, humanity is continually "advancing on a rising spiral" (213, 148). People of every age continue to use the evolutionary law of Attraction-Connection-Complexity-Consciousness to create a new future. The Renaissance provides a clear example. During that period, major advances were made in economics, industry, science, mathematics, art, education, and society.

This chapter shows that humanity is currently undergoing another "change of age" or advance in hominization. To prove that a change in hominization is truly an advance, Teilhard must demonstrate it in *thought* and *action*. He will show the following:

- The biggest change in *thought* that characterizes our age is *the discovery of evolution*. We have not only discovered evolution; we have also come to realize that it is the fundamental driving force of change in all domains of existence (216–26, 150–58).
- The biggest change in *action* that characterizes our age is accomplishing the *conscious transformation of the world* (226–34, 158–63).

1. The Discovery of Evolution (216–26, 150–58)

THE PERCEPTION OF SPACE/TIME (216–19, 150–53)

To recognize and realize the universal extent of evolution, humanity needed to develop a new mindset. This mindset includes three new abilities of thought:

- the ability to perceive physical space/time
- the ability to perceive biological (process) space/time
- the awareness that humanity is nothing other than evolution becoming aware of itself

These three points correspond to the three subsections of this section marking our achieved advances in *thought*.

To see how far humans have advanced in their perceptions of the universe, Teilhard says, we have only to go back and look at the scholarly and scientific books from as late as the eighteenth century to realize how nearsighted educated people were about the size and age of the universe. Teilhard asks, "Between them and us, what has happened?" (216, 150).

Consider how much our minds and consciousness had to open to move beyond eighteenth-century perceptions regarding the nearness of the stars and the youth of the universe. Some in those days believed that our planet was only about six thousand years old! Today, we know that the nearest stars are many light-years away and that the universe is already almost 14 billion years old.

Also, in the nineteenth century, some scientists saw space and time as two separate infinite entities. It took a long time, even for scientists, to grasp the fact that "time and space are organically joined so as to weave, together, the stuff of the universe" (218, 152).

Biologists confirm this organic joining. For they have come to realize "the irreversible coherence of all that exists." Each infinitesimal cell "is structurally so knit into the web of life that its existence cannot

169

be hypothetically annihilated without *ipso facto* undoing the whole network of the biosphere" (218, 152).

Evolution is not just a random series of transformations happening here and there in various parts of the world as some earlier scientists thought. Rather, it is a force that pervades everything. When grasped in its pervasiveness and power, evolution reshapes our consciousness so that we see the universe in a totally new way.

Not only has the universe been changed in our minds, but awareness of the prevalence of evolution has also had its transformational effects. Metaphorically, in the space of a few centuries, humanity has metamorphosed from a caterpillar to a butterfly.

THE ENVELOPMENT OF DURATION (219–21, 153–54)

When physicists think of space/time, they think of it as an integrated way of measuring each *single object* using yardstick *and* clock. In contrast, when biologists think of space/time, they think of it as measuring a *biological process* by stages of development. Process is measured by duration.[1] So, until we learn to think in process terms and the biological unity of all things, we are only halfway there.

In a long-standing scientific tradition, scientists believed that observers were unconnected to the object of their study, as if subject and object were somehow distinct from each other in the act of knowing. "It did not occur to the first evolutionists that their scientific intelligence had anything to do in itself with evolution" (220, 153).

The fact is that our minds are just as much in evolution as are the objects of our research. New qualities of mind continue to emerge in us as we continue to observe. We are changed as we observe changes in what we study. "How indeed could we incorporate thought into the organic flux of space/time without being forced to grant it [thought] the first place in the process? How could we imagine a cosmogenesis reaching right up to mind without thereby being confronted with a noogenesis?" (221, 154).

Thought not only participates in evolution, but evolution tells the story of the cosmos' progress toward thought. Or the cosmos' progress toward *Homo sapiens*.

THE ILLUMINATION (221–26, 154–58)

The first two requirements for grasping the meaning and purpose of evolution's prevalence in the universe are, as noted, the ability to perceive both physical space/time and biological space/time (process).

The third requirement is *illumination*, in other words, the realization that *humanity is nothing other than evolution becoming aware of itself*. In Teilhard's words, "The consciousness of each of us is evolution looking at itself and reflecting upon itself" (221, 154). When we look from humanity backward in time, Teilhard says, human thought appears as the natural outcome of evolution.

A *Triple Unity*

From today's perspective and looking back in time, the evolutionary line leading up to "thought" presents a triple unity:

1. unity of *structure*
2. unity of *mechanism*, and
3. unity of *movement* (222, 154).

Teilhard expands on all three unities.

1. *Unity of Structure.* The structure of the universe remains consistent at every level: in each age of the universe's history, *from the stem* (or peduncle or verticil) *the branches stretch out in a variety of expressions*. Subatomic particles branched into a hundred or more atoms listed in the table of chemical elements. Atoms branched into scores of molecules, and molecules branched into millions of chemical compounds. The same branching structure continues with cells spreading and expanding into the various phyla of plants, insects, reptiles, animals, and birds. Humanity has produced the same branching structure in its *social milieu* by creating different "phyla" of groupings or relationships. As Teilhard italicizes it, *"The social phenomenon is the culmination and not the attenuation of the biological phenomenon"* (223, 155).

A similar branching pattern occurs in other evolutionary developments—"in the formation and dissemination of languages, the development and specialization of new industries (education, transportation, media), and in the formulation and propagation of philosophic and religious doctrines" (223, 155).

2. *Unity of Mechanism.* Elements of the universe have always used similar mechanisms to ensure progress and development such as *groping* and *invention.* Typically, biological species did groping using biological "mutations"—single mutations (birds mutating the size and shape of their beaks) and mass mutations (flocks of birds moving their nesting place to a new island).

Historically, groping has also been used consistently by humans to ensure species safety, health, and development. "Let's try this herb to see if it quiets your stomach pain." "Let's plant these seeds and see if they produce a better crop than the seeds we used last season." "Let's see if this new manufacturing process works better than the old one." In the pharmaceutical laboratory, intelligent groping is used as well to discover new medications, which are then scientifically tested in animal and human trials.

Invention is also used consistently by humans to ensure species development. Beginning with toolmaking among the most primitive humans, invention progresses to innovations such as the wheel, the axle, the lever, the screw, weaving, and sewing. Today, the U.S. Patent Office is daily flooded with new inventions.

3. *Unity of Movement.* As we trace the history of the universe—from subatomic particles to the human brain—the development has always been *a movement toward higher complexity and consciousness.* Teilhard does not see humanity as the center of the universe but as its leading edge into the future. This is an important insight. Evolution is not about us; it is always about the future. We are "the last-born, the freshest, the most complicated, the most subtle of all the successive layers of life" (224, 156).

Teilhard's "fundamental vision" is that we are not the termination of evolution, just the tip of its arrow moving forward. His vision remains incomplete until we can see our purpose as enriching and evolving "the laws and conditions of heredity" (224, 156–57).

We have enlarged the biological meaning of heredity, that is, what is passed on through genetic transmission. As humans, through education and training, we also "inherit" everything that previous generations have discovered, invented, or created.[2] Humans inherit the entire noosphere to use to develop new abilities. Humans have learned more about flight in a century than birds have learned in millions of years. Humans operate, not merely by genetics, but primarily by using and transforming "the thinking layer of the earth."

The more a human operates "by the radiation of his own consciousness, the greater becomes the part of his activity which can be stored up and transmitted by means of education and imitation" (225, 157).

The noosphere is central to our lives. While the transmission of acquired *biological* characteristics is the dominant mode of movement in the biosphere, in the noosphere, Teilhard observes, we have developed "the transmission of *acquired* spiritual characteristics" (Teilhard's emphasis; 226, 158). The diffusion of facts, ideas, skills, thought processes, beliefs, attitudes, and values in the noosphere are part of our heredity. They serve as resources for evolutionary development.

Our ancestors have bequeathed to us a tremendously rich heritage and an enlightened consciousness in the hope and expectation that we will build upon that inheritance and create the future. Our response will be seen in our choice of actions.

2. The Problem of Action (226–34, 158–63)

MODERN DISQUIET (226–29, 158–60)

The choice of how to act is always a problem. How shall I live my life? What shall I choose as my life's purpose? To what or to whom should I be committed? Big questions like these begin to surface in our minds at this transitional time in history. They challenge us to shift our focus from *consciousness* to *conscience*. Questions of life's meaning and purpose move us into the realm of spirituality and morality.

As we read Teilhard's *Phenomenon*, we realize that the universe is extremely vast, and we are tiny. The project proposed to us—to envision and create a better future—is daunting. We feel inadequate. People in a simpler age did not experience our confusion and anxiety about how to act. Their moral and social task was simple: Be nice. Do good. Enjoy life while you can. Help others less fortunate than you.

The choices for action that Teilhard puts before us are far more ambiguous and unclear. One thing we know for certain is that, despite our anxiety, the universe continues to evolve.

For Teilhard, the task that faces us is to keep evolution moving forward in the noosphere. This is the process he calls *noogenesis*. Noogenesis (fostering the maturity of the noosphere) is the process within geogenesis (the maturing of Earth) that specifically needs our generation's contribution.

Scientists and profound thinkers who accept the fact of evolution find the future troubling. What disconcerts the modern world, explains Teilhard, "is not being sure, and not seeing how it could ever be sure, that there is an outcome—*a suitable outcome*—to that evolution" (Teilhard's emphasis; 229, *160*).

Teilhard tries to answer their concern.

THE REQUIREMENTS OF THE FUTURE
(229–32, *160–62*)

Teilhard understands we will never give our all to creating the future, except "on condition that the effort demanded of us has a chance of succeeding and of taking us as far [forward] as possible" (231, *161*).

All requirements for trusting in the future boil down to one: we want to be "assured of the space and the chances to fulfill ourselves, that is to say, to keep progressing until we arrive (directly or indirectly, individually or collectively) at the utmost limits of ourselves" (231, *161*).

We know that consciousness has no limits or ceiling in its ability to grasp reality. Limiting consciousness or going backward is impossible. The simple reason is "that every increase in internal vision is essentially the germ of a further vision which includes all the others and carries still farther on" (231, *161–62*). Humanity can move only "toward that which is interminably and indestructibly new" (231–32, *162*).

The only alternative is if we—all humans collectively—consciously choose not to act. If we make that choice, "the whole evolution will come to a halt—because we are evolution" (232, *162*).

THE DILEMMA AND THE CHOICE
(232–34, *162–63*)

In this final subsection, Teilhard issues a strong ultimatum. He says that we are at a crossroads, confronted with only two ways to go. We can choose to go forward or to stop trying. We can choose to stop trying by claiming that nature offers us no future. Or we can recognize that nature, based on billions of years of evidence, offers a wide-open future. Either pessimistically we see before us "a self-aborting and absurd universe," or we optimistically see "a super-soul above our souls" toward which we are moving (233, 163).

Remember that Teilhard was writing his *Phenomenon* in the 1930s, when many scientists and the church were denying the very evidence of evolution. We who live a century later are aware of the clear "choice" humanity has already made to explore that wide-open future. Back then, following World War I, Teilhard was not so confident of the choice that those in power would make.

Two Things Vitally Necessary

Teilhard ends book 3 with a few observations:

Once humans develop the power of seeing, they naturally desire to keep seeing more and more without limit. Once we develop the power of thought, nothing can stop the human desire to explore and create.

Teilhard says, "The best guarantee that a thing should happen is that it appears to us as vitally necessary" (234, 163). Do we not say, "Necessity is the mother of invention"?

Two things appear to Teilhard as "vitally necessary" beyond our mere survival as a species. We must begin

- to imagine a higher form of human life, and
- to create it (234, 163).

To make these two things happen, he says, we need to keep operating by using the laws of evolution that we have discovered: "Attraction-Connection-Complexity-Consciousness" and "Union Differentiates."

Spiritual Implications

If believers today need moral and social courage, a more crucial need is *creative courage.*

Creative courage calls for the discovery of new forms, new symbols, new patterns, new concepts, and new systems upon which a new society can be built.[3]

There are plenty of scientists and technology people today who show creative courage. There are also plenty of artists and musicians who show creative courage. There are plenty of writers and poets, too, who show creative courage. But where are the believers and saints who show creative courage?

We have saints who live lives of prayer, fasting, and suffering. We have martyr saints dying for their faith. But where are the saints who want to transform the world? Where are the believers who, like Teilhard, love both God and Earth with passion? Where are the believers who want to push anthropogenesis forward and present their effort as a gift to God? Where are the saints who pursue a human future beyond their own personal tasks and challenges?

These are the ones who, Teilhard would say, are willing to encounter the full reality of the human experience. They are the ones who want to forge a yet uncreated theological and moral consciousness worthy of the divine space/time experiment that began in the mind and heart of God and was initiated at the Big Bang. This is a consciousness that strives to look forward to the human phenomenon a hundred, a thousand, even a million years into the future.

When faced with the new unassailable scientific evidence of evolution, Teilhard dares to be the first to rewrite the story of creation in a new way and to reinterpret biblical symbolism in evolutionary terms. He did it during a time when almost everyone took the creation stories in Genesis literally and almost everyone believed that the universe was fixed and unchanging. Any changes they acknowledged were cyclical ones, like the rotation of the seasons and the paths of planetary orbits.

At the same time, modern science was revealing that everything was evolving, and that Earth was emerging in new and diverse ways revealing new and different properties and abilities.

In the face of a threatening and punishing church, Teilhard had the creative courage not to deny the facts discovered and verified by science. Instead, he attempted to integrate the two apparently contradictory positions of science and religion.

Even today, most believers and scientists hesitate to really "see" and acknowledge the truths of both science and religion. Each—believer and scientist—find it easier to conform to the traditions and beliefs of their respective positions.

It is also possible that in some cases apathy wins out over the effort it takes to form—and live—a true union of religion and science. In other cases, instead of being interested in searching for a greater truth at any cost, many are more interested in keeping peace at any cost—or making money or exploiting their power to control the status quo and spread mistrust of or disdain for the "other side."

Teilhard hopes to inspire an insurgent spirit in both scientists and believers. He wants them not to conform quietly to the status quo, but to push the community—and the congregation—forward. Teilhard wants to share his zest for the whole of life—the total human phenomenon—yet few scientists or religious experts want to exert the creative courage to forge a new synthesis.

He offers a spirituality that is focused on creating the future.

BOOK FOUR
SURVIVAL

Chapter 1

The Collective Issue

(237–53, 167–73)

Preliminary Observations

A T FIRST GLANCE, the title of book 4, "Survival," may be misunderstood. The title is not a question. Teilhard is not wondering whether humanity will survive. Teilhard assumes that we will continue to evolve. He takes a prophetic stance trying to picture that future and how to foster it. He proposes certain areas of development that we need to focus on in the next few millennia.

He envisions things and processes of which no one in the 1930s had ever conceived. He makes every effort to describe what he is imagining. He outlines the groundwork that present generations need to do to prepare for the humans of 2100, 2200, and 2300.

In my attempt to explain and simplify what he envisions, I may lose some of Teilhard's depth of insight. For this, I apologize.

To see the future that Teilhard envisions for humanity, we need to grasp important new concepts that Teilhard has invented, including the following:

- *planetization* (or *convergent phylogenesis*)
- *megasynthesis*
- *supraphysical humanity*
- the *hyperpersonal*
- *supercentration*

Each concept looks at our human future from a slightly different perspective. Together, they paint a fuller picture of our evolutionary potential.

WORKING TOGETHER

Teilhard titles his preliminary remarks "Isolation." He wants to point out that our species' survival will not happen individually. Progress primarily happens when we work together.

He acknowledges that some people would like to think that, "in light of the limitless future before them," they should seek their personal fulfillment in isolation (237, 167). Such people see themselves as the select few who have been called to full enlightenment. Such people often choose to live—and evolve *personally*—in isolation. Picture the cartoonist's wise man sitting alone on a mountain peak.

Teilhard warns that isolating oneself in this process is a "blind alley to be avoided." The evolutionary project needs everyone's help—working together.

1. The Confluence of Thought (239–45, 168–79)

Three natural factors ensure that humans will work together to achieve the evolutionary future that Teilhard envisions.

1. *The biosphere and noosphere are inseparable*; the two are symbiotically joined into a single evolving system.
2. *Forced coalescence*, one of the fundamental factors of life on Earth, requires people to think and work together.
3. The *connecting noosphere* provides a milieu of mind and heart that enables the entire human family to stay connected.

The first of these factors—(1) *the inseparability of the biosphere and noosphere*—was developed in book 3. Teilhard here discusses the other two.

FORCED COALESCENCE (239–43, *168–71*)

Coalescence, or joining together, is one of the "fundamental characteristics of the cosmic nature" (239, *169*). Coalescence is a natural evolutionary process. It is the way the universe works in its innate drive of Attraction-to-Connection. At every level of evolutionary development—particles, atoms, molecules, compounds, cells—elements mutually join with each other and form new unities. They coalesce.

At the human level, Attraction to Connection works in much the same way, but adds a new dimension. Human coalescence integrates both the *without* and the *within*. Groups "coalesce" to create new wholes and new systems.

In their *withouts*, groups of humans work together side by side. In their *withins*, they "combine their radial energies in bundles" (239, *168*). That is, ideas and thoughts are shared among group members and form bundles of energy available to each and all group members. Coalescence fosters the mutual development of a team's members. For example, mutual development happens in a scientific research team. By participating on the team, each researcher has access to the bundle of radial energy created by team interaction. In this sharing, the members mutually develop their skills and their union.

Teilhard observes that human coalescence happens continually and is multiplied millions of time each day worldwide whenever humans come together to plan together or work together. Coalescence is unavoidable. We are forced to coalesce. Coalescence is "forced" simply because we live confined on a spherical planet with a limited surface. Much of that sphere's livable surface has been populated.

Although human coalescence is *forced* because our planet cannot be enlarged, the ways in which coalescence can happen are *unforced* because of the freedom and flexibility of the human species. We can choose the groups to which we belong. We can choose what we share and how much we share.

THE CONNECTING NOOSPHERE (241–42, *170–71*)

The products of the coalescence of many groups are brought together and integrated in the noosphere, the thinking layer of mind and heart covering our planet. Tapping into the noosphere allows and encourages the entire human family to stay connected and grow. The internet makes this easy. Teilhard says that the noosphere provides the milieu that makes it easy for the various human branches to "become welded together before they have managed to separate off" (242, 171).

In earlier stages of mammalian evolution, species continued to split apart and branch into different subspecies. We might expect the same branching process to occur with humanity, but it does not happen. Portions of humanity do not separate, even though they seem like different branches. Despite gene variation, different races, many ethnic groups, and conflicting political parties, humans manage to remain "joined in a common tissue" (241, 170).

We continue to achieve something no other previous species has been able to do. "The human verticil as it spreads out remains entire….With man we find indefinite interfecundation on every level" (241, 170).

Apparently, human evolution tends to continue to improve its way of operating, while its members manage to live together, think together, and work together. In humanity, the universe has learned how to coalesce an entire phylum upon itself (242, 171).

Teilhard says that evolution's new ability to coalesce an entire phylum may be attributed to the "birth of reflection," or more precisely, to the ability of humans to create the noosphere. The noosphere supplies a "universal framework or support" to facilitate the forces of human coalescence.

Teilhard sees human history (anthropogenesis) as "a movement of convergence in which races, peoples, and nations consolidate one another and complete one another by mutual fecundation" (242, 171). This ongoing process of cohesion of a bundle of potentially distinct species into one species reveals a "completely new mode of phylogenesis" (development of the human phylum).

Planetization, or Convergent Phylogenesis

Before *Homo sapiens*, *phylogenesis* was the term used to describe the evolutionary *branching outward* of a phylum into many distinct species. In humanity, phylogenesis reverses its movement. For the first time, phylogenesis becomes a convergent and coalescing process, effecting the unification of many *potentially different* species into one species.

Teilhard calls this new mode of phylogenesis *planetization.* By *planetization* he means *creating a single thinking and flexible species that can cover the entire planet and unify it.*

Megasynthesis (243–45, 172–73)

Teilhard asks, "But why should there be unification in the world and what purpose does it serve?" (243, 172). What brings about this shift in phylogenesis—a shift from branching outward into many species to coalescing into a single species? The answer is Earth's very shape.

For Teilhard, the spherical shape of Earth together with humanity's flexibility and consuming mind counterbalance the ancient evolutionary forces of dispersion. Instead, these two factors bring about unification. The unification into a single thinking-and-flexible species is what Teilhard describes as a *megasynthesis.*

To explain this megasynthesis, he proposes what he calls "two equations."

Teilhard expresses his first equation as this:

Evolution = Rise of Consciousness

This equation says that evolution's process is simply another way of telling the story of the "rise to consciousness." In other words, to describe the process of evolution from the Big Bang to today is to describe the continuous rise of complexity and consciousness.

Teilhard's second equation states,

Rise of Consciousness = [Planetary] Union Effected

The second equation says that the rise to consciousness is, at the same time, the story of bringing about planetary unification. In other words, to describe the history of the rise to consciousness is to describe the history of planetary union.

He says that planetary unification is achieved by the "correlated actions of the *without* and the *within* of the earth." In other words, "the totality of thinking units [*within*, i.e., human minds] and thinking forces [*without*, i.e., human bodies] are engaged" in guiding this planetary unification process. The process goes forward despite the efforts of some individuals and groups who are determined to separate and divide us (243, 172).

Teilhard sees this process of human unification—or planetization—as inevitable because it is "the natural culmination of a cosmic processus[1] of organization" (243, 172). Human self-reflective consciousness naturally brings about the unity of the species *Homo sapiens*.

This driving process toward complexity/consciousness has been going on since the birth of the universe—from atoms to molecules to cells to living plants and animals to humanity. Thanks to humanity adding a thinking layer (the noosphere) to the biosphere, the planet "develops and intertwines its fibers, not to confuse and neutralize them but to reinforce them in the living unity of a single tissue" (244, 172).

A Larger Megasynthesis

For Teilhard, Earth's evolution describes "a gigantic psycho-biological operation, a sort of *mega-synthesis*" happening all over the planet (244, 172). Humanity's synthesis of the biosphere and noosphere affects more than collective humanity. It makes Earth as a whole evermore complex and evermore conscious. Teilhard calls this process *geo-genesis*. The planet itself continually carries on its own megasynthesis, which is larger than the synthesis of humanity. It is always the whole Earth evolving, not just humanity.

Geogenesis is a single global process to which everyone and everything contributes. There can never be "an egocentric ideal of a future reserved for...a few of the privileged." No element [individual human] can grow into this higher consciousness—become the superhuman—"except with and by all the others with itself" (244, 173).

2. The Spirit of the Earth (245–53, 173–79)

HUMANITY (245–48, 173–75)

Teilhard poses an interesting question: How early in civilization did humans conceptualize the idea of *man*, or *mankind*, or *humankind*, or *humanity* as a single entity? It had to be a concept that recognized the unity of all the apparently different branches of *Homo sapiens* on the planet. Just to grasp that single concept requires a deep awareness and an all-embracing consciousness.

For Teilhard, there are other important concepts that emerged, which require an all-embracing consciousness. For example,

- Who first evoked the idea of *human progress?*
- Who first envisioned a *human future?*
- Who first imagined an *unlimited future* for humanity and its *perpetual growth?*
- Who first realized the need for a *universal and integrated humanity* to achieve this future?

Teilhard notes that, to many prophets of the eighteenth century, "the world appeared really as no more than a jumble of confused and loose relationships" (245, *173*). Those four questions might never have occurred to them. Today, all reflective people think about them — or are at least aware of them. People see Earth as a single, well-integrated evolving process. Most acknowledge that a universal and integrated *humanity* is needed to keep it developing.

Not only fellow humans but also the totality of Earth in its many layers is "required to nurture each one of us" in our effort to coordinate and organize the work before us (246, *174*). We need matter — metals, minerals, and gases as well as plant and animal life along with technology's tools and products — to accomplish our evolutionary work. We are born of cosmic stuff and the product of cosmic evolution. We have a cosmic-sized task ahead of us, individually and collectively.

Supraphysical Humanity

Teilhard develops another of his new concepts, *supraphysical humanity*. This concept offers a fuller meaning of and adds content to the word *humanity*. For some, humanity is nothing more than an abstract idea or a mere conventional expression. Others characterize humanity as a closely knit biological group, an organic group, or social group. For others, humanity is a vague idea, a legal entity, or even a gigantic collective. To choose any of these definitions, Teilhard says, leads us to a dead end. Teilhard sees humanity as *a living reality in itself.* He boldly states that *humanity* belongs in a category of the "super-individual" (247, *175*).

Recall that for Teilhard, a collective—a group, a team, humanity itself—*has a unique reality, a life of its own.* He can only describe a group's life as being like that of an individual person, except that it is a super-individual person. A collective reality—any true relationship—has a life of its own. That life cannot be reduced to the sum of the lives of the elements in that relationship. For example, a sports team is a relationship that has a life of its own. Its life cannot be reduced to the lives of the individual players.

Besides having its own life, a sports team has *its own primary function or purpose.* That propose—to compete with other teams and win games—cannot be reduced to the function or purpose of any individual on that team. The same holds true for the functions or purpose of any group. Each group has its own life and its own purpose. So does humanity. Humanity has its own function and purpose, which is beyond that of any individual or group.

Teilhard wants us to begin seeing *humanity* no longer as a handy concept to describe the collection of people on Earth. He wants us to see humanity "directly, exactly as it is, without attempting to put it in terms of anything simpler" (248, *175*). Humanity, he says, is unlike anything we already know. Humanity itself is *a personal, living, evolving superindividual with its own functions and purpose.* It is a collective reality, sui generis (a thing unique unto itself, a one of a kind), a living "conscious synthesis…a common power of knowing and doing…an organic super-aggregation of souls" (248, *175*).

Teilhard says that, because humanity is supraphysical—physical, yes, but something more than merely physical—it is properly "only definable as a mind" (248, *175*). Humanity, as a living entity, possesses an evolving mind, a mind that is unique in the entire universe. It cannot be reduced to any individual's mind, nor is it simply the sum of all minds on Earth. This evolving mind is humanity's most defining quality.

Teilhard's exploration here in book 4 is focused on the future of this supraphysical living being we have named *humanity.* He sees two ways by which we can "picture the form mankind will assume tomorrow." We can see it either through the eyes of *science* or through the human experience of *unanimity.* Each viewpoint gives us a sense of and reasons for believing and hoping in our future.

SCIENCE (248–50, 175–77)

Modern science offers the ability to establish an overall and coherent perspective on the universe, its beginnings and history (*cosmogenesis*). Science lights up "for our speculative pleasure the objects ready made and given" (248–49, 176).

Every science is by nature creative, Teilhard asserts, because it is focused on making discoveries. Teilhard points out that every scientific "discovery" reveals "something new." Creativity is the process of bringing something new into existence that has never been in the world before. Each scientific discovery adds to our knowledge of our universe and ourselves. Each discovery also enriches the noosphere and us. "From this point of view, intellectual discovery and synthesis are no longer merely speculation, but creation" (249, 176). Discoveries create new content and interconnections in the noosphere.

Humanity as Hyperpersonal

Once we acknowledge that humanity is a superbeing with its own life and purpose, we ask, *But what is the nature of this superbeing?*

In the previous section, we looked at humanity as *supraphysical*. Here, Teilhard takes us one step further and shows that humanity is also *hyperpersonal*. *Supra* means "bigger or beyond," *hyper* means "a greater or higher amount of a certain quality." So, *hyperpersonal* means "personal to a greater or higher degree."

We are continually making and remaking ourselves and our minds. We are creating ourselves, individually and collectively. More precisely, the collective superbeing we call humanity is continually creating and recreating itself as a living being. In this sense, humanity acts like a person, except that humanity is superpersonal or, as Teilhard prefers, "hyperpersonal," which means something higher than simply personal or interpersonal.

This superbeing doesn't wait for the future to happen. It envisions ("imagines") it and creates it. Collectively, we not only imagine and create how we evolve. We imagine and create the *purpose and the goal* of our evolution. We do this "in a supreme act of collective vision obtained by a pan-human effort of investigation and construction" (249, 176). In effect, *humanity acts as one hyperpersonal person.*

Humans have learned to seek knowledge not merely for their own sake, but for its power to create the future, especially humanity's future. If the ancient alchemists sought to transform lead into gold, the ambition of today's scientists "is no longer to make gold but to make life" (249, 177), to deepen and transform our experience of life.

In this regard, scientists are no longer using random groping to make progress. They are using "calculated efforts" (250, 177). To do their exploring, they are using millennia of collected energy of human thinking, scientific methods, imagination, and reflection.

When you watch such people at work, says Teilhard, each of them in their own way, individually and in groups, are trying to find "the mainspring of evolution, seizing the tiller of the world." If others could see the human phenomenon as he sees it, Teilhard says, they would have to take only one small step to move from research into adoration (250, 177). If they truly realized the cosmic movements in which they are involved, they would be awestruck.

Unanimity (251–53, 177–79)

For Teilhard, unanimity, not uniformity, is evolution's goal. *Uniformity* means that everyone thinks the same thing and the same way. *Unanimity* describes the richness of all individualized minds sharing the mind of all. Unanimity is what "the gradual combination of individuals, peoples, and races will bring into existence" (251, 178).

The Unanimity of Supraphysical Humanity

The unanimity that is our destiny must also be *supraphysical*, not *infraphysical*. By this assertion, Teilhard means that humanity's final unanimity will produce a collective being that is "beyond physical," yet it will not be "pure mind." Rather, in this supraphysical state each of us will still manifest identifiable features of our human individuality, though those features will no longer be tangibly physical. How does Teilhard describe this apparent paradox?

When we enter this supraphysical stage of union far in the future, says Teilhard, this great gathering will feel like the "living reunion of reflective particles," in which each human is a "reflective particle." The union achieved may be a new union, but Teilhard says it will feel more like a "reunion."

Before the appearance of humanity, says Teilhard, the biosphere continued to split into many different living forms. It was "no more than a network of divergent lines, free [to branch out] at their extremities" (251, 178). In contrast, the noosphere "tends to constitute a single closed system in which each element sees, feels, desires, and suffers for itself the same things as all the others at the same time." The noosphere provides a "harmonized collectivity of consciousnesses equivalent to a sort of [single] super-consciousness" (251, 178).

In describing the process toward global unanimity, Teilhard pictures it as "the plurality of individual reflections grouping themselves together and reinforcing one another in the act of a single unanimous reflection" (251–52, 178). We are on our way to "a new step in the genesis of mind" (253, 179), where noogenesis drives and supports geogenesis.

Supercentration

Supercentration is another of Teilhard's new concepts meant to help us see the process of humanity's future stages. *Supercentration is a process that speeds up global unanimity.*

Teilhard understands, at present, we are far from global unanimity. Empires still wage war. There is vast economic inequality. Poverty and hunger pervade the planet. Teilhard acknowledges all the conflict, confusion, frustration, disagreement, rejection, and lust for conquest and control happening on Earth, yet he is ever optimistic. Within these unwelcome and even evil factors, he sees being revealed immense, untapped, *unused* sources of power and *wasted* power.

Despite humanity's vast amounts of unused, misdirected, and wasted energy, Teilhard continues to hold a vision of final unanimity. He also firmly believes that humanity can achieve this "great goal"—a single collective "spirit of the earth" (253, 179).

Teilhard says that we will achieve that goal by a process of *supercentration*. In this process, each of our individual "centers" (or *withins*) will find their fullest meaning in a higher "center," humanity's own center. Humanity's center is a center of centers. Teilhard explores these ideas in the following sections.

Chapter 2

Beyond the Collective: The Hyperpersonal

(254–72, 180–94)

Preliminary Observation: Discouragement (254–57, 180–82)

TEILHARD INSISTS that humanity is on its way to developing a collective global mind, but he acknowledges that there are groups of skeptics that would challenge his optimism.

One group of skeptics claims that only a very few enlightened individuals will evolve. Others declare that the universe itself is radically absurd. Others laugh at the idea of people universally agreeing on anything. Others are impatient. Others say we are too stuck in our values of competition and war that perpetuate conflict. Still others say we are too obsessed with "materiality" and power to even seek higher consciousness. Others believe that evolution has stopped with *Homo sapiens*; they say we have reversed it and are in devolution. Teilhard sees the rest of his book as a response to most of these skeptics.

First, he introduces a *radically new way of looking at our planet*, which he calls its *personalization*. Recall that book 3 dealt with *hominization* (the making of the thinking, self-reflective human species). The previous chapter dealt with *planetization* (the spreading of humans all over Earth and creating a thinking planet symbolized by the noosphere). Teilhard now begins discussing Earth's *personalization* (the making and the shaping of the *planet's personality*).

1. The Convergence of the Person and the Omega Point (257–64, 183–88)

THE PERSONAL UNIVERSE (257–60, 183–85)

The ancients tended to *personify* everything including oceans, trees, and animals. They invented a pantheon of gods, all of whom they symbolized as human persons. Teilhard claims that we humans have given our planet Earth a unique personality among all planets.

Today, in our age of science we tend to *depersonalize* everything. Using the techniques of analysis, we take apart every whole and dismantle every system. Scientists like to break things down to their most basic elements and study these elements (257, 183). In doing so, they take the life out of them.

Teilhard acknowledges that analysis provides a powerful tool in fostering tremendous advances in many fields, such as medicine, communication, commerce, chemistry, toolmaking, transportation, archaeology, or astronomy. All of it wonderful!

In the following pages, Teilhard is doing something no one else has ever done. He is exploring our *planet's evolutionary process* as something different from *humanity's evolutionary process*.

ENERGY, SPACE, AND TIME

Everyone, including scientists, works with *energy*. The secret to all progress is energy. Energy is a unifying factor of all advancing fields of modern life. Energy is what enables innovations to occur. Without energy, little can be accomplished. Energy is the only reality that "seems to survive and be capable of succeeding and spanning the infinitesimal and the immense" (258, 183).

Energy spans not only *space*, it also spans *time*. It pervades everything. Energy was there at the first moment creating the Big Bang, what Teilhard calls "Alpha." Energy will be there at the end of time, creating a final synthesis and unanimity that Teilhard calls "Omega."

According to Teilhard, science seems to have made energy into "a new spirit; the new god." For science, this energy god is *impersonal* (258, 183). Science sees all energy as impersonal—electricity, magnetism, gravity, fission, fusion, nuclear forces.

Scientists even view humanity and the human personality *impersonally*. Personality, they say, is a useful concept, a very changeable and "ephemeral property" of life. Everything, including humanity and personality, may be broken down into impersonal matter and energy.

In contrast, Teilhard believes his study of the human phenomenon points in the opposite direction. It leads toward seeing each person, humanity as a whole, and the planet itself as having a personality. A personality represents the synthesis of a living, evolving, complex, and conscious reality.

The trajectory of evolution has always been toward the development of personality. That is, toward *synthesis*, which, for Teilhard, is personality's main characteristic. Personality is shaped and grows as the person continually unites and integrates ongoing experiences, decisions, and actions. Personality synthesizes.

Teilhard notes that, though scientists are skilled in *analysis* (breaking down wholes into parts), they are also skilled in *synthesis and organization*. They synthesize and organize (and publish) their discoveries as well as write textbooks that synthesize and apply their principles and theories. He suggests they really know what he is talking about in this section.

THE MILIEU OF SPACE/TIME

But Teilhard takes a further step. As he reflects on the very concepts of space/time that science has discovered, he sees "space" and "time" not merely as concepts but as *realities*. The union "space/time" is also something real. It's as real as the water in a fish tank, even though the fish are unaware of it. It is as real as the transparent atmosphere in which we live and breathe, although we are mostly unaware of it. Space/time is the milieu that supports all that exists. It is as real as the atmosphere or the oceans. It too is alive and evolving.

Teilhard points out that the reality of space/time provides the necessary conditions for *hominization, planetization,* and *personalization*. All three of those processes need the milieu of space/time to keep evolving. Space/time is not dead or inert. It is a living milieu. Like the amniotic fluid in the mother's womb that provides the necessary vital milieu for the growth and development of the fetus, space/time provides the nourishing vital milieu for evolution.

INVOLUTION AND SUPREME CONSCIOUSNESS

When Teilhard traces the paths of those three processes — *hominization, planetization,* and *personalization* — he sees their evolution as nothing other than the story of "an ascent to consciousness" (258, 183). And he asks, Why should evolution cease advancing upward along the same ascending path into the future?

He predicts a continuous advance, one that "should culminate forward in some sort of supreme consciousness" (258, 183). If this consciousness is supreme, it must "contain in the highest degree the perfection of our consciousness — the illuminating involution of this being upon itself" (258, 183).

Involution is an integrative process that helps create and shape personality. Involution helps create and shape personality in individual humans. It helps create and shape the personality of groups such as families, sports teams, and nations. It also helps create and shape Earth's personality.

Note that *involution* is not the same as *devolution. Devolution* describes breakdown, diffusion, confusion. *Involution is a higher form of evolution.* It follows a path of continual convergent integration. It supports continual reconstruction, reorganization, and reclarification that integrates new material and information into the same limited space.

By its very nature, Teilhard says, consciousness cannot move toward breakdown and diffusion. Reflection must move "only in the direction of hyper-reflection," which is in fact hyperpersonalization (259, 184). Certain individuals may develop Alzheimer's disease, but the consciousness of the superpersonal being, which is "humanity," continues to expand and transcend itself. This expanding consciousness is reflected in the growth and development of the noosphere.

To some thinkers, the advance in consciousness that Teilhard envisions is laughable. These people would say that he is trying, in effect, to integrate one's Ego (individual consciousness) with the All (supreme consciousness).

Teilhard says that if you reflect on the evolutionary process, a supreme consciousness is precisely what must come about. The supreme consciousness integrates individual consciousnesses in its *within*. He explains the process.

Looking at the Ego, Teilhard observes three of its properties:

- Ego centers everything "partially" upon itself. It interprets whatever it experiences in terms of the effects on itself.
- Ego can constantly recenter upon itself. That is, it can self-reflectively reobserve itself and recenter itself as it deals with the many new experiences of life.
- Ego keeps being brought "into association with all other centers (Egos) surrounding it" (259, *184*). As one's Ego unavoidably relates to other Egos, it must deal with the content and thought processes of other minds.

As all Egos carry out these three processes constantly, Teilhard says, the entire universe itself is gradually being gathered up more and more in each one of us. As each of us influences others and we are influenced by the words and actions of others, we are interpenetrating and complexifying each other's Egos. The products of all these interactions are helping build and shape the noosphere. At the same time, they are supercentrating.

INVOLUTION, SUPERCENTRATION, AND THE NOOSPHERE

The noosphere is not a garbage dump of ideas or a pile of confused thoughts. Just as the biosphere continually self-organizes life on the planet, the noosphere continually self-organizes thought. The noosphere is constantly assimilating, adapting, adopting, adjusting, reorganizing its contents, its processes, its values, and its aims. In this, the noosphere is acting like superperson. It is performing a process of *supercentration* of all our individual centering processes. Since each of us has access to that supercenter, it *has its effects upon us, individually and collectively*.

Teilhard asks, Are we not daily experiencing "the first symptoms of an aggregation of a still higher order, the birth of some single center?"

(259, 184). Are we not watching the gradual convergence of billions "of elementary centers dispersed over the surface of the thinking earth?" (259, 184).

Teilhard insists that such a convergent integration process creates a whole that is not only enclosed but *must be centered*. In the process of the Earth's personalization, evolution—now as *involution*—has become a process that is centering all centers into a single supercenter, creating a *within* of all *withins*.

Notice that Teilhard envisions four supercentration processes happening simultaneously. Involution is happening on all levels.

- The noosphere as a whole is supercentrating.
- Humanity as a whole is supercentrating.
- Earth as a whole is supercentrating.
- All three supercentration processes are supercentrating into one "being" within space/time.

Teilhard sees space/time providing a milieu for all four centering processes. Each of the four is essentially of a "convergent nature." The noosphere's continuous convergence "must somewhere ahead become involuted to a point." So, too, humanity's continuous convergence must become involuted to a single center. So, too, Earth's continuous convergence must converge toward a single unity (259, 184).

THE PERSONALIZING UNIVERSE
(260–64, 185–88)

Just as each individual becomes a person (is personalized) through the development of his or her own "center," so planet Earth becomes a superperson (is personalized) as it develops its own center. Teilhard gives *personalization* a unique meaning as he applies it to the planet. For him, personalization becomes a *global process.*

The development of a *planetary center* (*personalization* of the planet) is an evolutionary stage that follows naturally from two previous evolutionary processes, *hominization* and *planetization.* Here's how Teilhard sees it.

In the *hominization* process, the universe through evolution produces *Homo sapiens from prehominid species,* so that humans now enjoy the emergent properties of thought and self-reflection.

In the *planetization* process, evolution produces (1) *a single species that can cover Earth* and (2) a layer of mind and heart covering the planet, which is the noosphere uniting with and enriching the biosphere.

The planet's *personalization* process emerges from the first two and goes beyond them. According to Teilhard, evolution is currently *creating a collective supreme personal center*, so that the planet itself is becoming a single-centered, thinking, self-reflective being within space/time.

OMEGA POINT

So far, Teilhard has merely described the personalization of planet Earth. His vision of Omega involves much more than the personalization of Earth. In Omega, he also envisions all other planets in the universe—wherever consciousness exists—becoming personalized. He then sees all these planets converging and becoming a personalized universe.

There will come a far distant moment, he says, marking the complete convergence of all consciousness in space/time into a single center. Teilhard sees personalization as an evolutionary process moving humanity as a whole toward this universal convergence point.

Teilhard named the space/time moment marking the complete convergence of all centers to a higher-order center the *Omega Point*. For Teilhard, Omega is not merely a culminating moment or "point" in space/time. Omega also represents the supreme consciousness itself. Omega is the center of all centers. In Omega, all other convergences are fused and consumed integrally into one great convergence (259, 184). The purpose of a universe of space/time is precisely to provide the "space" and the "time" for the evolutionary process of convergence to Omega to occur (259, 184).

The mind has always been seen as "essentially the power of synthesis and organization" (260, 184). "The Universal and the Personal grow in the same direction and culminate simultaneously in each other" (260, 184). In the end at Omega, each person's Ego (individual consciousness) will be integrated with the All (supreme consciousness).

Teilhard says that the convergence to occur at Point Omega is *integral*. By integral, he means that in Omega's involutive process it does not eliminate a single individual conscious center, or Ego, but recenters each of them integrally in its universal center. The identity of each individual human that ever lived will remain recognizable to others in Omega.

In Omega, says Teilhard, individual consciousness does not become mixed, or confused or lose its identity. In Omega, "the centration of a conscious universe would be unthinkable if it did not reassemble in itself all consciousnesses as well as all conscious beings. Each individual's particular consciousness remains conscious of itself at the end of the operation" (261–62, 186).

In fact, says Teilhard, as we approach Omega, each conscious center will become more and more itself and thus grow "more clearly distinct from the others" (262, 186).

"Union Differentiates"—Another Evolutionary Principle

Teilhard can make the claim that no individual conscious center will be lost in Omega. His claim is based on the evolutionary principle that *Union Differentiates*. This principle states, *As each conscious element (person) participates actively in the purposes of a relationship, group, or system, it becomes more clearly individuated.* For example, any individual on a sports team who is committed to the purpose or aim of that team will, in fact, become more fully himself or herself.

This principle also implies that, to the degree that members of a union participate actively in the purposes of that union, the participating members "perfect themselves and fulfill themselves" (262, 186). The more fully they participate, the more they become uniquely themselves.

Teilhard applies this "Union Differentiates" principle to the whole integral system of consciousness. At Omega, Teilhard says, the billions of consciousnesses present there become a "paroxysm of harmonized complexity" (262, 186).

Teilhard says that it is a mistake to confuse the philosophy of individualism with personality. In philosophy, individualism says you can most fully develop yourself *by yourself. Personalism* says you most fully develop yourself by involvement with others.

The evolutionary principle "Union Differentiates" supports personalism. It says that if you want to become most individualized and uniquely yourself, it can only happen as you commit yourself to joining relationships, teams, and other human systems—and fully participating in them. That is the way to fully develop personality.

Paradoxically, says Teilhard, "The element becomes personal when it universalizes itself" (263, 187). You become supremely personal as you universalize yourself in Omega.

Teilhard notes that not all unions personalize, but only those where the elements unite center to center. His point is easy to grasp when you compare two sports teams. One in which all teammates are united center to center and are committed to the success of the team; the other in which each player during a game is competing with other teammates to score the most points and promote his or her own success. Members of the first team are personalizing; members of the second team are not.

2. Love as Energy (264–68, 188–91)

Teilhard recognizes something that science has never considered. For Teilhard, *love is the energy driving all evolutionary processes.* Love is the energy that drives Attraction and Connection. Love is the energy that creates relationships and unions that bring about Complexity and Consciousness. Love is the energy that personalizes individuals, groups, and planets. Love is the energy driving everything toward Omega.

Here, Teilhard is not talking about sentimental and superficial expressions that some have mistakenly called "love." The love Teilhard discusses here has "natural dynamism and evolutionary significance" (264, 188). This kind of love has the power to determine "the ultimate phases of the phenomenon of man." Such love is the only kind that can carry us forward to the Omega Point.

Teilhard acknowledges that "love—that is to say the affinity of being with being—is not peculiar to man." Such love is "a general property of all life" (264, 188). He applies this love principle not only to all life-forms but also to all beings in the universe. For Teilhard, love is defined as *the essential expression of the fundamental property of all elements to unite.*

Attraction leads to Connection. Without Attraction operating at all lower levels, "it would be physically impossible for love to appear higher up [in human love]" (264, 188). Attraction to form Connections (unions) is the deepest and simplest form of love energy governing the universe's evolution from the beginning. "Driven by the forces of love, the fragments of the world seek each other [to form unions] so that the world may come into being" (264–65, 188).

Union—loving union—"alone is capable of uniting living beings in such a way as to complete and fulfill them" (265, 189). Today, we form loving unions in friendships, families, sports teams, research teams, communities, and even nations. If we can form center-to-center unions on a small scale and locally, why can't we achieve loving union "on worldwide dimensions?" (265, 189).

UNIVERSAL LOVE

At this point in human evolution, Teilhard admits, such a large-scale target seems like "invoking the impossible" (266, 189). He answers, "A universal love is not only psychologically possible; it is the only complete and final way in which we are able to love" (267, 190). Only when we are consciously integral participants in a suprahuman union will each of us become fully human and know how to love in a fully human way. Only such a higher-level union will truly differentiate us and make us everything we can be.

Teilhard is optimistic because he sees certain perspectives surfacing in our day that bring with them new levels of possibility in this loving quest. Teilhard sees inklings of a global mind emerging all around us that give him hope that we will be able to glimpse Omega in our lifetime, even though we may not yet be ready to attain it. A universal love is what will get us there.

3. The Attributes of Omega (268–72, 191–94)

Achieving Omega may take humanity a thousand or a million more years. It is a very long-term quest. It is not something that can be achieved in a lifetime, like finding a cure for cancer or starting a colony on Mars. Therefore, Teilhard can merely describe Omega in the most general terms. It is important for him to do so, since Omega represents the culmination of his exploration of the human phenomenon.

Teilhard's genius in envisioning Omega lies in the fact that he does it by using the same evolutionary principles and laws that he has already uncovered from observing the human phenomenon starting from its embriogenesis. The universal evolutionary laws operating since the Big Bang are the same laws that will bring humanity to Omega. The two principal evolutionary laws are: *Attraction-Connection-Complexity-Consciousness* and *Union Differentiates*.

Using those laws, Teilhard can identify four attributes of life and love at Point Omega:

Autonomy. "Omega must be independent of the collapse of the forces with which evolution is woven" (270, 192). At Point Omega, evolved humanity will have transcended the limitations of materiality. Humanity will no longer be "burdened by the perishable." Omega as a reality in itself must be an autonomous center of all centers. Although Omega is the final term in an evolutionary series, it also *outside all series*.

Actuality. Omega as an entity is actual and real. Awareness of it emerges thanks to the rise of consciousnesses. Omega has already been present to us and awaits us.

In its final form, Omega does not escape from time and space, nor does it do away with time and space. It gathers time and space together and integrates them in itself (271, 193). Recall that by the evolutionary principle *Union Differentiates*, nothing will be lost at Point Omega. Omega will somehow integrate time and space within itself.

Irreversibility. Omega ensures that there will be no relapse into multiplicity. "Once formed, a reflective center can no longer change except by involution upon itself" (272, 194). Involution keeps making us even more centered as we approach Omega.

Transcendence. Omega allows an escape from the laws of entropy. At Omega, it's as if a new universe gets created. Instead of using sub-atomic grains of matter to build itself, Omega uses "grains of thought" as the new "indestructible atoms of the universe" (272, 194). Persons become the principal "atomic elements" that make up the universe at Omega.

The universe is a collector and conservator, not of mechanical energy, as we supposed, but of persons. All round us, one by one, like a continual exhalation, "souls" break away, carrying upwards their incommunicable load of consciousness. One by one, yet not in isolation....The noosphere... will reach collectively its point of convergence—at the "end of the world." (272, 194)

Chapter 3

The Ultimate Earth

(273–90, 195–208)

I N THIS CHAPTER, Teilhard deals with questions reflective people typically ask about the final days of our planet Earth. He discusses some of the "ultimates" and "inevitables," such as the end of all life on Earth, the death of the planet, and the "ultimate phase of the phenomenon of man."

He acknowledges that all these events defy the powers of our imagination to grasp. It seems absurd to try to describe them. Even *his* mystical imagination fails in this enterprise (273, 195).

Therefore, Teilhard does not focus on describing *details* of the eschatological events themselves. Rather, he first chooses to explore their *significance*. And, second, he wants *"to circumscribe the forms"* by which these events can happen. He asks himself,

- How will "ultimate Earth" take its shape? (*significance*)
- What shape is most likely? (*form*) (274, 195)

1. Prognostics to Be Set Aside (274–76, 196–97)

In general, when ordinary people think about the end of the world, they envision a fiery catastrophe, a sidereal cataclysm, the heavens exploding, burning stars hurtling toward Earth.

Science pictures the end of the world quite differently. According to the laws of physics, Earth will slowly grow darker and colder. As a consolation, science also assures us that we have several hundred million years before Earth's dark and cold finale is likely to occur (274, 196).

Other, more pessimistic, scientists allow that, by chance, Earth can be struck by a giant meteor tomorrow. Such a cosmic blow would cause the end of humanity very quickly, much as happened 65 million years ago when a huge meteor caused the end of the dinosaurs. People who hold this pessimistic view have no motive for undertaking "the task of ascending higher toward union" (275, 196).

Teilhard is more optimistic regarding these dire predictions. He thinks that "we have higher reasons for being sure that they will not happen" (275, 196). Such a catastrophic event would be like "the universe committing abortion on itself" (276, 197). For Teilhard, humanity is irreplaceable. "However improbable it might seem, [humanity] must reach the goal, not necessarily, doubtless, but infallibly" (276, 197). Teilhard is an optimist and a probabilist.

2. The Approaches (276–85, 197–204)

Before exploring the two issues of *significance* and *form* of ultimate Earth, Teilhard lists a few assumptions that he deems important to point out.

- *Life on Earth still has long periods of time in which to develop.* Humanity is so young at present that it could easily be described as "newborn" (277, 198). During our period on Earth, humanity's maturation is not slowing down but speeding up. Humanity has boundless energy.
- During this period, *progress is developing in collective and spiritual forms.* With humanity, Earth is at present primarily involved in mental and social transformations (277, 198).

The question now is this: Based on optimistic predictions, on what lines of advance are we most likely to proceed? Teilhard identifies three principle lines:

A. The *organization of research*
B. The concentration of research on *the human phenomenon*
C. The *conjunction of science and religion*

He discusses each of these three themes.

THE ORGANIZATION OF RESEARCH (278–80, 199–200)

As far as Teilhard is concerned, research today is sadly characterized by three things: "pettiness of spirit, poverty of means, and general haphazardness" (278, 199). Remember, Teilhard is writing this in the late 1930s.

First, he says, only a small proportion of energy is devoted, here and now, to the pursuit of *truth*. Research is mostly committed to our materialistic values, so that "everything is subordinated to the increase in industrial production and to armaments" (279, 199).

As for money, he says, "less is provided annually for all the pure research all over the world than to build one capital ship." No wonder some philosophers consider us as still "barbarians" (279, 200).[1]

Regarding the haphazardness of research, it seems research is more interested in producing leisure material for pleasurable consumption (games, entertainment, sports) or for manufacturing or warfare. There seems to be no truly coordinated and organized research program for moving humanity into a new future, which is what we need.[2]

THE DISCOVERY OF THE HUMAN OBJECT (280–83, 200–202)

Teilhard believes that we are moving toward a humanity-focused era of science and research. He says, "It will be eminently an era of human science. Man, the knowing subject, will perceive at last that man, 'the object of knowledge,' is the key to the whole science of nature" (281, 201).

Yet, Teilhard is baffled about the lack of interest in developing a true "science of humanity." He says, "We find man at the bottom, man at the top, and, above all, man at the center—man who lives and struggles desperately in us and around us. We shall have to come to grips with him sooner or later" (281, 201).

Teilhard says that as an object of study, humanity is of unique value to science for two reasons. First, humanity "represents, individually and socially, the most synthesized state under which the stuff of the universe is available to us" (281, 201). Second, humanity "is at present the most mobile point of the stuff in course of transformation" (282, 201). Humanity is resilient, flexible, adaptable to almost any environment, capable of almost any achievement. And it is readily available for study.

Teilhard says that the study of the human phenomenon provides the best way "to find out how the world was made and how it ought to go on making itself" (282, 201). He says he might subtitle such a discipline "a science of human energetics" (283, 202).

Regarding the issues that he thinks need to be studied in his science of humanity, he mentions specifically the distribution of Earth's resources, protecting currently unpopulated areas, the optimum use of machines, development of new technology, geo-economy, geopolitics, geo-demography, geo-environment, and the organization of research (283, 202).

If science concentrates on developing a science of humanity, it will also find itself increasingly face-to-face with religion, which he discusses next.

THE CONJUNCTION OF SCIENCE AND RELIGIONS (283–85, 203–4)

Teilhard suggests that the current tension between science and religion needs to be resolved using an entirely different form of relationship, "not in elimination, nor duality, but in synthesis" (283, 203). So far, he says, neither science nor religion has been able to discredit its adversary. Neither side is ever going to "win." So, it is time for an integrative approach.

The synthesis of both fields is inevitable. Looking at science, he says, "Neither in its *impetus* or its *achievements* can science go to its limits without becoming tinged with mysticism and charged with faith" (284, 203).

Regarding science's *impetus*: when we observe dedicated people continuing to work and to do research, we notice that they are driven by a passionate interest in the outcome. Their impetus comes from their inner conviction that the universe has a purpose and a direction. They usually call this a "belief in progress" (284, 203). Teilhard calls it faith. Whether sacred or secular, faith is the belief in something hoped for, an outcome that is yet unrealized.

Regarding science's *achievements*, science can envision "an almost indefinite improvement in the human organism and in human society." Whoever envisions a better future for oneself or for the community, says Teilhard, counts on the "convergent properties" of humanity, and thus holds a "belief in unity" (284, 203).

Teilhard asks, What is the special binder or glue "that will bind our lives together, vitally, without diminishing or distorting them?" His answer: *religion and faith.*

Teilhard describes religion as "belief in a supremely attractive center which has personality" (284, 203). This is a definition of religion that most people have never heard. It is necessary to grasp *his* meaning of each word to catch the significance of his description.

As a *center*, religion organizes and integrates everything within it. As *supremely attractive*, it draws all other centers toward union with it and within it. Since it has *personality*, it can build conscious relationships and can act on its own. If this sounds to you like he is describing Omega, you are correct.

He then offers another fresh insight. He says, "Religion and science are the two conjugated faces or phases of one and the same complete act of knowledge — the only one which can embrace the past and future of evolution so as to contemplate, measure and fulfill them" (285, 204). Only the combined knowledge of science and religion can produce a complete act of knowing.

Only in the mutual reinforcement of "reason and mysticism," that is, of science and religion, can humanity do the work of bringing us to Omega. Or, as Teilhard puts it, only in mutual reinforcement will humanity be able to achieve "the uttermost degree of its penetration with the maximum of its vital force" (285, 204).

3. The Ultimate (285–90, 204–8)

Once evolution reached the threshold of reflection, says Teilhard, it entered an entirely new domain of evolution, that of *involu-*

tion. Humanity began this process of self-unification "thanks to the prodigious power of thought to bring together and combine in a single conscious effort all the human particles" (285, 204). We created the noosphere to maintain unity or oneness in our widely dispersed human family.

As we continue to create the noosphere, Teilhard adds, we have no idea of the possible magnitude of evolutionary effects that it can bring about (286, 204). He asks us to consider some of the marvelous technological advances in communication, already achieved using the noosphere, that foster the union of individuals, nations, and races. I leave it to the reader to carry out this suggestion.

Teilhard says that the noosphere has also revealed and recognized the need for the emergence of "an autonomous and supreme personal focus to bind all elementary personalities together" (287, 205). To do this, humanity will have to stop searching for this supreme personal focus in the physical or biological Earth and began looking elsewhere for "the transcendent center of its increasing concentration" (287, 206). Religion offers ways to help find this transcendent center, especially regarding the purpose of the universe and the "end of the world."

Science, by its knowledge alone, describes Earth's final years as growing progressively darker and colder. Religion offers a more hopeful outcome. For Teilhard as a believer, the "end of the world" refers not to a death but to a culmination of life. He describes the end as "the wholesale internal introversion upon itself of the noosphere."

Point Omega describes the moment when the "noosphere of the universe" (not merely of Earth) has reached its ultimate complexity and its total centeredness. That is the point when humanity (and all other forms of consciousness in the universe) can go no further in degree of complexity or breadth of consciousness (287, 206).

Somewhere in the far future, at Point Omega, Teilhard predicts, humanity will detach itself from its "material matrix" (the physical planet and human bodies). This will allow humanity's mind (the fulfillment of Earth's noosphere) to come to rest "in God-Omega" (288, 206). On the final page of book 4, Teilhard uses the word *God* for the first time.

Omega is no longer merely Point Omega, a singular culminating moment for the thinking universe. Omega has become the "supreme personal Being" who is the Center of all our centers.

POSSIBLE FINAL OUTCOMES

Looking at the whole of humanity at the "end of the world," Teilhard can see two possible outcomes for the human phenomenon, neither of which can be guaranteed.

The first is that everything will be gathered into Omega in peace and love. This fits Teilhard's theory. In this scenario, theology's hell is empty.

But there is another possible outcome, where hell is quite full. Teilhard describes this outcome. "Evil may go on growing alongside good, and it too may attain its paroxysm at the end in some specifically new form. There are no summits without abysses" (288, 206). If in the end there is a group that accepts living in Omega and another group that rejects living in Omega, then we will have *ramification once again, for the last time* (289, 207).

If bifurcation of final humanity into good and evil becomes the ultimate outcome for the human phenomenon, says Teilhard, three processes would achieve their ultimate at the same moment. First, it would mark the death of our materially exhausted planet. Second, a "percentage of the universe" would go into Omega. Third, the rest that synthesize themselves in evil would enter the Abyss.

Summary

Throughout his book, Teilhard has been using scientific observation to study the human phenomenon. Specifically, he has tried to show that the emergence of thought and self-reflection in humanity is not an evolutionary aberrance, but the most logical and natural evolutionary step for an evolving universe to take. Teilhard defends his observations against those who consider him a dreamer of fanciful ideas. He sums up his reasoning in this conclusion to book 4:

> To make room for thought in the world, I have needed to "interiorize" matter: [1] to imagine an energetics of the mind; [2] to conceive a noogenesis rising upstream against the flow of entropy; [3] to provide evolution with a direction, a line of advance and critical points; and [4] finally to make all things double back upon *someone*. (290, 208)

He says he has done his best to make these four points and hopes others will do better. At least, he says, he has made the problem clear, especially the need to develop a *science of humanity*.

Here is his last statement: "The only universe capable of containing the human person is an irreversibly 'personalizing' universe" (290, 208). This insight becomes a fundamental tenet of such a science.

If anyone but Teilhard had been writing *Phenomenon*, the book might end here. As a Jesuit priest, however, Teilhard feels he must add an epilogue and discuss another "phenomenon," one that significantly enriches his study of the "phenomenon of man." His epilogue discusses the "Christian phenomenon."

Spiritual Implications

If Teilhard's analysis of the human phenomenon is correct, then the task of spirituality for a believer in an evolving world becomes quite clear. God has created an evolving universe. At the moment of the Big Bang, God sent out an explosion of countless subatomic particles and photons of light. Each and every particle was imbued and implanted with a generative force, which Teilhard called the evolutionary law of Attraction-Connection-Complexity-Consciousness. God creates from the inside out. Teilhard would say that God put a *within* in every single particle. It's as if they were preprogrammed to grow and develop from within.

God set the particles free to interact—and they did. It was God's experiment. God's project. We can imagine that God kept watch to see if creation would ever discover what it was, how it came to be, and what its purpose was.

Stage by stage, the implanted law of evolution got particles to join to form atoms. Immense numbers of hydrogen and helium atoms began to form the stars. Other particles joined to form more complex atoms, and these joined to form compounds. Stars, like our Sun, became solar systems, holding and warming planets like our Earth in orbits around them. God watched, blessed, and managed the divine project as it continued to move forward. God saw that it was good.

The evolutionary law of Attraction-Connection-Complexity-Consciousness kept transforming God's project from within, and eventually it produced life-forms. As these forms grew in complexity, they manifested abilities and properties that earlier forms did not possess—awareness, movement, reproduction, sensation, memory. In the last half million years, mammals that enjoyed consciousness evolved into *Homo sapiens*, who possessed self-reflective consciousness. The principle that "Union Differentiates" was working.

God was breathing life and love into God's project. It was moving at full speed. But would creation ever discover what it was, how it came to be, and what its purpose was?

As humanity grew into the twentieth century, people slowly began to discover that creation has always been evolving. Teilhard formulated the evolutionary law of Attraction-Connection-Complexity-Consciousness that could explain what God's project really was, how it came to be, and what its purpose was.

That purpose—the union or reunion of all things—was what God hoped would happen to God's Earth experiment. But that final achievement is still awaiting a future to be achieved.

God is inviting us to keep God's project moving forward. Our human task is simply to cooperate with God's work using the evolutionary law. By doing this, we are divinizing human action. There is no longer a need to perpetuate the separation between the work of faith and the work of science.

Furthermore, we now know where to look to see what needs to be done. Teilhard has given us the secret. As long as we keep using the evolutionary law, we will be fulfilling God's plan for creation. Omega becomes the focus of the contemplative's prayer.

The task of spirituality today is to find ways to keep applying the evolutionary laws: to practice its stages of Attraction-Connection-Complexity-Consciousness and to trust that "Union Differentiates." To do this, we all need generous and loving hearts that are full of faith, hope, and love. Above all we need creative courage to go forward—both knowing and not knowing.

God is up ahead; God awaits us. But God is doing more than that. For Teilhard, the force of evolution is the loving hand of God behind us slowly drawing us toward Omega. Teilhard identifies the energy humanity needs to go forward as *love*. He also points out that the four-stage law of evolution is also the law of love.

From his theology, Teilhard learned that the primary nature of God is Love. It was a loving divine mind that conceived of the great experiment, the creation of an evolving universe. As we contribute to the growth and development of human life and the life of the planet, we are revealing God's loving plan by what we create and how we act.

Though we live in a secular society, we are called to renew that society by spiritual means and motivation. As long as anyone or any group is working to promote life, love, or unity, they are contributing to God's project. Whether such people are Christian, Jew, Muslim, Hindu—whether they belong to any faith or reject all faiths—they are contributing to God's project for Earth and creation.

To love God's project is to love the universe. To love the universe is not only psychologically possible, says Teilhard, it is the only complete and final way in which we are able to love. It is to love what God loves.

If the universe ahead of us assumes a face and a heart, and so to speak personifies itself, then in the atmosphere created by this focus the elemental attraction will immediately blossom (267, *190*).

If you have a copy of Teilhard's *Phenomenon*, please read and reflect on Teilhard's own pages "Love as Energy" (264–68, *188–91*).

Epilogue
The Christian Phenomenon
(291–99, 209–15)

Perspective

EVEN THOUGH TEILHARD, as he writes, is a devout priest "living at the heart of the Christian world," he is still writing as a scientist. "It is not the convinced believer but the naturalist who is asking for a hearing" (292, 210). Teilhard has not shifted his viewpoint. He is still presenting objective evidence easily observed in the ongoing history of the "human phenomenon."

Teilhard concludes book 4 by exploring the idea that Omega must be a unique conscious living reality, a Being that is the Center of all our centers, a Presence having its own personality and its own emerging properties.

Here is his epilogue's argument:

Either this entire book's presentation is "vain ideology," or "somewhere around us, in one form or another, some excess of personal, extra-human energy should be perceptible to us if we look carefully, and should reveal to us the great Presence" (292, 209).

Teilhard claims that we should be able to recognize the active presence among us of the living Omega, the transhuman center that unites all other centers in itself. If Omega is already in existence and "operative at the very core of the thinking mass," he says, "then it would seem inevitable that its existence should be manifested to us here and now through some traces" (291, 209).

Teilhard believes that the phenomenon of Christianity provides some of these "traces" of evidence that reveal the living presence of

Omega in our midst. For scientists, this neglected evidence is the importance of *the Christian phenomenon* (292, 210). He looks at tangible data for the living presence of Omega in Christianity.

Teilhard says that Christianity is an observable fact so we can study it scientifically. He is certain that we can find in its beliefs and practices some traces of the great Presence of a living Omega. He explores three aspects of the Christian phenomenon:

- The substance of its creed (its "axes of belief")
- Its existence value
- Its extraordinary power of growth

1. Axes of Belief (292–94, 210–11)

In its key doctrines, Christianity's creed (its axes of belief) "contains an extremely simple and astonishingly bold solution of the world" (292, 210). Christianity professes,

- God as *personal*: "the uncompromising affirmation of a personal God"
- God as *providence* directing the universe with loving watchful care
- God as *revealer*, "communicating himself to man on the level of and through the ways of intelligence"
- A faith that holds a "tenacious personalism"
- Openness to "everything that is great and healthy in the universe"
- Possessing "the most cosmic of beliefs and hopes" (292–93, 210–11)

Teilhard then discusses how God, as understood by Christians, creates, fulfills, purifies, and unifies the world "by uniting it organically with himself" (293–94, 211).

How does God do this? God immerses his divinity in *matter* by the incarnation. In Jesus Christ, God takes on flesh and blood, experiencing what it means to be fully human. Jesus develops a physical body in the womb of a woman and is born as a helpless baby. Like all humans, he experiences life in a community and grows into adulthood. He reveals his divinity only to his special friends. Teilhard's point is that the divine Christ, just like an ordinary human being, lives in "the heart of matter" and in the biosphere.

More importantly for Teilhard, Christ enters the evolving human phenomenon *during the blossoming of the noosphere*. In entering fully both the biosphere and the noosphere, Christ assumes "the control and leadership of what we now call evolution." By becoming a human being, Christ puts himself in the position "to subdue under himself, to purify, to direct, and to super-animate the general ascent of consciousness into which he inserted himself" (294, 211).

Although Christ experiences physical death, he overcomes it and rises to new life—undergoing a change of state. Christ is more fully alive than ever. In Teilhard's language, Christ, still living, emerges as a supercenter, the human-divine center of all centers, uniting them into himself. For Teilhard, each of our human centers is recentered in Christ. In him, we reach the highest form of union or oneness. In him we experience the fullness of life.

Teilhard comments on this image of the Christ as unifier of all. He says, "This is indeed a superior form of 'pantheism.'" Teilhard scholars call it "pan*en*theism." In traditional pantheism, everything *is* God; God is all there is. In Teilhard's pan*en*theism, everything *lives in God*, each thing maintaining its own identity (or Ego, or *within*, or center) while living in God. In God, each enjoys the fullness of life.

These, says Teilhard, are the major axes—or lines—of Christian belief. They are evident and measurable in the beliefs and behaviors of Christians. They are part of the Christian phenomenon. They are vitally alive and observable in the noosphere.

2. Existence Value (294–96, 212–13)

A study of Christianity as a phenomenon reveals its existence value and its reality value.

Christianity reveals its existence and reality by virtue of the large-scale movements and advances it has contributed to the human phenomenon—in education, medicine, art, music, drama, architecture, astronomy, mathematics, biology, ethics, philosophy, and social justice. Fostering centuries of developments in each of these fields Christianity has given continuous impetus to the growth and evolution of the noosphere. Christianity's "stamp and its enduring influence are apparent in every corner of the earth today." It addresses itself to every human and to every class of humanity. Since these advances are observable and measurable phenomena, Christianity has *quantitative* value (295, 212).

It also has *qualitative* value inasmuch as it has introduced to the world "a specifically new state of consciousness." Teilhard is referring to Christian love (*caritas* in Latin, *agape* in Greek). Christian love calls for unconditional welcoming and care of others as well as limitless forgiveness of others. Not only does Christianity preach unconditional love, it also shows such love "to be psychologically possible and operative in practice [especially in its saints]" (296, 213). And the momentum for this all-embracing consciousness seems to be growing worldwide. The Christian consciousness is present and active throughout the noosphere.

3. Power of Growth (296–99, 213–15)

Christianity continues to grow and evolve. This is observable fact within the human phenomenon. Moreover, says Teilhard, Christianity's continuous growth "reveals itself as inherently more *vigorous* in itself and as more *necessary* to the world than it has ever been before" (296, 213).

When practiced according to its beliefs, Christianity needs and creates "an atmosphere of greatness and of coherence." Moreover, according to Teilhard, Christianity is ready to welcome the challenge of integrating evolution into itself and its beliefs.

> If the world is convergent and if Christ occupies its center, then *Christogenesis* [the becoming and fulfillment of Christ] is nothing else and nothing less than the extension, both awaited and hoped for, of that noogenesis in which cosmogenesis…culminates. (297, 213)

Epilogue

Evolution enriches Christianity. "Evolution has come to infuse new blood, so to speak, into the perspectives and aspirations of Christianity" (297, 213). At the same time, Christianity can use its evolved form of love (*caritas, agape*) in very practical ways to accelerate evolution's forward and upward thrust. Evolution allows Christianity and modern science to operate as symbiotic partners, each enhancing the other.

Teilhard argues that "at the present moment Christianity is the *unique* current of thought...which is sufficiently audacious and sufficiently progressive to lay hold of the [evolving] world at the level of effectual practice" (297, 214). In its doctrines, Christianity is already complete and all-embracing. In practice, it remains "capable of indefinite perfection, where faith and hope reach their fulfillment in love" (297–98, 214).

Teilhard says that "Christianity fulfills all the conditions we are entitled to expect from a religion of the future" and that the principle trajectory of evolution passes through Christianity (298, 214). Christianity is structured to keep evolution moving forward. It is a vital reality that offers humans powerful ways of moving our world toward higher consciousness and a supremely personal Someone in whom to place all our centers.

Postscript
(300–310, 216–23)

TEILHARD SIGNED HIS final completed *Phenomenon* manuscript "Peking, June 1938–June 1940." Ten years later, he added some pages that he called "Summing Up or Postscript." We might have expected to see some major changes or new perspectives, but he makes no major changes and adds only a few evolved perspectives.

He opens his postscript with these words: "Since this book was composed [but never published till after his death], I have experienced no change in the intuition it seeks to express. Taken as a whole, I still see man today exactly as I saw him when I first wrote these pages" (300, 216).

What evolved during those ten years was Teilhard's "vision" — not *how* he sees but *what* he sees. In June 1940, he recognizes that many advances have been made that enrich the contents of his evolutionary "vision." For example, in physics think of splitting the atom, nuclear energy, rocketry, and the validation of Einstein's theories. In medicine, think of antibiotics, breakthroughs in anesthesiology, and surgical techniques. In technology, think of plastics, automation, the laser, robotics, and mass-production techniques. Teilhard became aware of advances and new discoveries being made in geology, paleontology, and cultural anthropology. What Teilhard could now see, to his delight, was that the noosphere was growing at a faster pace than ever before.

He also acknowledges gradually refining the explanations he originally gave in his book. He finds "certain new formulations and articulations" for his ideas. As he put it, the *Phenomenon* in essence remains "unchanged though recogitated" (300, 216).

The postscript presents his views under three themes:

- *involution*
- *individual reflection*
- *the social phenomenon*

1. A World in Involution, or the Cosmic Law of Complexity-Consciousness (300–302, 216–18)

Considered in cosmic terms of stars and galaxies, the universe is in a process of spatial *expansion*, from the infinitesimal singularity of the Big Bang to the immense diversity of billions of galaxies and countless stars.

Considered biologically and psychologically, the universe shifted into reverse. It is in "a process of organic *involution* upon itself" (301, 217). Involution has moved from the extremely simple to the extremely complex. Though Earth, biologically and psychologically, is becoming bewilderingly complex, it is becoming more and more unified.

The growth in complexity parallels a growth in consciousness. The evidence for this cosmic process is irrefutable. Complexity invariably produces *involution* and a parallel increase in *interiorization*, in other words, both a deepening and widening in consciousness (301, 217).

Teilhard here redefines consciousness in terms of complexity. He sees consciousness "experimentally as the specific effect of organized complexity" (301, 217). He reasserts the power of the cosmic law of Complexity-Consciousness, but this time pointing out the law's centrality also in morality and spiritual practice. We can start using this cosmic law as a guide in living our daily lives.

2. The First Appearance of Man, or the Individual Threshold of Reflection (302–4, 218–19)

Here, Teilhard makes only one major point. He reinforces an insight made in his original text. In the prehuman world, changes were made by random groping and chance. Involution at that time proceeded "step by step by dint of billion-fold trial and error" (302, 218). Thought and self-reflection changed that pattern.

Self-reflection became a threshold into a new state, a new form of biological existence. Thanks to the abilities of reflection, changes could be made and implemented by conscious intention, not merely by random groping and chance. Changes could be made by invention and rational experimentation.

Reflection enables individuals to foresee a future, plan for it, and carry it out. This gives humans an "indisputable superiority" (304, 219). But also an indisputable social responsibility. Practically, Teilhard says, we need to "make up our minds to apply relentlessly and to the bitter end the experimental law of Complexity-Consciousness to the global evolution of the entire group" (304, 219).

3. The Social Phenomenon, or the Ascent toward a Collective Threshold of Reflection (304–10, 219–23)

In the text of *Phenomenon*, Teilhard places most of his emphasis on the threshold of reflection of the *individual*. In these final pages, he adds his observations on the threshold of reflection of the *collective* and its increasing rate of growth. Such collective reflection is a relatively new stage of consciousness. Just as each individual evolves, *society also evolves*. He calls it a social phenomenon. It shows the human phenomenon operating "in full impetus around us" (305, 219).

Most people view "society" as an abstract concept, a convenient category, a political or judicial construct, a superficial and extrinsic way of describing collections of individuals. Teilhard says that is not enough. Society is a functioning reality, enjoying its own life and purpose.

With the arrival of *Homo sapiens*, he says, "biological evolution has reached its ceiling." Humanity ushers in a new way of leaping forward as a collective. Evolution becomes a social phenomenon. Evolution is now focused on human groups and the whole evolving human family. The noosphere has assumed primacy over the biosphere as the new milieu of evolution. The noosphere is a collective invention, a social phenomenon that human society uses to advance itself. History is not the story of individuals, but of a species.

The same evolutionary force that challenges individuals to grow in complexity and consciousness is, today, also operating within the collective. That same evolutionary force operates and does it "in proportions and with a depth hitherto never attained" (305, 220).

Teilhard pictures evolution's force becoming a collective cyclone, driving the entire human society forward.

> How can we fail to see that after rolling on us individually—all of us, you and me—upon our own selves, it is still the same cyclone (only now on the social scale) which is still blowing over our heads, driving us together into a contact which tends to perfect each one of us by linking him organically to each and all of his neighbors? (305, 220)

The evolutionary process of the human phenomenon has three stages. Stage one establishes the primacy of *life itself* in the biosphere. Stage two, within the biosphere, establishes the primacy of *reflection* and creates the noosphere. Stage three, within the noosphere and through human socialization, is decisively pursuing *collective interiorization and involution* (306, 220).

To put it another way, hominization had an elementary phase culminating in the individual human. Now, "there is really developing above us another hominization, a collective one of the whole species" (306, 220–21). Teilhard predicts that in this new phase, human groups and societies will possess and use the same three properties that individuals have used to advance: *invention*, *attraction*, and *aspiration*.

First, just as individuals used *invention* to advance the noosphere, so now groups and research teams are using "collective invention" in the same way.

Second, just as individuals were *attracted* to each other, so now groups are attracted to each other to combine their group energies and talents.

Third, just as individuals have *aspirations* and dreams, so now groups are developing and imagining their own futures.

"The human group is in fact turning…toward a second critical pole of reflection of a collective and higher order; toward a point…

born of involution…of that transcendent force we call Omega." Omega, Teilhard points out, is "the principle which at once and the same time makes this involution irreversible and moves and gathers it in" (307, 221). Teilhard sees the Omega principle operating within us, individually and collectively. And he also sees Omega as ahead of us, waiting for us, as it were, beckoning us forward and upward.

TEILHARD'S OPINION ON THREE FINAL QUESTIONS

First question: What place remains for human freedom and hence for the possibility of a setback in the world?

Teilhard answers, "It in no way follows from the position taken up here that the final success of hominization is necessary, inevitable and certain" (307, 222). The universe at its beginning operated "by chance at the bottom" with subatomic particles. It now operates by "freedom at the top" with humanity. Therefore, anything can happen. But for a Christian believer, Teilhard observes in a footnote, "the final success of hominization (and thus cosmic involution) is guaranteed…but this takes us beyond the plan of phenomenology" (307n, 222n).

Second question: What value must be given to spirit as opposed to matter?

Teilhard answers, "Matter and spirit do not present themselves as 'things' or 'natures' but as simple related *variables*…in space and time." This is a radically new way of thinking about matter and spirit—as "simple related (measurable) variables." Thus, "matter" and "spirit" are related variables like "height" and "weight," or "temperature" and "pressure," or "velocity" and "time." The things that really exist are people, animals, plants, lakes, mountains, and so on. We use different variables to measure and compare their states. Thus, consciousness or spirit "presents itself and demands to be treated, not as a sort of particular and subsistent entity, but as an 'effect,' as the 'specific effect' of complexity" (308, 222).

> In the perspectives of cosmic involution, not only does consciousness become co-extensive with the universe, but the universe rests in equilibrium and consistency, in the form of thought, on a supreme pole of interiorization. (309, 223)

More simply, spirit as a variable takes primacy over matter as a variable.

Third question: What is the distinction between God and the world in the theory of cosmic involution?

Behind this question, as Teilhard recognizes, lurks people's fear that Teilhard is a pantheist, seeing no distinction between God and the world. He dealt with this question earlier, but apparently people still wonder if Teilhard's ideas qualify as Christian. He explains how his form of "pantheism" is very much Christian.

He replies, "For if, in the last resort, the reflective centers of the world are effectively 'one with God,' this state is obtained not by identification (God becoming all) but by the differentiating and communicating action of love (God is all *in everyone*). And that is essentially orthodox and Christian" (310, 223). If union differentiates, love certainly does.

Spiritual Implications

In his epilogue, Teilhard presents the powerful potential force for evolution that Christianity offers to humanity. Ironically, as he is writing these pages, his Catholic Church can hardly claim to be at the vanguard of evolution. He is, in fact, operating within a hierarchical institution that is moribund, proud, and mired in self-declared triumphalism, yet afraid to welcome the discoveries of modern science.

Sad to say, the official church in our own day has not progressed very far. It has not used or recognized the spiritual force that Teilhard envisions within it. Nor has it realized the new potential it would possess if it would integrate within it the knowledge that science offers to it.

Teilhard presents a vision of Christianity in its best dress. It is an ideal picture of a believing community that today's ordinary Christian hardly recognizes—or hears preached from the pulpit. Yet Teilhard's vision of Christianity is there, potentially. The Holy Spirit is continually prompting Christians—and others—to live up to their inherent greatness, to push forward the boundaries of knowledge and love.

In all ages, there have been Christians with an insurgent spirit. Paul of Tarsus, Origen, Augustine, Aquinas, Catherine of Sienna, Luther, Joan of Arc. Such spiritual visionaries refused to conform quietly to minimum expectations or to live in fear of authorities. Rather, they pushed the believing community forward. They made people aware of what was possible. Teilhard is one of these. He says we need many more prophetic voices that possess this "zest for life," as he calls it.

Postscript

These religious rebels refused to be stifled. In their attempt to move Christianity forward, they "died" in many ways—rejected, ostracized, abandoned, imprisoned, martyred. Despite the strongest resistance, they continued to push for transformation and reform.

Another way of presenting Teilhard's spiritual challenge is to find what theologian Paul Tillich calls the "God beyond God." In each age, we have a conviction of who God is and what God expects of us. Teilhard says that the fact of evolution forces us to look to a God of the Future. Some insurgents have begun living in this new way, but the new way has not yet been fully articulated.

These insurgent Christians challenge us to find the creative courage to look and "see" the God of Tomorrow, the God of the Future. Teilhard does this in describing the living Omega, who is God Up Ahead, beckoning us. Omega is not the God Above, who lives in a faraway "heaven." Omega is with us on Earth, but ahead of us, beckoning us forward, challenging us to evolve our minds and hearts and to build a new Earth. For Teilhard, evolution is the loving hand of Omega up ahead drawing us toward him.

The spirituality question Teilhard puts to us is this: Since, in many ways, you and I can influence humanity and the noosphere, what specifically is Omega asking of us? What is to be our unique active role in creating the human future? Ours must be an active, creative role, since we humans have the power to shape the future.

To create is to bring something new into being. For Teilhard, creative people are those who enlarge and enrich human consciousness. In an evolving world, exercising one's ability to bring something new into the world becomes the basic way an individual or group fulfills their own being and purpose in the world.

When Teilhard talks about creativity, he is not referring to hobbies or activities that take up leisure time or the things people do to amuse themselves on weekends. For him, creating—whether in science, technology, society, art, philosophy, or religion—represents the highest level of emotional and mental activity.

Creativity is an open and responsive encounter with reality, whether it happens in a scientific lab, an artist's studio, a philosopher's study, at a writer's desk, or in a saint's vision. Creativity enlarges consciousness. It enriches our experience of life.

If to create is to bring something new into being, what kinds of things are truly "new"? There are three basic ways to create.

The first is to *bring something into the world that has not been here before.* For example, the light bulb, the telephone, the radio, television, the rocket ship, the robot. One might say that this first kind of creativity "fills an empty space." An artist's blank canvas, a blank page of music paper, a sculptor's uncut stone, a blank sheet of paper in a novelist's type-writer, an empty Word file in a computer.

The second way to create is *to give form, meaning, direction, order, or structure to things that seem complicated, confusing, or chaotic.* Teil-hard's integration of the apparently contradictory systems of science, evo-lution, and Christianity is one example of this mode of creativity. Another is Thomas Aquinas's *Summa Theologica* integrating Aristotle's scientific logic with the theology of his day.

The third way to create is to *make connections between things never previously connected.* Connecting astronomy and physics to create astro-physics. Or connecting paleontology and biology to create paleobiology.

Teilhard strongly challenges the assumed dichotomy between subject and object that has been a central characteristic of Western thought for the past five centuries, especially in science. Teilhard insists that we can-not really "see" an object unless we have some emotional involvement with it. We cannot see the human phenomenon in the process of anthro-pogenesis unless we "see" it with emotional involvement, with love. Michelangelo loved the piece of marble and loved the "David" in it, which was waiting to be released. Jonas Salk loved the people and loved the chemicals that he believed held a polio vaccine within them. When Salk was asked why he did not claim a patent for the polio vaccine as his own property, he said it belonged to the people.

For Teilhard, the essence of an evolutionary spirituality is to love both God and Earth passionately. Leonardo da Vinci understood this principle many centuries earlier. He expressed it this way: "Perfect knowledge of the Universe and perfect Love of God are one thing and the same."

Teilhard challenges Christians to develop an ever-deeper knowledge of the universe by a commitment to all fields that can advance our knowl-edge of creation and our love for it. If he prayed for vocations to the priesthood and religious life, he would pray that those who commit-ted themselves to God would be the ones most strongly committed to research and advancement in every field, secular and sacred.

Appendix

Some Remarks on the Place and Part of Evil in a World in Evolution (311–13, 224–26)

SOME READERS POINT out that nowhere in his *Phenomenon* does Teilhard talk about suffering, pain, or wrongdoing. Does that mean he believes that evil and its problems have disappeared and no longer influence the progress of the world?

Teilhard is no cockeyed optimist or Pollyanna. As he says, "My aim in this book has been limited to bringing out the *positive essence* of the biological process of hominization....I have assumed that what I have omitted could nevertheless be seen...as part of the cosmic drama." Surely, evil "inevitably seeps out through every nook and cranny, through every joint and sinew of the system" (311, 224).

He lists several kinds of evil:

- *Evil of disorder and failure.* The world has always proceeded by means of groping and chance, producing disorder and failure along the way. Even at the level of spirit, we find wickedness and suffering, as well as mistakes being made always and everywhere (312, 224–25).

- *Evil of decomposition.* Sickness, corruption, and death, "the regular, indispensable condition of the replacement of one individual by another" (312, 225).

- *Evil of solitude and anxiety.* The result of "waking up to reflection in a dark universe...a universe we have not yet succeeded in understanding either in itself, or in its demands on us" (312, 225).

- *Evil of growth*. The demands of synthesizing "make all progress in the direction of increased unity express itself in terms of work and effort" (312, 225).

We are living in "a universe which is involuted and interiorized, but at the same time and by the same token a universe which labors, which sins, and which suffers."

Teilhard ends his manuscript with the mystery of the cross.

In one manner or the other, it remains true that, even in the view of the mere biologist, the human epic resembles nothing so much as a way of the Cross.

Notes

Preface

1. Charles Darwin's *On the Origin of Species* was published in 1859.

Pre-Notes

1. Sarah Appleton-Weber's *The Human Phenomenon* is not merely a new translation or an attempt to make Teilhard's language more politically correct. It is what scholars call a "critical edition."

Teilhard's Preface

1. See *Activation of Energy*, 286, 325.

2. More recently, scientists have come to recognize the psychological impossibility of the researcher being totally "objective," or of the object of research remaining unaffected by the researcher and the setting, conditions, and atmosphere of research, whether in laboratory or field.

3. Brian Swimme and Thomas Berry, *The Universe Story* (San Francisco: Harper, 1992). Quoted in "Teilhard Perspective" newsletter with no page reference cited.

4. These thoughts resonate with Teilhard's book of spirituality, *The Divine Milieu*. If *Phenomenon* is about teaching people to look at humanity in all its dimensions, the *Divine Milieu* is all about teaching people to see God's kingdom at work among us in all its dimensions. Both books are about learning to *see*.

Book 1: Chapter 1

1. The *Big Bang* was a term first coined in the 1940s, two decades after Teilhard began putting *Phenomenon* together. He would have used the term later in his life.

2. Since Einstein, the speed of science's "clock" is governed by laws of relativity.

3. *Future of Man*, 34.

4. Teilhard writes of "a Christianity re-incarnated for the second time…in the spiritual energies of Matter." *Heart of Matter*, 96.

Book 1: Chapter 2

1. For a study of the evolution of subjectivity, see John F. Haught, *The New Cosmic Story: Inside Our Awakening Universe* (New Haven, CT: Yale University Press, 2017).

Book 1: Chapter 3

1. C. S. Lewis, *Mere Christianity* (New York: MacMillan, 1943), 65.

Book 2: Chapter 1

1. Typically, most megamolecules are made up of sixty carbon molecules each, typically shaped like soccer balls or geodesic domes.

2. New data from astronomy suggest megamolecules developed *everywhere* in the universe. Earth was not the only setting in our galaxy where megamolecules emerged.

3. Teilhard's theory of cellular emergence was based on the biology and geology of the 1930s. But he wasn't far off, predicting microfossils thriving around volcanic hydrothermal vents in oceans worldwide. Eric Betz, "When Did Life Appear?" *Discover*, Jan/Feb 2018, 71.

4. Betz, "When Did Life Appear?," 71.

5. Humberto Maturana and Francisco Varela, *Autopoiesis and Cognition: The Realization of the Living* (Basel, Switzerland: Springer, 1973; 2nd ed., 1980).

6. See my paper "Expanding Teilhard's 'Complexity-Consciousness' Law," *Teilhard Studies*, Spring 2014.

Book 2: Chapter 2

1. Interestingly, roughly 80 percent of the human genome arrived sideways through Horizontal Gene Transfer (HGT) by viral infection. This new dimension in the evolution of life entangles the traditional "tree of life."

2. The dispersion of masses of early cells into groups reflects the dispersion of subatomic particles into more than a hundred species of atoms that branched into identifiable atomic groups such as gases, metals, and minerals.

3. Mya = million years ago.

4. In *Phenomenon*, regarding the diagram on page 123, 77, using an older naming system, Teilhard calls the Cenozoic Age the "Tertiary."

5. A paleogenetic study in *Nature Communications Journal*, July 2017, found that modern humans had been interbreeding with Neanderthals 220,000 to 470,000 years ago. This pushes back human interbreeding at least 100,000 years earlier than previous research suggested.

6. This is the classification system in use at the time of Teilhard's writing.

7. Teilhard understood people reading his book defending human evolution would know that he was not merely a scientist but also a Roman Catholic priest.

8. Geologists and paleontologists, however, are now beginning to find fossils from the Precambrian, now called the Ediacaran period (from 635 mya to 540 mya). It became an official geological period only in 2004. David Quammen, "When Life Got Complicated," *National Geographic*, March 2018, 88–107.

9. Almost all animal life-forms Teilhard would know about appeared in the Cambrian, that is, after 540 mya.

Book 2: Chapter 3

1. Teilhard first proposed this insight in book 1, chapter 3. Spiritual Energy, section B.

2. Modern scientists are coming to recognize Teilhard's using *Complexity* as a legitimate form of measurement. Biologist Wang writes, "The complexity of the interacting network [of brain fibers] likely determines intelligence." Hurng-Yi Wang et al., "Rate of Evolution in Brain-Expressed Genes in Humans and Other Primates," *PLoS Biology* 5, no. 2 (February 2007): 13.

3. New primate species are still being discovered. More than twenty-five species were taxonomically described in the first decade of the 2000s and more have been described since.

4. In 1 Cor 13, Paul lists many characteristics of love. All of them are characteristic of God and meant to be characteristics of the ways we treat each other.

Book 3: Chapter 1

1. This is Teilhard's own peculiar definition of involution, that is, the process of continually reorganizing more and more complexity into the same space (as in increasing neuronal complexity in the human brain). In traditional biology, involution simply describes an organism growing smaller (as in old age) or shrinking (as in a uterus after birth). Involution has different meanings also in mathematics and in Eastern religions.

2. In other writings Teilhard describes the evolution of the noosphere using terms like *psychogenesis* and *noogenesis*. Cf. *Future of Man*, 34.

3. The phylum from early hominin lines to the modern human reveals a process. Among the hominin (members of our family tree) before us—and for a time overlapped with archaic *Homo sapiens*—we know of the Neanderthals, the Denisovans, and *Homo naledi*. Evidence of the latter two species was discovered only in the twenty-first century.

4. Some earlier evolutionary examples in the phylogeny of the species homo include the subspecies *Homo erectus*, *Homo habilis*, *Homo heidelbergensis*, *Homo floresiensis*, *Homo rudolfensis*, *Homo neanderthalensis*.

5. Teilhard was involved in the discovery of Peking Man, one of these prehuman species.

Book 3: Chapter 2

1. Teilhard calls this period the Late Quaternary. In geology, this term is now used only informally.

Book 3: Chapter 3

1. Biological process, measured in process time, was introduced in book 1, chapter 1, subhead "Duration," pp. 41–42.

2. Certain animal species have evolved the meaning of "heredity" as well. In their own way, adult animals can "teach" their young new abilities they have spontaneously discovered or developed. Animals can also observe and copy new behaviors they observe in others of the same or different species.

3. Rollo May, *The Courage to Create* (New York: Bantam Books, 1973), 15.

Book 4: Chapter 1

1. Teilhard uses the Latin word *processus* here, which has a richer meaning than the English "process." *Processus* includes the course, progression, progress, and advance of a process or system.

Book 4: Chapter 3

1. For perspective, in 2018, one fully loaded aircraft carrier costs about $15 billion, while the government provides about $30 billion for basic research to colleges and universities.

2. Teilhard died in 1955, before international space programs began. The Hubble Space Telescope, photographing the cosmos, wasn't launched until 1990.

Glossary

Aggregating molecules: groups or networks of the same molecule.

Anthropogenesis: humanity's beginnings and developmental or evolutionary process. Teilhard proposes the creation of a new science called *anthropogenesis*.

Arrangement: the process of continually organizing and reorganizing of contents; a process that organisms must undergo as their complexity grows.

Arthropods: (invertebrates, i.e., without spines): snails, squids, octopus, crabs, lobsters, barnacles, and shrimp.

Atmosphere (from the Greek *atmos*, meaning "vapor"): the layer of gases, commonly known as air, that surrounds the planet.

Atom: a system made up of subatomic particles, primarily electrons, protons, and neutrons. The periodic table of chemical elements lists and classifies all known atoms.

Attraction: a fundamental evolutionary energy or drive in the universe; *individual elements attract other elements to join to form connections or unions*; the force that built and shaped the universe into what we experience today.

Barysphere (Greek *baros*, meaning "heavy"): the central core of Earth made up of a heavy solid iron center surrounded by a hot liquid nickel-iron alloy.

Biosphere (from the Greek *bios*, meaning "life"): the entire layer of living things in the sea, on land, and in the air.

Big Bang: a term coined to describe the first explosive moments of the universe's birth; the beginnings, or the

237

first phase, of both cosmogenesis and anthropogenesis; the moments when humanity was first conceived in the womb of space/time.

Center: the nucleus or *within* of a thing, animal, or person that guides its inner movements and outer actions. Each person has a center. Each group has its own center, which becomes a *group center of the individual centers* of its members.

Coalescence: a joining together of different elements to form a new union; a fundamental characteristic of cosmic nature that creates elements such as animals and humans who Attract and Connect; such coalescence connections occur in both the *without* and the *within*. (See **Convergent phylogenesis** and **Forced coalescence**.)

Complexification: an evolutionary drive that moves things to become concentrated into evermore complex organized forms of matter; a process that produces a union of elements.

Complexifying molecule: see **Compounds**.

Complexity: a concentrated and well-ordered system of elements; a new basis of measurement for the scientific field of natural history—in addition to measurements of space and time.

Compounds: chemical structures that are more complex than molecules; a larger molecule made up of a union of two or more different molecules.

Conjugation (or horizontal gene transfer): the transfer of genetic material between bacterial cells by direct cell-to-cell contact or by a bridge-like connection; a mechanism that happens among protozoa and some algae and fungi.

Consciousness: capacity for awareness plus an appropriate response; capacity that develops in proportion to complexity of structure; a variable of nature.

Conservation of energy: a physics concept about how we use and spend the quantity of fuel available on the planet.

Controlled additivity: an organism's ability to continuously accumulate properties, thereby providing a vertical component to the evolutionary process.

Convergent phylogenesis: coalescence of all humans into a single planetary species; in contrast to branching outward into many distinct species among plants and animals.

Cosmogenesis: the universe in its beginnings and process of becoming what it is meant to be.

Dissipation of energy: A law of physics that says that once you use (e.g., burn) a physio-chemical fuel, it *cannot be reconstituted or reused.*

Duration: the amount of time taken to complete a process; evolution's way of measuring an event.

Emergent properties: new capacities or functions of an evolved element (species) that are not possessed by any of its predecessors or its parts.

Endomorphism: a mapping of one set of objects onto another set of the same object, so that the new mapping reveals what could not be recognized in the first mapping.

Evolutionary law: Teilhard proposes two evolutionary laws: *Attraction leads to Connection, which builds Complexity and expands Consciousness,* and *Union Differentiates.*

Faces of matter: The three "faces of matter" that Teilhard studies as phenomena at each level of evolution are (1) *plurality,* (2) *unity,* and (3) *energy.*

Forced coalescence: Although human coalescence is *forced* because our planet cannot be enlarged, the ways in which coalescence happens are *unforced* because of the freedom and flexibility of the human species.

Genesis: a process of conception, birth, and development to maturity. When you see a word ending in *genesis,* think of its "beginning and becoming." For example, see **Geogenesis** below.)

Genotyping: a way of *classifying species using DNA and other genetic markers.* The phenotype of a dinosaur might not look like that of a chicken, but genotyping will clearly verify their common roots. (Compare **Phenotype**.)

Geogenesis: Earth's beginning and becoming; Earth's developmental or evolutionary process; the *sequence of appearance* of life-forms on Earth and the emerging properties and abilities of each new life-form.

Groping: directed chance; a form of learning through trial and error; a primitive way of expressing the drive to evolve.

Hominization: the lengthy process of making or forming what today's human phenomenon looks like and is capable of; *humanity taking shape*; an important later stage of anthropogenesis.

Homogeneity

Basic homogeneity: among subatomic particles, each proton, neutron, and electron throughout the universe enjoys the same properties as every other proton, neutron, and electron.

Specific homogeneity: structural consistency of each of the hundred or more chemical elements. For example, any atom of hydrogen can substitute for any other atom of hydrogen, since every hydrogen atom is structured identically.

Structural homogeneity: the similar basic makeup or structure of every atom in the universe. Each atom is made up of electrons orbiting around a nucleus of protons and neutrons.

Human phenomenon: includes not only all humans and all human groups but also *everything observably human*, including all the things on Earth that humans have invented, assembled, created, manufactured, and use to carry on their lives; everything that nature by itself could never have produced including living and nonliving items that allow us to express thought and ingenuity in innumerable ways.

Hydrosphere (the Greek *hydro*, meaning "water"): the combined mass of water and other liquids found on or under the planet's surface.

Hyperpersonal: humanity itself (all human beings collectively) as a personal, living, evolving superindividual with its own functions and purpose; a commonly shared power of knowing and doing; an organic superaggregation of souls.

Involution: the process of continually increasing complexity within a limited physical space.

Lepidopter: an order of insects that have four broad wings, such as butterflies and moths.

Lithosphere (from the Greek *lithos*, meaning "rock"): the rigid outermost shell of the planet including its mantle and crust; the basic source of Earth's metals and minerals.

Macromolecules: larger and more complex molecular unions that make up the world of organic compounds, e.g., proteins, DNA.

Megasynthesis: the planetary synthesis of the biosphere and noosphere being carried out by humanity; the totality of thinking units (*within*) and thinking forces (*without*) engaged in guiding planetary unification.

Metamorphosis: a change *in the form, state, or nature* of a thing or a person into a completely different state, usually from a lower state to a higher (*meta*) state, e.g., a caterpillar morphing into a butterfly.

Molecules: unions formed of two or more distinct kinds of atoms.

Morphology: the scientific study of changes of shapes, forms, and configurations among individuals in a species or between species.

Noogenesis: the formation and building up of the noosphere; fostering the maturity of the noosphere; the process within geogenesis (the maturing of Earth) for which humanity is responsible.

Noosphere (from the Greek *nous*, meaning "mind"): the sphere or layer of continuously accumulating totality of human thought, consciousness, and mental activity throughout history that is available to all; a domain of knowledge that could be created only by humans; a stage of evolution crucial to humanity's role in Earth's evolutionary future.

Ontology (ontological): study of development at the *individual* level from fetus to infant to adult. (Compare **Phylogeny**.)

Orthogenesis: proper development or developing in the right way; the overall force or law that governs the masses of cells in their process of diversification into a restricted number of dominant directions.

Peduncle: in botany, *the main stalk of a flower or a fruit*; the peduncle gives birth to the flower; the first cells are the "peduncles" of all terrestrial life.

Personalization: the process of making and shaping a planet of persons and personality.

Phenomenon: something that can be seen, observed, and measured; something *apparent and tangible*.

Phenomenon of Man: see **Human phenomenon**.

Phenotyping: classification by appearance and physical evidence; in mammals and reptiles it involves comparing observable features, such as cranial shape and size, number and structure of teeth, nature of the spinal cord, and size and shape of feet and limbs.

Phylogeny (phyletic): evolution at the *species* level, e.g., an evolving series of mammal species evolving over time. (Compare **Ontology**.)

Phylum: in biology, *a living bundle of bundles of species, a line of lines*; a *collective reality*, a *living union*, not just an artificial category for the sake of classification; a "verticil of consolidated forms."

Planetization: a new mode of phylogenesis by which a single thinking species covers the entire planet and unifies it. (Compare to **Hominization**.)

Psychism: any activity related to the human mind, heart, and spirit.

Quantum: the energy potential of a system; a system's

emergent qualities and functions that can express forms of energy that none of its parts alone possesses.

Radial energy: energy that drives things toward unions of greater complexity; an energy that is not depleted but that continually increases with use. (Compare **Tangential energy.**)

Ramification: as life expands, it splits spontaneously into many branches or hierarchical units. Among large living masses, ramification serves as a form of "reproduction."

Socialization: the organized formation of groups of animals or humans to provide shared ways of growth, protection, and survival; an essential law of organized matter or groups of individuals; a sign of species maturity.

Stratosphere (from the Latin *stratum*): the covering or blanket that stretches out over, or covers the atmosphere.

Subatomic particles: the particulate nature of the original universe that came forth at the Big Bang; common subatomic particles include electrons, protons, neutrons, and photons of light.

Sublimation: a form of phylogeny that gradually transforms what is primarily physical into something psychic or spiritual; the progressive spiritualization happening in human civilization of all the forces contained in the animal world.

Supercentration: humanity seen as center of centers; a conscious synthesis of a superaggregation of souls; a collective process that can imagine and create the purpose and goal of evolution; a process that speeds up global unanimity.

Supraphysical humanity: humanity as a living reality in itself; humanity's ongoing life as being like that of an individual person, except that it is a superindividual (collective) person.

System: two or more parts that interact for the benefit of the whole; a system is not simply the sum of its parts, but the *product of its interactions.*

Tangential energy: energy that can get used up or burned, like spent fuel. Tangential energy dissipates with use. (Compare **Radial energy.**)

Taxonomy: a branch of zoology that classifies forms of life based on shared physical characteristics; a convenient system for cataloging biological and botanical data for easy retrieval; zoological classification names: *kingdom, class, order, family, genus,* and *species.*

Total matter (*totum,* Latin for "whole" or "all"): all matter in the entire physical universe viewed as one being; the anatomy of a living universe.

Tree of Life: a metaphorical diagram created to display the branching of species over time. All living things on Earth today may be traced back in time to a few main branches that emerged from a single trunk.

Unanimity: a supraphysical stage of union where humanity is of one mind and one heart; in contrast to *uniformity,* where everyone thinks and says the same thing.

Union Differentiates: an evolutionary principle that states that as each conscious element (person) participates actively in the purposes of a relationship, group, or system, that person becomes more clearly individuated or more fully himself or herself.

Vertebrates: creatures with spinal cords, such as fish, reptiles, birds, and all mammals.

Verticil: any branch or stem from which emerge a series of smaller branches sharing similar characteristics. If a tree's trunk is its *peduncle,* its main branches are its *verticils.*

Within: a thing's *inner life*; those actions and events that are intangible and invisible to others, such as thoughts, intentions, emotions. For Teilhard, everything has a *without* and a *within.*

Without: A thing's *physical, tangible, visible, dimensions* such as size, shape, weight, density, structure, movement, velocity, and lifespan.

Index